# FROM DANIEL BOONE TO CAPTAIN AMERICA

From
# DANIEL BOONE
to
# CAPTAIN AMERICA

Playing Indian in American Popular Culture

## CHAD A. BARBOUR

UNIVERSITY PRESS OF MISSISSIPPI / JACKSON

www.upress.state.ms.us

Designed by Peter D. Halverson

The University Press of Mississippi is a member of the Association of
American University Presses.

Portions of chapter 4 appeared as "Playing Indian and Performing Gender in 1940s and
1950s United States Comics," *International Journal of Comic Art* 15:2 (Fall 2013): 278–97.

Portions of chapter 5 appeared as "When Captain America Was an Indian: Heroic Masculinity, National Identity, and Appropriation," *Journal of Popular Culture* 48.2 (Apr. 2015):
269–84.

First printing 2016
∞
Library of Congress Cataloging-in-Publication Data

Names: Barbour, Chad A., author.
Title: From Daniel Boone to Captain America : playing Indian in American
popular culture / Chad A. Barbour.
Other titles: Playing Indian in American popular culture
Description: Jackson, Mississippi : University Press of Mississippi, 2016. |
Includes bibliographical references and index.
Identifiers: LCCN 2015046485 | ISBN 9781496806840 (hardback)
Subjects: LCSH: Comic books, strips, etc.—United States—History and
criticism. | Indians in popular culture—United States. | Masculinity in
popular culture. | Superheroes—History. | Comic strip
characters—History. | Courage—Mythology. | Frontier and pioneer
life—West (U.S.)—Mythology. | West (U.S.)—In popular culture. | BISAC:
SOCIAL SCIENCE / Popular Culture. | LITERARY CRITICISM / Comics & Graphic
Novels. | SOCIAL SCIENCE / Ethnic Studies / Native American Studies.
Classification: LCC PN6725 .B33 2016 | DDC 741.5/352997073—dc23
LC record available at http://lccn.loc.gov/2015046485

British Library Cataloging-in-Publication Data available

# IN MEMORY OF MY FATHER

# CONTENTS

# ACKNOWLEDGMENTS

THIS BOOK HAS BEEN IN PROGRESS FOR THE PAST FEW YEARS, AND OVER those years I have presented its ideas and arguments at various conferences: American Studies Association, Nineteenth Century Studies Association, Southwest Popular/American Culture Association, and Popular Culture Association. The feedback and questions received at these conferences have been of much assistance. Joe Sutliff Sanders and David Bennett also provided helpful feedback on an early version of the Captain America article.

A number of online resources have been quite useful in writing this book. Two websites have been invaluable in their collecting of and making available scans of public domain comic books, many of which are integral to this research: *The Digital Comic Museum* and *Comic Book Plus*. The *Grand Comics Database* has been a constant source of technical and publication details. The *Comix Scholars* listserv has provided me with a profound education in comics studies and its academic nuances.

At the University Press of Mississippi, the two anonymous readers provided insightful critique for the proposal and manuscript. Craig Gill has been most supportive and kind during the proposal and drafting process. As the book has entered its later stages, other staff at the University Press of Mississippi have proven most helpful, including Katie Keene, Courtney McCreary, and John Langston. I am grateful also to Lisa Williams for her meticulous copyediting.

In my formative years as a scholar, Dana Nelson provided guidance and advice that has resonated throughout my life and career. Dale Bauer was also a supportive mentor in those early years. Further back, I would also recognize Gail McDonald, Christopher Hodgkins, and Tom Kirby-Smith for encouraging me toward a life in scholarship.

At Lake Superior State University, my colleagues in English, Communication, and Language Studies have demonstrated ideal collegiality throughout the years. A sabbatical awarded by the university provided me with much-needed time toward the end of the manuscript's composition. The staff of Shouldice Library has assisted me in obtaining books and articles through interlibrary loan and ordering books when needed; their service cannot be overstated. My students over the years have provided me with the opportunity to try out some of these ideas in the classroom, but I would especially recognize the students in my honors seminar, "Superheroes and American Culture," for their enthusiasm and ideas, as well as the Honors Program for allowing me to teach this course.

My mother, Beth, with her unconditional encouragement and love, has made more possible for me than she knows. My in-laws, Nelson and Cindy, treat me as one of their own, and to them I am grateful for their love and support. When I was an undergraduate, I met Julie through a shared love of poetry. As our friendship became something more, we shared and nurtured our respective passions, and then careers, in English. I cannot imagine my life in writing and scholarship without her, my iceblink luck. My daughter, Eleanor, with her questions, her positivity, and her grace pushes me to do better, to be better.

This book is dedicated to the memory of my father, Mike Barbour (1950–2005), whose light shines on.

# FROM DANIEL BOONE TO CAPTAIN AMERICA

# INTRODUCTION

ON MAY 29, 2014, WASHINGTON, DC'S NFL TEAM DECIDED TO EXECUTE a publicity maneuver in which Twitter users were encouraged to address Senator Harry Reid (a vocal opponent of the NFL team's mascot): "Tweet @SenatorReid to show your #RedskinsPride and tell him what the team means to you." As some Twitter users immediately surmised, this was not a good idea. On Deadspin.com, Barry Petchesky collected some of the responses, which included the likes of this one from Twitter user @JamilSmith: "#RacialSlurPride RT @Redskins: Tweet @SenatorReid to show your #RedskinsPride and tell him what the team means to you." Or this one from user @xodanix3: "Dakota 38 were called redskins b4 largest mass hanging in us history. No #redskinspride here @SenatorReid." This tweet included an image of a newspaper article on the hanging that used the "redskins" name. Many other tweets expressed similar sentiments. While there were certainly tweets that supported or defended the use of the name, those that expressed resistance to and critique of the name illustrate the role that social media has come to play in protesting appropriation and racist depictions of Native Americans.

Not only have Twitter and Facebook, among other platforms, provided a medium to discuss publicly matters of Native American issues that have largely been marginalized from mainstream awareness, these platforms provide concrete proof of survivance.[1] Rather than historical relics or ghosts of the past, Native Americans are living, contemporary individuals, a fact made concrete and real via social media (as well as many other facets of culture and life). While social media is not the only area in which such survivance can be witnessed, the presence of many Native American voices on Twitter, Facebook, websites, and blogs draws widespread attention to the wrongful appropriations and depictions of Native Americans and their cultures, articulating an awareness and critique of Native American appropriation that continues to gain energy and attention. Blogs like Adrienne Keene's *Native Appropriations*, Twitter hashtags like

#notyourmascot during the 2014 Super Bowl, and groups like Eliminating Offensive Native Mascots (EONM) are among the many voices calling attention to the rampant appropriation occurring in popular culture.

Popular culture, then, is a particularly vivid area of dialogue and debate about the limits and justifications for cultural appropriation. Given the parallel course of playing Indian[2] as a cultural trope and phenomenon in US history (as most concisely traced by Philip Deloria), it is no wonder that popular culture would be such a fertile ground for questions about cultural appropriation. While much brilliant analysis has been devoted to multiple areas of US life and culture concerning appropriations of "Indian-ness" (such as literature, film, and sports mascots), one area has yet to have received such extended study: comics. This book aims to apply the cultural and literary criticism surrounding questions of cultural appropriation and Native representations in American culture to comic books, tracing the lineage of that usage from the nineteenth century.

A foundational concept for this discussion derives from Philip Delo-ria's influential study *Playing Indian*. Deloria examines the significance of the Indian in constructing and performing a national identity by (mostly) white American males. "Indians" serve a dual, yet contradictory, function for white Americans: "Savage Indians served Americans as oppositional figures against whom one might imagine a civilized national Self. Coded as freedom, however, wild Indianness proved equally attractive, setting up a 'have-the-cake-and-eat-it-too' dialectic of simultaneous desire and repulsion" (Deloria 3). The Indian, in this context, is an imagined projec-tion of white culture, a malleable symbol or image: sometimes a fierce and courageous warrior, at other times a wretched and villainous monster, or, as needed, a primal connection to the land and to prehistory.

Deloria's work participates in a rich scholarly tradition of examining cultural appropriations of Native cultures by whites. Leslie Fiedler offers an early examination in his analysis of American literature and what he sees as a renewed fascination with Indian symbolics. Roy Harvey Pearce, Richard Slotkin, Robert Berkhofer, and Richard Drinnon offer analyses of white appropriations and conceptions of Indians throughout US culture and politics. S. Elizabeth Bird, Dana Nelson, and Susan Scheckel brought the idea of "playing Indian" into a fuller critical parlance. In addition, Jacque-lyn Kilpatrick, Renee Bergland, Shari Huhndorf, and Armando Prats have analyzed white imaginings of Natives in literature and in film, especially in the twentieth century. Michael Sheyahshe has cataloged stereotypes of Native Americans found in comics. This study follows in the footsteps of these scholars.

A recurring argument in this scholarship is that Indianness is a mul-tivalent tablet upon which white culture inscribes its ideals and its fears. Even more vital to my argument is not just the imagined Indian as an embodiment of whatever heroic or villainous quality desired by a white audience, but how that imagined Indian is conjured through material or visual symbols, specific objects, designs, or props that transmit this ideal-ized projection of Indianness. In other words, an efficient metonymy is at work here in which the mere presence of, for instance, a headdress bears a complicated and contradictory host of associations.[3] This metonymy relies upon the inclusion of key signature items or visuals that connote qualities associated with Indianness. Furthermore, this amplification of the visual signs of Indianness marginalizes or even erases actual Native presence.

In comics this metonymic logic functions pervasively and powerfully. In his work on racial identity in superhero comics, Marc Singer argues, "Comics rely upon visually codified representations in which characters are continually reduced to their appearances, and this reductionism is especially prevalent in superhero comics, whose characters are wholly externalized into their heroic costumes and aliases" (107). Scott McCloud's influential dissection of icon in comics is relevant here, as well. He argues, "By stripping down an image to its essential 'meaning' an artist can amplify that meaning in a way that realistic art can't" (30). The "essential 'meaning'" of Indianness is transmitted via key and recognizable icons: the tomahawk, the headdress, or buckskins. Moreover, these icons evoke a dense and complicated web of popular and imagined associations of "the Indian," associations that bear little accuracy or particularity (they are not realistic), and with that disconnect from realism, they evoke powerful affect.[4]

In their examination of visual literacy and construction of Indian iden-tity, Dànielle Nicole DeVoss and Patrick Russell LeBeau observe,

This pervasive view of the Indian as a commodity and as a romantic reflec-tion of America's cultural past often relies on an absence of an understand-ing of Indian culture. Images of Indians in headdress and tomahawk rarely are created or interpreted with an understanding of the cultural and tribal conventions explaining dress and custom. Thus, Indians become both icon and archetype—a singular, static motif—of a glorious American past. (55)

The combination of comics' iconic fluency and Indians as "icon and arche-type" produces in the texts being examined in this book an intensification of the appropriation of Indianness as imagistic motif. Playing Indian is a su-perficial masquerade, a performance of an Indianness, usually originating from non-Native sources, with little connection to or regard for genuine history, ongoing traditions, and particular peoples. In fact, the power of Indianness lies in its divorce from actual indigenous peoples. Jennifer Dyar contends that "as one extracted Indianness from the Indian, one also acquired or collected power" (830). Likewise, as Richard Slotkin argues, as "the threat of real Indians was removed from proximity to American civilization . . . Indian virtues could be symbolically exaggerated and Indian values accepted as valid for American society" (*Regeneration* 356–57). The process of appropriation, then, "extract[s] Indianness from the Indian" and preserves the former in visual signs and material objects, while the latter is abandoned and marginalized. The tomahawk, buckskins, and the headdress, among other objects, signify Indianness without any particularized association with historical or cultural contexts. Sierra S. Adare, in her study of TV science fiction and Indian stereotypes, articulates this point thusly: "With the symbolic trappings of a drum, a pipe, a feather fan, and a few 'Indian' words, non-Natives can instantly be transformed" (76). When the visual signs are unattached from actual peoples, then anyone can be "Indian." In addition, with such flexibility in racial performance, playing Indian, in the comics examined below, acts as a convenient narrative device to attach nobility and/or savagery to a character, to represent a character's transformation from weak to strong, and to authenticate the character as a representative American.

To understand better the interpretative process that is operational in the playing Indian dynamic, I turn to Charles Peirce's semiotic theory on icon, symbol, and index. Charles Hatfield astutely illustrates the applicability of Peirce's ideas to the reading of comics.[5] Importantly, Hatfield argues concerning Peirce's "three relationship terms": "Each term could be defined not as an objective entity but rather as a way of *reading*, a way that privileges a certain assumption on the reader's part. An iconic reading privileges assumptions of likeness; a symbolic reading privileges assumed codes or conventions; an indexical reading privileges assumptions of presence, past presence, or direct connection" (43). Daniel Chandler confirms the significance of the relationship between the sign and the signified: "Although it is often referred to as a classification of distinct 'types of signs,' it is more usefully interpreted in terms of differing 'modes of relationship' between sign vehicles and what is signified" (36). Therefore, a discussion of a sign ("the whole meaningful ensemble" [Chandler 30]) recognizes that both a relationship of reading and a relationship of signifying are occurring: the way we read the sign and the way the sign expresses its signified are both significant processes that affect the sign's function in expressing its object.

To focus directly on Peirce's model itself, here are his own definitions of each of these modes of signs:

> An *Icon* is a sign which refers to the Object that it denotes merely by virtue of characters of its own, and which it possesses, just the same, whether any such Object actually exists or not. . . . An *Index* is a sign which refers to the Object that it denotes by virtue of being really affected by that Object. . . . A *Symbol* is a sign which refers to the Object that it denotes by virtue of a law, usually an association of general ideas, which operates to cause the Symbol to be interpreted as referring to that Object. (102)

To bring this discussion into more immediate relevance to this book's area of study, let us consider the tomahawk as icon, symbol, and index. Moreover, to be more precise, let us consider a drawing of a tomahawk in a comic. The tomahawk acts as a potent sign in the rendering of the Indian–white racial line. This utilization of the tomahawk is readily apparent, for example, in the introductions of Chingachgook and Hawkeye in *The Last of the Mohicans*. Cooper shows that Chingachgook possesses a "tomahawk and scalping knife," while Hawkeye "bore a knife in a girdle of wampum . . . but no tomahawk" (32–33). The presence or absence of the tomahawk in this scene subtly marks a racial and cultural difference between the Mohican and the white frontiersman. The possession of the tomahawk, along with a "*scalping* knife," designates the Mohican as Indian, as other to Hawkeye's whiteness. Later in the novel, Hawkeye accords the tomahawk to the Indian: "I leave the tomahawk and knife to such as have a natural gift to use them" (216). Hawkeye reiterates this notion a few paragraphs later: "[F]or 'tis their gift to die with the rifle or the tomahawk in hand; according as their natures may happen to be, white or red" (217). The tomahawk is the signifying weapon of the Indian, the weapon he uses according to his "nature," which, as Hawkeye states, "should not be denied" (162). Another example that illustrates the tomahawk's function as racial marker is the fact that Tom Hawk, in his Indian adoption, becomes "Tomahawk" in the DC comic. As well, the tomahawk's rhetorical power exists vividly in the film *The Patriot*, as Prats demonstrates (239–43). Taken together, these examples provide an appropriate point of departure to consider the tomahawk as icon, symbol, and index.

Tomahawk as icon refers to the actual weapon; the drawing is a pictorial representation of an object that we identify as a tomahawk. Tomahawk as symbol invokes associations of Indianness and its various associations of courage, savagery, bloodthirstiness, the warrior, or the primitive.

Tomahawk as index: the drawing points to the artist who drew it; the style of the drawing is an index, so that we say this tomahawk was drawn by X, while this one was drawn by Y. The indexical mode of the drawing of a tomahawk will change: different artists with different styles leave their marks; the drawing refers to their past presence in various ways as the tomahawk reappears in comic books. Yet the fact of this change perhaps does not possess significant interpretative weight. The iconic reading (based upon conventions for a "tomahawk") remains usually persistent: a drawing of a tomahawk done well (or even not) will function effectively enough to express likeness to the object. The symbolic mode undergoes varying permutations and is of most interest to this study, especially in its richness of multiple valences.

The symbolic mode of the drawn tomahawk changes according to who holds it, where it appears in the comic, and the narrative exigencies that press upon it. The tomahawk in the hand of a white man might variously mean a regression to savagery, a reinvigoration of the male's martial spirit, or the exacting of vengeance. In the hand of an Indian, the tomahawk corroborates his perceived savagery, a frightful thing on one hand; or affirms his fierce warrior spirit, doubly frightful and admirable; or adjudicates his primitivism.

The iconic mode of the tomahawk may at first glance seem obvious: a drawing of a tomahawk is taken to resemble an actual tomahawk. Questions of accuracy most obviously assail the drawing's iconicity. Our invocation of conventionality would assert a correspondence between the tomahawk drawn and the tomahawk in actuality. On the other hand, to what actual material object might we compare the drawing? The question to be asked on this point: Have you seen an actual tomahawk? Readers' experiences will vary on this point, and whether or not one has seen an actual tomahawk may be splitting hairs, because one knows what a tomahawk "looks like." Or one knows what a drawing of a tomahawk *should* look like. Or one is acquainted with the conventions of a "tomahawk."

The visual *representamen* of the tomahawk as sign is at the forefront of this discussion, but the word itself—"tomahawk"—possesses its own symbolic mode as well. One might describe an object as an "axe" or "hatchet" or "tomahawk." Iconically, these three words might be read to describe different objects or, if shown the object and then given the name, one might agree that all three are accurate terms that describe the object in question. Without a visual, one might read each of these three words differently: a tool or a weapon, a weapon exclusive to a certain group, a certain status, or a certain value judgment. The word itself—"tomahawk"—implies a variety of connotations.

In all, these various theoretical understandings of the symbolic function of the image in comic books reveal not only the complexity of discussing the comic image itself, but the complexity of cultural and ideological connotations attached to the image. As the specific example of the tomahawk shows, when examining the trope of playing Indian in comics, one must contend with not only the cultural and the ideological, but also the image.

Also at stake in the performance of Indianness by white males is the maintenance of whiteness. Playing Indian both problematizes and affirms the construction of whiteness. This point finds one of its best articulations from Richard Dyer:

> The concept of racial blood came to dominate definitions of race by the end of the nineteenth century in the USA, just as genetics has in the twentieth. 'Blood' and genes have been said to carry more of the purely mental properties that constitute white superiority. In these discourses, all blood and genes carry mental properties, but invisibly, white blood and genes carry more intelligence, more spirit of enterprise, more moral refinement. Thus our bodily blood or genes give us that extra-bodily edge. (24)

Following Dyer's argument, such a conception of tangible versus intangible traits for race becomes troublesome "for the representation of white people"(24). Tangible signs of race produce a stronger corporeality for nonwhites (which means that whites, in order to define their whiteness, must depend on that nonwhite corporeality), while dependence upon intangibles like spirit or genetics creates difficulties in visualizing whiteness (24). To visualize whiteness is a precarious endeavor, one that Dyer also illustrates when he argues: "Whites must be seen to be white, yet whiteness as race resides in invisible properties and whiteness as power is maintained by being unseen. To be seen as white is to have one's corporeality registered, yet true whiteness resides in the non-corporeal" (45).

Playing Indian registers the corporeality of the white male; he becomes a body that can be seen, whose identity is being predicated upon visual signs of dress; he no longer enjoys the privilege of invisibility possessed in whiteness. His body exposed, the white male is in danger of losing the superiority afforded him by his whiteness, according to Dyer. The white male body in these playing Indian comics commonly is on display when the hero changes from the white clothing that tends to cover much of the body to the Indian clothing that tends to expose the body. On one hand, such exposure stresses the physical strength and superiority of the hero, drawing the audience's attention to his musculature and bodily signs of strength. On the other hand, as Dyer argues, such exposure threatens the white body in producing it as an object of the audience's gaze (as understood in the power dynamic of the gaze—see John Berger, for instance) as well as the commonality of the white body to other bodies (146). The negotiation of the white body playing Indian can be articulated in the following analysis from Dyer: "The built body in colonial adventures is a formula that speaks to the need for an affirmation of the white male body without the loss of legitimacy that is always risked by its exposure, while also replaying the notion that white men are distinguished above all by their spirit and enterprise" (147). As Dyer also points out, the embodiment of the white male is also tempered by the evidence and demonstration of his resourcefulness, "the intelligent, improvisatory use of his environment" (160). The white hero playing Indian often displays resourcefulness, especially in manipulating his surroundings, in dealing with his adversaries, as someone like DC's Tomahawk often demonstrates. Furthermore, the ability of these characters to take on different identities indicates their control and authority. Friedrich Weltzien examines "masculinity as a masquerade" in comic books and concludes that "[t]he ideal masculinity . . . is not signified by one costume or the other but by the ability to change the role at will and according to specific situations" (246). Playing Indian in these comics connotes not only a racial superiority (the acceptability of whites "passing" as Indian is seen as "normal," while the reverse would be viewed as transgressive) but also a sign of masculine power and strength. Such control of identity might even be linked to the ability of the white male to maintain his whiteness while adopting Indianness in his dress and outward abilities (think of Hawkeye in *The Last of the Mohicans* and his constant reminder of his being a "man without a cross"). Control of racial identity merges with the control of costumed identity in these comic books in a way that intertwines heroic masculinity, civic duty, and playing Indian.

Playing Indian, then, as many critics have shown, is extremely attractive to white audiences in American culture. As this book will discuss, playing Indian fulfills multiple desires and fantasies for a white audience or participant: affirmation or strengthening of manhood, freedom from perceived urban weakness, liberation from domestic obligations, and the fantasy of the individual as hero, to name a few. On this latter point, Matthew Costello identifies "[t]he persistent rhetorical power of the individual in

American culture [that] is represented in the American vision of heroism, ranging from Daniel Boone and Natty Bumpo through the cowboy on the frontier and the private detective in urban America to the superhero in comic books" (42).

Playing Indian must be viewed also within the larger frame of the frontier myth whose lineage extends from the nineteenth century forward in American culture. This frontier myth encapsulates fantasies and desires revolving around heroic manhood, self-reliance and self-determination, physical strength, hybridity of the "civilized" and the "savage," and adventure and battle, with the notion that these qualities combine to form an exceptional American character. For example, Mervi Miettinen identifies the relationship between masculinity, the frontier myth, and popular fictions: "As a representative of a particular brand of twentieth century American hegemonic masculinity, the superhero usually embodies the tough, uncompromising masculine virtues of the American nation, virtues that originate from the Frontier myth and which can be located in other popular fictions of America, such as westerns and detective fiction, which tend to embrace the idea of a masculine essence instead of a plurality of masculinities" (105). This lineage is readily apparent. Peter Coogan also identifies this transmission of the frontier myth, namely, through the concept of "permeability" between civilized and savage states:

> Throughout the tales of Doc Savage and the Shadow, the criminal class maintains some permeability as people can pass in and out of it. That permeability would be mostly removed in the comics of Superman and Batman. Removing that permeability reestablishes the line that separates the civilized world from the savage one, omnipresent in Westerns, and reproduces the idea of an alternative culture. Like the alternative culture of the Indians that seduced white men like captains Simon Girty and James McPhee into becoming "white Indians" and which tempted Daniel Boone and Natty Bumpo, the alternative culture of the criminal class tempts young people and other weak-minded citizens into a life of crime, and this alternative culture must be fought as the savagery of the Indian was fought. (187)

Coogan's study draws attention to the link between American frontier fantasy and comic books, as does Lorrie Palmer when she relates the superhero to the Western in her analysis of *The Punisher*, especially noting the terms of the opposition between the domestic and the wilderness and civilization and savagery found in the superhero story, echoing the same dichotomies of Westerns and playing Indian stories. One of the goals of this book is to further examine this linkage between the frontier myth as it is transmitted from nineteenth-century sources to the comic books of the twentieth century and after. The texts under examination in this study affirm, and sometimes revise or modify, the frontier myth, and the playing Indian trope takes on a particularly potent role in that affirmation and revision.

Chapters 1 and 2 focus on nineteenth-century themes and texts in order to establish their influence upon later cultural products in the United States. Two notable figures are significant in their enactment of the frontier myth: the Indian male and the white frontiersman. Chapter 1 examines the existence of the Indian male body as object of admiration and repulsion. On one hand, the Indian male body is glamorized as a specimen of classical beauty, an ideal of physical and aesthetic form. On the other hand, that Indian body possesses the potential for danger and physical harm. This chapter shows how American art and literature in the nineteenth century attempt to neutralize the perceived threat of the Indian male body through artistic objectification of that body. Chapter 2 focuses on what might be considered the foil to the Indian: the white frontiersman. Specifically in the form of the Daniel Boone figure, the white frontiersman portrays a complementary ideal of white manhood to the Indian male, an ideal that may appear safer in terms of racial purity but, like the contradictory dynamic of the Indian male body's potential for attraction and repulsion, possesses a threat of perceived regression into wild or savage conditions. Boone represents a shining ideal of white manhood, yet his adoption by the Shawnee demonstrates a permeability of racial and national identification. While the Boone figure is fully reclaimed by writers and biographers for the American cause, other white frontiersmen might remain solidly on "the other side." Simon Girty, for example, represents that even a white man can be "lost" to the Indians; thus, white settlers and citizens must be on guard to protect their sense of racial and national "loyalty." These two chapters lay the groundwork of the fantasy and ideology so important to understand for the remainder of the book.

Chapter 3 follows the lineage of frontier and Western fantasies from the nineteenth century to the twentieth via the comic-book adaptations of novels such as *The Last of the Mohicans* and comic depictions of frontier figures such as Boone and Girty. Following in the line of late-nineteenth-century dime novels and early-twentieth-century film, comic books inherited many of the tropes and conventions of the Western and frontier genres, including the white Indian and playing Indian tropes. Multiple adaptations of *The Last of the Mohicans* from the 1940s to the 2000s testify to that story's persistent appeal. The flurry of Boone comics in the 1950s demonstrates his popularity as an American hero while engaging in many of the themes and cultural implications that are essential to this book's focus.

Chapter 4 engages more directly with playing Indian in comic books, examining a host of titles from the 1940s and 1950s and afterward that feature a white hero adopted by Indians or appropriating Indian ways. This depiction implements specific recurring characteristics: adoption by Indians, the white hero with Indian clothing or weapons, Indianness as strength and valor, the Indianized hero as upholder of justice on the frontier, and, in some cases, echoes of superhero conventions in a secret identity or sidekick. These stories not only engage in the frontier lineage discussed in previous chapters but also potentially reveal cultural values of the United States in the postwar years, especially concerning the construction and performance of gender, representations of nationalism and loyalty, and the construction of race and difference.

Chapter 5 continues the discussion of playing Indian in comic books with the focus on superheroes in particular. In the late 1940s and early 1950s, Plastic Man, Captain Marvel, Superman, and Batman play Indian. This chapter then examines Green Arrow's Indian masquerade and its interaction with the social consciousness of Dennis O'Neil's *Green Lantern*. There follows a consideration of Captain America as Indian, and the repercussions of playing Indian for his role as national superhero and representative of US identity. In Neil Gaiman's *1602* (2003–2004) and Tony Bedard's one-shot story *What If? Featuring Captain America* (2006), these reimagined visions of the Captain America mythos appropriate and perform Indianness in order to possess virile masculinity and physical strength. Furthermore, that appropriation of Indianness to produce heroic masculinity accompanies the comics conventions of superheroism. The white superhero as Indian encapsulates the major themes of this study and provides a fitting resolution for this book.

## CHAPTER ONE

# THE INDIAN MALE BODY AND THE HEROIC IDEAL

*Tecumseh and the Indians of Parkman and Cooper*

---

IN VARIOUS INSTANCES IN EARLY-NINETEENTH-CENTURY US CULTURE, the Indian male is cast as a heroic, yet tragic, figure: John Galt's anecdote of Benjamin West and the Apollo Belvedere, the figure of Tecumseh (especially in Ferdinand Pettrich's sculpture *The Dying Tecumseh*), Uncas in *The Last of the Mohicans*, and Francis Parkman's depictions of Oglala warriors. The Indian male body functions in four ways: 1) as an ideal of admiration, especially by white viewers; 2) as dangerous, with the attendant menace of the body; 3) as a figure of dying, specifically in the trope of the vanishing Indian; and 4) as stasis, the artistic freezing of the body in print, sculpture, or art. The Indian male body represents an attractive physical ideal often hollowed of historical particularity yet also maintaining a degree of menace or violent potential. In other words, the Indian male body is a contradictory blend that inspires admiration and fear.[1] By examining these examples from the nineteenth century, one will see many of the precedents for later incarnations in American culture of playing Indian, as well as some of the rationale behind the attraction to being like an "Indian," especially in terms of masculine rhetoric and ideology. This chapter describes a rhetorical and ideological dynamic of depicting idealized Indian male bodies in American literature and art that gains purchase in the nineteenth century and will carry on into the twentieth century.

The anecdote of Benjamin West and the Apollo Belvedere provides an early significant example within an American context of the valorization of the male Indian body. In 1760 Benjamin West visited the Vatican in Rome on his grand tour of Europe. While there, his Italian hosts took him to see the Apollo Belvedere, the sculpture that resides in art history's pantheon as one of the pinnacles of art and of human beauty. As the story goes, upon seeing the statue, West proclaims, "My God, how like it is to a young Mohawk warrior!" This anecdote would find circulation in antebellum US culture via the biography by John Galt (1816–1820). Galt's anecdote, coming as it does in the early nineteenth century, depicts an Anglo white identity that identifies with the physical vigor of American "savages." Galt recodifies West's "Mohawk" as a model of Anglo white manhood, a "Mohawk Apollo" that obfuscates Indian racial features while maintaining the admirable physical strengths and masculine virtues of courage and strength. The West anecdote brings into focus the somewhat convoluted racialized negotiation of ideological qualities drawing on imagined Indians and white manhood. The conflation of the Apollo Belvedere with a Mohawk warrior performs a kind of pentimento of the Native "savage" in order to preserve from him those admirable, mythic qualities that can fortify an Anglo white manhood.

In considering the Indian male body as found in the neoclassical style of sculpture and art of the nineteenth century, an ideological negotiation emerges between admiration and objectification. The audience may admire the physical prowess and athleticism of the Indian male but must maintain an objective distance to maintain an appropriate racialized distinction. One way to understand this negotiation is through viewing the depiction of the Indian male body as simultaneously embodiment and disembodiment. This symbolics of male Indians performs two primary functions: 1) disembodied Indians are "safe" Indians in white male imaginations, and 2) disembodied Indians are a blank slate onto which white males can inscribe their symbolics of manhood.[2] Yet, while this disembodiment takes place, there is still the need for those bodies, for the embodied part of the equation. This figurative process strips the Indian of any historical particularity while simultaneously preserving the figure of his body, a figure that takes on a metonymic function in which the Indian male is both disembodied (emptied of actual agency and presence) and embodied (his figure made a symbol or vessel of desired qualities). This metonymic physicality maintains an Indianized ideal of manhood for a white audience without that Indian ideal's potential for encroachment upon white male authority through competition or conflict. Metonymic Indian male bodies provide an ideal object of male physicality that white males can identify with and admire. Indian male bodies are such objects of identification because of their perceived "untouched" masculinity; Indian male bodies represent a manly physicality that has not been tempered or softened by the luxury of "civilized" living. For this reason, male Indian bodies present admirable models of physicality, while also representing that "savagery" to which whites must not succumb.

Imagined Indians like Cooper's Uncas or Pettrich's version of Tecumseh provide ideal Indian bodies with which white males identify, yet the classical aesthetic form empties them of political and historical specificity. White males idealize an Indian (for his impressive physical strength and build) but identify with a de-Indianized male body (to avoid the potential of cross-racial sympathy). The power of this strategy lies in white males' affective detachment from the Indian body in its objectness, which receives emphasis through its marginalized status in white imaginations structured upon the "vanishing Indian" trope. These figurative Indians, then, prop up white manhood through erasing racial difference by classicist reproduction of Indian bodies. Instead of seeing Indian bodies as already passed away, the visualizing and imagining of Indians as examined in this chapter seek to reveal the physical presence of those bodies, although emptied of sociopolitical force.

The problem of Native bodies becomes apparent in Nancy Shoemaker's analysis of Indian and white metaphors of the body in treaty language. She argues that the body worked to help Indians and Europeans "circumnavigate a larger sphere of obscure and cultural differences" (212). What began as a way to communicate from a common ground became a troublesome contact zone. The image of one flesh and one blood shared by whites and Indians, which formerly allowed different cultures to communicate with each other, becomes a troubling thought for whites who would see themselves as racially separate from Indians. As Daniel Richter shows, the "parallel lives" of Indians and Europeans, held together by an "Empire of Goods," would ultimately collide, especially in the 1760s with the "parallel campaigns of ethnic cleansing" led by Pontiac and the Paxton Boys (190–91). The common ground gives way to increasing perceptions of both whites and Indians of their racial opposition. As Richter articulates this point, the growing perception of "ethnic diversity" in the eighteenth century "wrought an increasingly pervasive view that 'Indians' and 'Whites' were utterly different, and utterly incompatible, kinds of people who could never peacefully share the continent" (180).

In terms of this chapter's analysis, this oppositional diversity creates a contradiction in that white males seek to extirpate Indians yet find that their male bodies can provide a symbolics of white manhood. This conflict drives an iconology of Indians into that realm between the corporeal and the spectral, not fully ghosts and not fully flesh and blood.[3] It is this flux of corporeality that allows whites to imagine Indians as either embodied or disembodied, according to whatever cultural or racial imperative needs to be fulfilled. For example, a white model of virile masculinity might evoke the image of a muscular Indian male body, such as Uncas with his classical features. On the other hand, a white model of expansion might evoke a decorporealized Indian that aligns more closely with the spectral Indian; another example from Cooper is Chingachgook as the lone surviving Mohican after his son's death and his appearance as a "spectral-looking figure." A rhetorically powerful device of embodiment/disembodiment exists in the Indian as statue. Literally and figuratively, a host of examples illustrate the presence of the Indian body as a physical entity while being removed from historical presence via a figuration as statue.

A striking figurative example of the Indian as statue appears in an obscure epic poem by George Hooker Colton, *Tecumseh* (1842). Colton relates Tecumseh's initial appearance in this way: "He yet revealed a symmetry / Had charmed the Grecian sculptor's eye, / A massive brow, a kindled face, / Limbs chiseled to a faultless grace" (37). On one level this statue imagery communicates the manly stoicism of Tecumseh, his physical perfection. These lines are meant to convey praise and admiration for the Indian leader. Colton's choice of the epic poem speaks to the classicizing of Tecumseh as epic hero. Colton transforms the Indian leader into an American hero, suitable for epic treatment. On the other hand, this rhetoric of classical sculpture and epic poetry makes Tecumseh a static figure, a statue or artifact of some ancient past, not a sentient near contemporary. Folded into the archaic potential of this description is the distancing of the audience from the object of description. Through likening Tecumseh's features to sculpture, Colton marginalizes or preempts any potential intimacy that might arise through the male gaze fixed upon a male subject. Colton's description of Tecumseh as statue makes the person an artifact, and such objectification channels any potential subjective identification into a safer rhetorical alignment with the Indian disembodied of physical particularity and agency and embodied with symbolic or figurative meaning.

When Tecumseh is rendered as statue, he is a dead Indian frozen in the past, and his incorporeal status marginalizes him from flesh-and-blood existence, displacing him as a political entity and rendering him as a static body, a statue. Nowhere is this more vivid than in Ferdinand Pettrich's *The Dying Tecumseh* (1856).[4] Sculpted in white marble, Tecumseh lies supine, upper body exposed, muscular though submissive in his dying position (Fig. 1.1). He grasps his tomahawk in his death as he exhales his last breath. The most literal reading of this statue is as the Vanishing American. Julie Schimmel argues that "Pettrich's marble, which creates for Tecumseh the

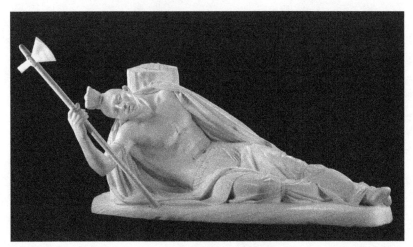

Figure 1.1. Ferdinand Pettrich. *The Dying Tecumseh*. 1856. Marble with painted copper alloy tomahawk. 36 5/8 x 77 5/8 x 53 3/4 in. Smithsonian American Art Museum. Transfer from the US Capitol.

role of a dying Roman general, passes judgment on all Indian 'heroes' who die in battle against whites. Their courage and skill, Pettrich maintains, were devoted to the wrong cause. Their deaths argued not for Indian rights but for the triumph of expansionism" (169–70). Within the popular Vanishing American tradition of this time, this interpretation is accurate. *The Dying Tecumseh*'s contemporary and stylistic peer, Thomas Crawford's *The Indian: Dying Chief Contemplating the Progress of Civilization* (1856), extends this particular reading of the Vanishing American theme (Fig. 1.2). As Vivien Fryd describes, *Dying Chief* "is frozen in melancholic thoughts" (116). Like *Dying Tecumseh*, *Dying Chief* represents the impotence and lack of force of an Indian race in its inevitable decline. This interpretation gains resonance in this statue's inclusion in Crawford's *Progress of Civilization* (1855–1863), the Senate pediment in which the chief appears on the right beside a grave and a grieving Indian woman. As the eye travels from the chief to the left, one sees the "progress of civilization," culminating in the figures of the white businessman and mechanic. Crawford's statue complements Pettrich's in the representation of the Vanishing American. Yet their compositions are striking differently: *Dying Chief* sits, bending forward with head propped in right hand,[5] while *Dying Tecumseh* lies supine and visibly dying. This particular pose occurs in other instances of classical and neoclassical sculpture. *Dying Tecumseh* follows in this tradition and demonstrates a concern or fascination with such aesthetic representations of the dead or dying male.

Figure 1.2. Thomas Crawford.
*The Indian: Dying Chief
Contemplating the Progress
of Civilization.* 1856. Marble.
Height 55 in. New York Historical
Society, New York City.

A number of sculptures featuring the dying-male pose provide another possible reading of *Dying Tecumseh* that is more attuned to the white male's stake in viewing this statue. From antiquity, such sculptures as the *Dying Gladiator (Dying Gaul)*, the *Son of Niobe* (of the *Niobe Group*), and the *Pasquino* depict the dying male. Preceding and contemporary to Pettrich are Jean-Baptiste Giraud's *Achilles* (1789), Antonia Canova's *Endymion* (1819–1822), and Paul Akers's *Dead Pearl Diver* (1857).[6] Samuel F. B. Morse's *The Dying Hercules* (1812) offers one instance of this pose in US painting.[7] The frequency of the dying-male pose might owe to an early-nineteenth-century sentimental fascination and preoccupation with death and mortality.[8] Yet, while this may be more the case in images of women and children, the image of a dying male in antebellum US culture raises a set of issues concerning white male authority and power. On this point Abigail Solomon-Godeau's argument is useful: "It may well be the case that the manifest preoccupation with perfect male bodies that are at the same time threatened, symbolically castrated, or dead speaks both to (and of) a defensive aggrandizement of masculinity and the concomitant acknowledgement of its vulnerability—the threats that assail it both materially and psychically" (97). In the case of *Dying Tecumseh*, and its stylistic and cultural peers, the white male fear of vulnerability would find origin in the forces of market change, democratization, and domestic realignments especially prevalent in the early nineteenth century. Kasson argues that the power of such images of vulnerability "spoke to the concerns of both an older economic elite and a rising business class on the brink of a period of social and economic transformation" (18). The image of the dying male, then, not only conveys a fascination or confrontation with mortality but captures a potent symbol of masculine vulnerability. With an Indian male as the subject, such vulnerability might be displaced onto the other, insulating the white male audience from anxieties of disempowerment or weakness. The dying Indian functions as a projection of white male anxieties, as well as effecting the abstraction of a concrete threat into the realm of aesthetics and the imagination.

While such ideological functions of the dying Indian make this figure an attractive symbol for white males, the physical presence of that Indian male body raises a troubling relationship between it and the male spectator. The statue's three-dimensional concreteness as a physical entity supplies a physical presence that is not as available in painting. The physical presence emphasized by the sculpture's own presence implies the actuality of the Indian's physical self, that ever-looming threat constantly depicted and imagined in American culture, a physical threat of violence or of disruption of a national mythology of "progress" and "manifest destiny." Such implications of the sculpture's physicality become muted, though, via the form and operation of the gaze upon the sculpture. The form of marble or stone freezes the Indian body, creates a stasis that hollows the Indian subject of agency. The operation of the gaze further removes agency of the subject, because the sculpture makes the Indian male's body accessible and available to the white male viewer's gaze. In this aspect the male is "nude" in the sense that John Berger describes it: "To be nude is to be seen naked by others and yet not recognized for oneself. A naked body has to be seen as an object in order to become a nude. . . . Nudity is placed on display" (54). The Indian male body is nude in this sense: it is on display as an object, not as a subject. In this way the Indian male is available to white males' gaze and possession. Thus, *The Dying Tecumseh* erases the physical threat and particularity of an Indian male body (his potential aggression and/or attractiveness) while making that same body available as a symbolic object of white manhood and its own sense of entitlement. This simultaneous erasure and objectness of the Indian male body demonstrates the dynamic of embodiment and disembodiment discussed above.

This artistic dis/embodiment found in sculptures by Pettrich and others detaches and obfuscates white male attraction to an Indian male body. Russ Castronovo's model of "necro citizenship" is especially relevant in this regard. Castronovo argues that "necro citizenship" is "a logic of incorporation and discorporation hostile to some historical bodies, but also erotically bound to the rigidity and corporeality of others" (17). As incorporeal historical bodies, Native persons possess no political weight and thus become available as symbolic figures. But as symbolic models for white manhood, these Indian male bodies become bound, erotically or sympathetically, to white males in a connection that alleviates the troubling exigencies of an Indian's, like Tecumseh's, corporeal existence while maintaining enough of his reality to form a stable and comprehensible symbol for white manhood. Similarly, one could look to Judith Butler's "derealization of the 'Other,'" in which "it is neither alive nor dead, but interminably spectral" (qtd. in Byrd xviii). In her examination of the function of indigeneity in American colonialism, Jodi Byrd modifies Butler's "derealization" (originally conceived in regard to post-9/11 conditions) to argue that "this process of derealization . . . has been functioning in Atlantic and Pacific 'New Worlds' since 1492" (xviii). This dis/embodiment paradigm is not isolated to any one period of US history. The representations of Indianness existent in the nineteenth century persist in their power and their reach into the wide array of fictions of Indians and the frontier that populate American culture into the twentieth century and beyond. These examples from sculpture vividly illustrate the dynamic of Indian symbolism that erases and preserves, disembodies and embodies. This symbolic dynamic finds potent life in literature, too, especially in the work of James Fenimore Cooper and Francis Parkman.

The examples of Indians depicted as sculpture in the neoclassical style in the early nineteenth century demonstrate the power of such depiction to simultaneously embody and disembody the subject. This same dynamic is also present in the literature of the period. Two prominent works, among many, that focus on the Indian during this time are Cooper's *The Last of the Mohicans* (1826) and Parkman's *The Oregon Trail* (1849). In one vivid example, Cooper implements the rhetoric of classical sculpture to describe Uncas. When the travelers have settled in the Glenn's Falls hideout, they are able, for the first time, "to view the marked lineaments of either of their Indian attendants" (61). Uncas receives an extended portrait in this section that accentuates his aesthetic appeal with "the bold outline of his high, haughty features, pure in their native red; or the dignified elevation of his receding forehead, together with all the finest proportions of a noble head, bared to the generous scalping tuft" (61). Preceding this description of his face are terms connoting an aristocratic physiognomy: "high, haughty," "dignified elevation," and "noble"—Uncas appears in a white man's hunting shirt that "more than usually screened" his body. The concealed body paradoxically emphasizes a potential revealed body, since Cooper implies that usually Uncas's body would be uncovered. The viewer's curiosity is aroused, then, in the suggestion of what is concealed but could be revealed. To circumvent this spectatorial curiosity, the narrative shifts the gaze from Uncas's concealed body to his bare face. All the while, this description of Uncas invokes characteristics associated with classical physiognomy. Alice sees Uncas with the "free air and proud carriage as she would have looked upon some precious relic of Grecian chisel, to which life had been imparted by the intervention of a miracle" (61).

Cooper's depiction of Uncas in this way appears to have been a predictable choice. D. H. Lawrence quotes Mrs. Cooper on her husband's depiction of his characters: "It was a matter of course . . . that he should dwell on the better traits of the picture rather than on the coarser and more revolting, though more common points. Like West, he could see Apollo in the young Mohawk" (54). According to Lawrence, Uncas was "Adonis rather than Apollo" (62). Cooper's classicization of the Indian is not a secret.

The obviousness of the classical in Cooper's description of Uncas does not lessen the rhetorical impact of the Indian as sculpture. Likened to a "precious relic," Uncas figures as a rare or ancient artifact of a forgotten or antique past. Aligning Uncas with classical sculpture freezes him in a prehistory; this living Indian male body finds articulation in the text only as a static body of the past. This stasis of Uncas's body finds life, then, only in the "intervention of a miracle"; that is, an Indian body is a priori lifeless or immobile and requires the intervention of an external force to provide that body with life, humanity, or civility. Most importantly, this association of Uncas with Grecian sculpture aligns him with a white classical aesthetic. As Kirk Savage has demonstrated, scientific racism of the early nineteenth century appealed to classical sculpture as a model of evolved, white superiority, "an authenticating document of a normative white body" (9). Cooper casts Uncas's facial features in this classical mold. One incentive for doing so is the idea of the "noble savage," that in an uncorrupted state, humans possess an aesthetic perfection. Another important aspect of Uncas's appearance as a "relic of Grecian chisel" applies to Heyward's participation as spectator.

Heyward's view articulates itself through the lens of Alice's gaze. Succeeding Alice's gaze, Heyward sees Uncas as even above the "perfection of form" that he was accustomed to seeing among Indians, such that he "openly expressed his admiration at such an unblemished specimen of the noblest proportions of man" (61). It is important and necessary that Alice's linkage of Uncas to classical sculpture comes before Heyward's admiration. Alice, as a female, safeguards Heyward's observation of Uncas's beauty. Alice "gazes"—recognizes the male beauty—while Heyward merely corroborates what Alice has seen. Alice acts as an intermediary between Uncas and Heyward in terms of the gaze. In addition she frames the gaze in terms of classical structure so that this white admiration of an Indian body occurs in the language of aesthetic commentary. This process of gazing at the Indian male, then aligning him with classical aesthetics, performs a disembodiment. That is, Uncas appears as a physical body whose actual physical presence is mediated by aesthetic discourse and a focus on "the finest proportions" of his form. In short, Heyward is able to "openly express" his admiration because Alice's female gaze intercedes for his own, while the aesthetic frame pardons his idealization of another male, who is also an Indian.

To see more clearly how Uncas's classical appearance makes him an object of suitable admiration, one might refer to Magua's first appearance and how Cooper presents this villainous Indian to the viewer. Magua has "an air of neglect about his person" (20). This neglect of appearance devolves into an appearance of chaos:

> The colors of the war paint had blended in dark confusion about his fierce countenance, and rendered his swarthy lineaments still more savage and repulsive than if art had attempted an effect, which had been thus produced by chance. His eye alone, which glistened like a fiery star amid lowering clouds, was to be seen in its state of native wildness. For a single instant, his searching and yet wary glance met the wondering look of the other, and then, changing its direction, partly in cunning and partly in disdain, it remained fixed, as if penetrating the distant air. (20)

The racially inflected "swarthy lineaments" connotes Magua as aesthetically unpleasing. He has not the classical order and proportion of Uncas. Instead, his war paint spreads over his face in "dark confusion." The racial inflection of "dark" compounded with "confusion" creates Magua as an image of Indian "savagery": his appearance works as a code of his "savagery" and thus his villainy. Whereas Uncas's ability to rise above such "savagery" is codified in his "Grecian chisel[ed]" features, Magua is a vivid example of Indian "savagery." In fact, Magua's face is incomprehensible by art: "still more savage and repulsive than if art had attempted an effect" (3). Art, even if attempting to represent disorder, still possesses order. Magua's painted face represents a disorder that not even art can replicate. Unlike the plain view of Uncas's face, the paint upon Magua's face conceals his visage, thus creating a barrier between this Indian and the viewer. This sense of barrier between Magua and his viewers heightens in the Indian's anonymity: he stands out only to "much more experienced eyes," and his adversarial gaze—his "wary glance"—meets and deflects the viewer's gaze. Magua is not a visual object of admiration. Therefore, Magua is neither described as a piece of sculpture nor aligned with classical beauty. The ideal Indian male is Uncas, and Cooper determines this idealization through the classical figuring of the heroic Uncas versus the disordered figuring of villainous Magua. Their physical features code their value. The villainous Indian is submitted to an aesthetic detachment, as if Cooper's description were an attempt to exorcise Magua via an appearance that refuses to adhere to artistic order. On the other hand, the heroic ideal is embodied in the physical ideal. The male body's physical perfection (here conveyed via classical form) signifies the male's heroic status. This point bears remembering as this study progresses later into its examination of comics and superheroes.

The Indian as physical ideal possesses much power in its embodiment of such admirable form. The physical ideal depicted as an Indian male body also presents a precariousness in its representation of admirable masculine qualities along with the threat of regressing to savagery. The admiration of the embodied ideal is accompanied by a reciprocal need to disassociate from that body so as to neutralize its potential threat. This tension between attraction to and rejection of the Indian body is apparent in Parkman's description of the Oglala that he visits in his journey west in *The Oregon Trail*.

The tension especially resides in two contrasting images that Parkman employs in describing Indian males: the dignity and beauty of "superb, naked figures" (254) and the more ominous "dark naked forms" (256). Robert Sheardy, for example, offers insight into this duality of the Indian body, arguing that "the visible native body" can represent dignity and strength along with barbarity and violence. His analysis of John Vanderlyn's painting *The Death of Jane McCrea* (1804) demonstrates how white depictions of Indian male bodies emerge in the early nineteenth century as markers of "savagery" and of freedom. The bare Indian physique operates as both attraction and repellant. Indian bodies can be both "superb" and "dark," admirable and threatening, in their naked forms. One aspect of the Indian male body that Parkman focuses the reader's gaze upon is the signs of the violent manhood (that is both "superb" and "dark") found upon that body.

The body of a male Indian not only acts as an attractive model of physical beauty but can display, too, marks of violent manhood: scars. Kongra-Tonga's scarred body, for instance, presents to Parkman a model of strength and bravery. He details the scars themselves, then their origins:

> I felt some curiosity to learn the history of the numerous scars on his naked body. . . . Each of his arms was marked as deeply gashed with a knife at regular intervals, and there were other scars also, of a different character, on his back and on either breast. They were the traces of those formidable tortures which these Indians, in common with a few other tribes, inflict upon themselves at certain seasons; in part, it may be, to gain the glory of courage and endurance, but chiefly as an act of self-sacrifice to secure the favor of the Great Spirit. (295)

Other scars, the reader learns, were received in war, since Kongra-Tonga "was one of the most noted warriors in the village," having killed fourteen men (295). The gashes and scars stand as markers of ritualized manhood that demonstrate the male's fortitude as well as the conscious decision by which the scars were obtained. As if noting the scars' existence is not enough, Parkman then continues to describe the making of those scars in graphic detail:

> The scars upon the breast and back were produced by running through the flesh strong splints of wood, to which ponderous buffalo-skulls are fastened by cords of hide, and the wretch runs forward with all his strength, assisted by two companions, who take hold of each arm, until the flesh tears apart and the heavy loads are left behind. (295)

The graphic nature of this passage performs a few functions: 1) demonstrating Kongra-Tonga's endurance and strength, his manhood; 2) possessing shock value for the prim Eastern readers that Parkman knew to be his audience; 3) affirming a perception of savagery among these Native peoples; and 4) demonstrating Parkman's own fortitude in being able to write down these gory details.

Kongra-Tonga's torture scars represent both an exalted manhood (the ability to endure pain and suffering) and degraded savagery (in terms of a perception that only barbaric peoples would commit themselves to such torture or that in their "uncivilized" state they do not feel pain as a white person would or are desensitized to violence). The mention of torture here also suggests a stock image of the Indian male who undergoes severe torture until death but mocks and derides his persecutors, singing his death song as flames lick about and consume him. Accounts of Indians and their behavior under torture circulated widely among white purveyors of Native cultures and were met with a mixture of shock and admiration. On this point, Uncas's own fortitude in the face of torture and death comes to mind within the context of this chapter. The Indian body that undergoes torture exemplifies a savage manhood, conveying by its scarred flesh the memento of its toughness and courage.

This tour of an Indian body full of the scars of battle and torture depicts a strong and fearless masculine body. Kongra-Tonga's body offers a "history" of endurance through torture and violent warriorship that garners Parkman's admiration while he notes the innocence of this Indian in describing his murderous exploits. This paradox of fierceness and simplicity suggests a sense of Parkman's ideal of manhood: a "man" is able to feel emotion while not expressing it. This ideal becomes clearer in a comment on the Hail-Storm: "[H]is handsome face had all the tranquility of Indian self-control; a self-control which prevents the exhibition of emotion without restraining the emotion itself" (325). The concept here is not to extinguish emotion but to restrain the expression of it. Kongra-Tonga can detail his scalpings and violent acts with the air of a child, and the Hail-Storm can feel an emotion while not exhibiting it. This emphasis on self-control of emotions offers a model for Parkman to identify with, a template of masculinity that is stoic but passionate.

While the Hail-Storm represents a manly ideal of self-control, he also suggests to Parkman a disturbing aspect of Indian male manhood: predation upon other men. Parkman says that upon first seeing the Hail-Storm he had just emerged from boyhood to manhood (325). Since then the Hail-Storm's hunting prowess had gained him a favorable reputation among the women and the men. The one milestone that the Hail-Storm has yet to perform is killing another man. This act, it seems, keeps him from enjoying full manhood. Parkman observes that "the handsome smooth-faced boy burned with a keen desire to flesh his maiden scalping-knife and I would not have encamped alone with him without watching his movement with a distrustful eye" (326). The physical threat of the Hail-Storm is evident here. While he is physically admirable, he is also bent on gaining his first kill. Parkman combines in the Hail-Storm an ambiguous mixture of admiration and fear. To counteract this ambiguity, or to mitigate the threat, Parkman employs language that objectifies Indian male bodies, specifically in the language of art and sculpture.

The objectification of Indian male bodies allows Parkman to detach himself from their real presence, the disembodiment through embodiment that has been evident in this chapter's examples. Mahto-Tatonka the younger finds "favor in the eyes of the fair, [yet] he was no dandy" (206). He does not dress extravagantly in "gaudy blanket and glittering necklaces" but allows "his statue-like form limbed like an Apollo of bronze, to win its way to favor" (206). This description of Mahto-Tatonka's physicality embodies both intimation and detachment: Parkman's language conveys admiration of this Indian's handsome and manly form, but he is "statue-like," and so these words then take on the aspect of objective art criticism. This comparison to statues continues in another passage, when Parkman observes warriors on horseback and describes them as "equestrian statues" (210) or when, upon observing a warrior standing by a tree, he describes a visual tour of that Indian's body:

> Your eyes may trace the whole of his graceful and majestic height, and discover no defect or blemish. With his free and noble attitude, with the bow in his hand, and the quiver at his back, he might seem, but for his face, the Pythian Apollo himself. Such a figure rose before the imagination of West, when on first seeing the Belvidere in the Vatican, he exclaimed, 'By God, a Mohawk!'" (211)

Parkman both creates an intimate connection, visually, with this Indian, and at the same time detaches himself as viewer through the use of the second person. On the printed page, it is not Parkman himself whose eyes trace the height of this Indian male body (although in actuality, it was). In this description, Parkman assigns the gaze to the reader: "your eyes." This gaze creates intimate visual contact with the Indian warrior, scanning his whole body, but Parkman sublimates that intimacy by diverting attention to the Pythian Apollo and West's Apollo Belvedere statement. Parkman's allusion to West draws on the patterns of embodiment and disembodiment of the Indian male body in art that are central to this analysis.

In his work on monuments and race in the United States, Savage shows how the Apollo Belvedere "constituted nothing less than a benchmark in the concept of the human" (9). In terms of race, Savage argues that the Apollo Belvedere in US culture served as an ideal of whiteness, especially as opposed to the animalistic qualities of the "Negro" (9–10). When Indians appear in sculpture, however, this racial division does not hold. Indians were often based sculpturally on classical models: for instance, Henry Kirke Brown's *Choosing of the Arrow* (1849) and the sculptures by Pettrich and Crawford discussed above. Savage attributes this difference of treatment between Native Americans and African Americans to the dividing line of slavery (14). Werner Sollors argues that this portrayal of Indians was "connected to republicanism, and it conveyed to American culture a touch of Roman antiquity" (117–18). I would argue from these two critics that Indian sculpture worked to indemnify white manhood. The very whiteness of many of these Indian sculptures reflects the traversing of racial lines between Indian and white. This blurring of the racial line, though, effects a greater need to detach further and objectify Indians. As statues, Indians work as completely symbolic figures with no flesh-and-blood exigencies that might adversely affect white imaginings of Indians. Aligning Indian males with the Apollo Belvedere does not ultimately elevate them racially, although that potential might exist, but it works to align white US males with a classical past and an ideal whiteness. When Indian bodies are whitened through sculpture (literally, in some cases), they work to represent white manhood and its connection to a Romanesque model of life and governance.

Parkman seeks to align and identify himself with these Indian models of manhood, yet in so doing he must acknowledge their admirable qualities. Such acknowledgment, however, blurs the line between objective observation and attraction. Therefore, the safest route through this conundrum is to turn these Indians into artifacts or artistic objects, into statues. Kim Townshend too notices this move in Parkman and points to it as "the image of manhood [that] Parkman finally set before himself, one with no life in it, that of the heroic man as statue. It was the best form to take in the face of danger from without or in response to the irritability within" (110).

Ultimately, a fantasy about Indian manhood emerges here that in one way might be best described by Bernard DeVoto. He writes, "Weakness did not enervate their knees, an objectless panic did not surge up in them, their minds had no depths of self-suspicion, they felt no dread that they might not be whole" (297). These depictions of Indian male bodies redeem white manhood through offering an alternative to the emasculating world of white US culture, with its materialism, domestic entanglements, and democratic leveling. As Parkman famously declares in *Conspiracy*, "the Indian is hewn out of rock" (389). He is "stamped . . . with a hard and stern physiognomy. Ambition, revenge, envy, jealousy, are his ruling passions; and his cold temperament is little exposed to those effeminate voices which are the bane of milder races" (387). The Indian male body represents a hard manhood that withstands those influences that might weaken it. This imagery of rock and sculpture also produces "the Indian" as changeless; "he" will not take to "civilization," and "it is this fixed and rigid quality which has proved his ruin" (389). So while the Indian male's stony ruggedness makes for an admirable model of manhood, it also separates Indians racially. They must be left behind in their archaic ways, because they cannot change and adapt to the times. This depiction justifies Indian removal and genocide. If Indians are "destined" to disappear, what, then, of their bravery and strength? How might the white society that views itself as following in the wake of the vanishing Indian preserve those qualities of the Indian viewed as worth preserving? Playing Indian seems to be the solution, but this performance occurs through a carefully orchestrated dynamic of connection and detachment, of ironic performance of Indianness enacted by a circuitous dynamic of embodiment and disembodiment.

Thus far, this chapter has explored the depiction and utilization of the Indian male body as a vehicle of attraction and rejection, of admiration and disdain. To further view this dynamic at work, I return now to the figure of Tecumseh as an example of the heroic Indian that embodies the sought-after qualities of white manhood developed in the absence of the actual person of Tecumseh. Tecumseh's actual absence gives rise to his figurative presence. The wealth of literature and art that surrounds the Tecumseh figure attests to its power in US culture. Tecumseh's significance to this chapter's argument has been touched upon above, but this section will explore more deeply the function of the Tecumseh mythos in US culture and its implications for the significance of the Indian male as ideal of white manhood.

A storied procession of Tecumseh iconology exists in US culture following his death in the War of 1812, so it would be helpful to survey his presence in white US culture. In doing so, I will briefly analyze William Emmons's play *Tecumseh* (1836), which depicts Tecumseh as a foil to white male heroism. Emmons's play presents an anti-Tecumseh, as it were, dispelling the heroic stature of the man that circulated so widely in the mainstream culture at the time. This negative treatment provides a telling contrast to the more typical heroic representation of Tecumseh in works such as Colton's poem.

Tecumseh's appeal in white US culture operates based on an erasure of the historical Tekamthi, who, as a British ally, opposed the United States during the War of 1812, and who sought an Indian confederacy that could potentially challenge US expansion. Yet Tekamthi's efforts for an Indian confederacy also supply one reason for the appeal of Tecumseh. As R. David Edmunds observes, "His attempts at political and military unification seemed logical to both the British and the Americans. . . . Although such a system of centralized leadership seemed foreign to the Indians, it was common within the framework of Anglo-American political traditions" (224). Tekamthi's advocacy of such a centralized and strong leadership causes another biographer, John Sugden, to title one of his sections "The Federalist." Tekamthi's efforts possessed nuanced and complex political intricacies for Native tribal governance and British and US plans.[9] Yet the mythical Tecumseh that emerges in antebellum white US culture is stripped of these historical complications and comes to represent a hero, an ideal man, and a true patriot (though for the "wrong" side). Tekamthi's historical dissonance is painted over by that Tecumseh iconology.

Tekamthi's reputation was considerable during his lifetime and only increased after his death as a Tecumseh iconology developed. Benjamin Drake in the 1841 biography wrote that Tecumseh was "uniformly self-possessed and with the tact and ease of deportment which marked the pact of the heart, and which are falsely supposed to be the result of civilization and refinement only" (qtd. in Seelye 157). In 1878 Elizabeth Eggleston Seelye called Tecumseh "the finest flower of the aboriginal American race" (318). For Seelye, Tekamthi's greatness came at the wrong time: "[H]ad his lot fallen to him in a more favorable time, [he] might have produced results more permanent than a confederacy of savages" (327). Seelye acknowledges his patriotism but deems it "mistaken" (326). Bil Gilbert cites an *Indiana Centinel* editorial written soon after Tekamthi's death that trumpets his greatness: "Every schoolboy in the Union now knows Tecumseh was a great man. His greatness was his own, unassisted by science or education. As a statesman, warrior and patriot, we shall not look on his like again" (qtd. in "The Dying Tecumseh and the Birth of a Legend," 1). This excerpt offers another clue to Tecumseh's appeal to a white audience: this vision of a self-made man ("unassisted by . . . education") and combination of noble masculine roles ("a statesman, a warrior, and a patriot") creates a Tecumseh as symbol of American manhood: self-sufficient, noble, loyal, and strong. Edmunds offers two additional factors in Tecumseh's appeal: 1) his efforts for confederacy fit into white plans for Natives, and 2) he fulfills the conception of the noble savage (189).

As with other heroes detached from their historical actuality, much apocrypha (all false) has built up around Tecumseh: that he was lighter colored than other Shawnee and that he had a romance with a white woman are not true (Edmunds 190). These two elements of the Tecumseh myth obviously indicate an attempt to accept an Indian as a hero for whites by minimizing racial difference. This effort to Europeanize Tecumseh appears in this statement from E. G. Randall, a nineteenth-century historian: "Tecumseh, though a savage of the forest, evidenced in his character a rare combination of Italian craft, Spanish revengefulness, German patience and Anglo-Saxon fortitude" (qtd. in Gilbert 212). This "whitening" of Tecumseh is an essential part of stripping away the historical dissonance of race in order to create Tecumseh as an appropriate white hero. A process that has obviously succeeded, given the amount of material that has been published about him in white culture: Sugden estimates at least one hundred full-length treatments and even more shorter pieces (ix). Various literary titles in the United States during the antebellum period took up Tecumseh as their major character.[10]

One striking example of the power of Tecumseh in US political culture occurs in William Emmons's *Tecumseh.* This play was written solely as a campaign advertisement for Richard Mentor Johnson (who allegedly killed Tecumseh) in his successful run for vice-presidency. Sugden writes, "In Baltimore an Indian outfit, said to have been worn by Tecumseh in battle; a British standard captured on the occasion; and a pistol alleged to have belonged to Johnson were exhibited to accompany the drama" (397). In a very real way, Tecumseh's death fuels the career of this white politician. Furthermore, the conjoining of Tecumseh with the British through the artifacts of an Indian outfit and a British flag works to emphasize and strengthen Johnson's "Americanness" and Tecumseh's foreignness. In the same vein, William Henry Harrison ran his campaigns based on his battles with Tecumseh and the British.[11] An 1840 campaign poster features these events in pictures framing a portrait of Harrison in full military regalia upon horseback. Both Johnson and Harrison based their political influence upon their military reputations, and their encounters with Tecumseh formed a central moment for each man that proved his

American manhood.[12] Johnson's disputed claim as Tecumseh's slayer drove his political career, one of the slogans of his supporters being "Rumpsey, dumpsey, Colonel Johnson killed Tecumseh" (Richter 236). This political manipulation of Tecumseh's death affirms the power that white imaginings of dead Indians possessed (or the power of dead Indians to possess whites). Emmons's *Tecumseh* provides a striking example of the political weight that a dead Indian could carry, not for himself but for the furtherance of white men's political authority.

The representation of Tecumseh in this play contrasts remarkably from the epic heroic figure evidenced in examples discussed above, such as Colton's poem. Where Colton's Tecumseh speaks with eloquence and poetic elocution, Emmons's Tecumseh speaks in the broken English popularly imagined by whites as "Indian talk." In one exchange with the British Colonel Chambers, Tecumseh speaks: "Me hold my passion down, to hear what you shall speak.—Me—now (*he struggles to subdue his feelings*) say on" (I: ii, 86–88). Passionate and rash, quick to violence and difficult to subdue, the Tecumseh portrayed here is the worst villainous Indian. And while he occupies the role of villain, the British ally and American foe, he also conveys admirable masculine traits. In one instance he refuses an offer of a military sash and epaulets as "pale face trinkets," saying to the giver, General Proctor, "Give them to some squaw, for which *perhaps*, she'll hide thee in her wigwam. Me not the trash accept. 'Twould cramp my limbs in native wildness free. My father taught to cast a way such gifts" (IV: iii, 40–44). Following in a paternal tradition, Tecumseh rejects the decorations as seductions and as constraining to his "native wildness free." This particular comment asserts a savage masculinity, but it is not the preferred masculinity in this play.

Johnson, not Tecumseh, offers the preferred vision of manhood. Where Johnson is eloquent and noble, Tecumseh is savage and horrific. This excerpt from Johnson's speech details the enemy's atrocities: "See! Hath not the foe raised the murderous tomahawk against us! Violence! To nature! Sacrilege to Heaven! Deeds past a name! Our fathers massacred, —mothers butchered, while singing to their cradles. The snowy bosoms of our virgins stained with blood—the skulls of sleeping infants" (V: I, 23–28). Emmons routes Johnson's speech through familial terms here; it is for the murder of fathers, mothers, and infants, as well as virgins, that these men must fight. Johnson concludes the speech with a patriotic fantasy of death in battle, a death that would take the soldier to heaven to stand beside Washington— "saint his name with Washington on high"—and the final image is of an eagle screaming in the sky as these men "[c]harge on with death—charge on with chivalry!" (V: I, 34–38). Chivalric death-bringers, these men.

Tecumseh's speech contrasts in its savage language and blood-thirst and is short enough to quote in full: "Now, Red man, raise and pour thy spirit forth. Begirt the field with lightning! Glut thy wrath! Make drunk earth with blood! Let each his path choke with dead men's skulls! As thunder speaks above tempest—lift—so lift thy voice on high, and, to the shrieking ghosts hold converse!" (V: iii, 1–6). While Johnson and Tecumseh set out to do exactly the same thing (destroy the enemy), Emmons casts each of these men's goals in starkly different lights. Johnson invokes murdered family members and patriotic glory. Tecumseh, on the other hand, speaks of no higher purpose; his brief speech constitutes their purpose as only to spill blood and pile up skulls. While Johnson's men might commune with Washington in sainthood, Tecumseh's men will converse with "shrieking ghosts."

The play's end offers a remarkable contrast to the tragic death finales as famously seen in John Augustus Stone's *Metamora, or, The Last of the Wampanoags* (1829). Tecumseh's death offers a sensational tableau, and, like Metamora, he delivers a curse upon whites: "Great Spirit! Thy Red Children's cause avenge! Thick curses light upon the white man's head! Hold not thy thunders back! Blast him with all thy lightnings! May the hawk flap his wing over his steaming carcass! The wolf lap up his—his—blood! The Red man's course is run; I die—the last of all my race" (V: vi, 6–12). Unlike in *Metamora*, the curtain does not drop here. The white characters learn that Tecumseh is dead and that Johnson still lives. They then gather around Johnson, and the play's heroine, Lucinda, places an evergreen garland on his brow. All cheer, "The Champion of his Country!!" (V: vi, 35). In the finale the band plays "Hail Columbia" as the Goddess of Liberty descends, enveloped in the Revolving Star of Columbia, bearing in her hand the Star Spangled Banner. Tecumseh's dying words fade away as the strains of patriotic pageantry assert this play's message in no uncertain terms. While plays like *Metamora* that give its Indian hero the last words might be met with applause bordering on ambiguity,[13] Emmons makes sure that the audience gets the point here: white US men will triumph; the "Red man's course is run," and Tecumseh is the last of his race (as is every Indian who dies on stage or on page before and after).

The figure of Tecumseh exemplifies the convoluted dynamic of admiration and repulsion found in the depiction of the Indian male in US culture. Like Uncas, like Parkman's Indians, Tecumseh modulates between a threatening presence and a heroic absence. The Indian male's physical actuality must be marginalized because of its potential to challenge and resist white American hegemony, yet that physical actuality possesses admirable characteristics: strength, admirable physique, the body of an Apollo. The social physicality becomes disembodied then. The actual person, the historical actuality is absented: this is disembodiment. The figurative physicality remains in the form of art and writing, in the form of image and visual iconography: this is embodiment. It is this visual embodiment that is key to understanding the succession of the imagined Indian in the following years in the fictions of dime novels, film, and, most importantly for this book, comics. As the imagined Indian male body provides one track of rhetoric and ideology for white manhood, so too does the frontiersman, which might be considered a figurative counterpart to the Indian male. The white frontiersman, as exemplified in the figure of Daniel Boone, also possesses a sometimes contradictory complex of image and symbol articulating masculine American ideals. Whereas the imagined Indian works as an othered image of attraction and threat, the frontiersman operates as a more perceivably sympathetic image, although also possessing its own set of caveats and threats for an idealized American manhood.

## CHAPTER TWO

# THE WHITE FRONTIERSMAN, MANHOOD, DOMESTICITY, AND LOYALTY

THE PREVIOUS CHAPTER FOCUSES ON HOW THE INDIAN MALE BODY IS isolated as an admirable physical model, an exemplar of strength and beauty that finds expression through classical rhetoric and art. The heroic Indian male complements another powerful figure in American culture: the white frontiersman. This particular figure appears in many guises, but the one that is most significant for this study is the white frontiersman who has been adopted by Indians or who appropriates Indian ways. Following from the frontiersman mythos of Daniel Boone, characters such as Hawkeye, of *The Last of the Mohicans*, exemplify the white man who lives among the Indians and learns their ways. This living and learning is an appropriation, as opposed to assimilation. This appropriation is often expressed rhetorically as a strengthening of white masculinity, enabling the male to embody more fully the idealized traits that characterize manhood. This chapter takes a closer look at the white male protagonists in such stories and their relationship with the "Indian ways," examining Boone and Hawkeye as figures of the heroic and ideal frontiersman. The negative foil to this figure is the white renegade, with Simon Girty the most infamous example, and the chapter closes with an examination of how the white renegade challenges the notion of the white male playing Indian, especially in concert with the threat of crossing over into savagery.

Boone's symbolism has been interpreted in various ways, a fact that Henry Nash Smith draws attention to when he asks, "Which was the real Boone—the standard-bearer of civilization and refinement, or the child of nature who fled into the wilderness before the advance of settlement?" (55). Forty years after Smith, Elizabeth Johns reiterates this question: "The major interpretative question about Boone as symbol of American pioneers was whether he—and by extension, the nation—was civilization's 'advance guard' or whether in fact he was a natural man of the wilderness who could not stand to be 'hemmed in'" (133). Richard Slotkin reads Boone as an "archetypal hero of the American frontier . . . the man who made the wilderness safe for democracy" (*Regeneration* 268–69). Boone, here, is a "myth-hero" manifesting a national vision of the United States. Richard Drinnon sees Boone as straddling the line between white and Indian: "With the build-up of accretions the legendary Boone had become more definitely a double: half-empire builder and half white-Indian" (161). Daniel Herman argues that Boone's importance lies in his role as hunter, a role that carried with it important meaning for establishing an "indigenous identity" based on middle-class masculinity possessing self-reliance, singular individualism, and liberal competitiveness. As is evident, Boone as a representative or symbolic figure has undergone a variety of interpretations, a phenomenon that began even while he was still alive.

The multiplicity of "Boones" owes much to the tension that exists between the legend and the actual person. For example, the Boone *legend* figures an Anglo white identity that resists any intermixture or influence from non-British, nonwhite cultures. Yet Boone's life runs a very different course. His adoption by the Shawnees of the Ohio Valley in 1778 and his Spanish naturalization in 1799 are two vivid examples of the historical Boone's crossing cultural lines that resists the singular insularity of an Anglo white identity. Boone's life represents an amalgamation of multiple national and racial identities beyond the Anglocentric one that would come to define the "American." Boone's legend testifies to his significance as a central representation of American identity. From biographies to fiction to art and sculpture to dime novels to comics to television and film, Boone possesses a continuous figurative presence in US culture from the late eighteenth century into the twentieth century. How this figurative presence alters to meet the cultural expectations of American culture through the years provides a rich illustration of the persistence and adaptability of Boone as symbol.

Perhaps the seeds of the Boone legend can be found in John Filson's 1784 ghost autobiography and Henry Trumbull's 1786 abridgement. Afterward, a host of works on Boone appear in the early nineteenth century: Daniel Bryan's epic poem *The Mountain Muse* (1813), James Fenimore Cooper's Leatherstocking Tales (1823–1841), Timothy Flint's *Biographical Memoir of Daniel Boone* (1833), Robert Montgomery Bird's *Nick of the Woods* (1837), John Mason Peck's *Daniel Boone* (1846), and Emerson Bennett's *The Renegade: A Historical Romance of Border Life* (1848). Flint's popular biography is exemplary in its carving out a representative Boone from the historical figure.[1] John Mack Faragher shows that Flint's biography "went through fourteen editions before 1868, making it the most widely read biography of antebellum America, second only to Filson's narrative in creating the image of Boone in the popular imagination" (323). Another telling statement comes from historian Marshall Fishwick (1953): "Flint was Boone's Parson Weems" (qtd. in Faragher 324). This biography was republished in 1854 as *The First White Man of the West, or the Life and Exploits of Col. Daniel Boone.* This new title certainly lends a stronger racial character to the Boone ideal. Flint, following in the wake of Filson and Trumbull, makes the strongest contribution in setting the tone and character of the mythical Boone. Flint's biography offers a vivid example of the interplay between the disparate elements of Boone's historical life and the making of an iconic Boone.

Daniel Boone's status as a legendary and symbolic figure begins most notably with John Filson in 1784. Among others, William H. Truettner asserts that Filson's biography spawns the succeeding popular images of Boone (41). Filson's account, and Henry Trumbull's 1786 abridgement, sparked the popular circulation of Boone's story. Kent Ladd Steckmesser argues that Filson's "sketch made Boone the representative hero of the trans-Appalachian frontier and helped to define the tradition of the Western hero" (4). John Filson's *Kentucke* includes as an appendix "The Adventures of Col. Daniel Boon." Faragher states that it did not go into a second edition, but Willard Rouse Jillson states that "it found so widespread a demand that within a decade, in one form or another, in first, second, or third editions or reprints, it spread . . . across the civilized portions of two continents, Europe and North America" (15). Perhaps in Europe, as Faragher says, it had this demand, and perhaps in the United States its demand did not increase until much later. Filson's book sold reasonably well but did not gain the popularity that Trumbull's abbreviated edition would. Faragher relates that Trumbull's emendation "has rarely been out of print in the more than two centuries since [it was published]. During Boone's lifetime, when people spoke of reading his narrative, they invariably referred to Trumbull's Boone, not Filson's" (6). Trumbull cuts the page count of Filson's original biography nearly in half, thus concentrating the Boone narrative into a version that would be variously repeated in succeeding narratives and biographies: exploring and settling Kentucky, the captivity and rescue of Boone's and Richard Callaway's daughters, Boone's captivity, and then various Indian battles through the Revolution and its resolution. In the early nineteenth century, biographers and writers would take up Boone's life to produce interpretations that reveal much about the surrounding culture's concerns with settlement and expansion. As Faragher relates, the images of Boone in the antebellum period ranged from civilizer to natural man to Indian killer.[2] In addition to these depictions, Boone as white Indian emerges as a source of fascination and consternation.

Boone's capture and adoption by the Shawnee in 1778 highlights his significance as a figure of American culture. These few months of his life are not only a standard milestone in the Boone biography—one that is depicted by most, if not all, treatments of his life—but a cultural touchstone of national and racial understanding, one that can, depending on the depiction, challenge, problematize, or affirm notions of whiteness and American character. The perception of his captivity and adoption varies in tone from text to text but usually remains sympathetic to Boone. The early telling of Boone's captivity can be understood concerning how those writers depict Native Americans. Filson presents a favorable view of Native society in general, while Trumbull departs from this approach to establish more firmly a Boone in opposition to Indians. The appendix following the autobiography in Filson's *Kentucke* is "Of the Indians." Here Filson describes the various Indian tribes in the Ohio Valley and their qualities. Filson dictates a common perception of Indians concerning equality and community: "Among the Indians, all men are equal, personal qualities being most esteemed. No distinction of birth, no rank, renders any man capable of doing prejudice to the rights of private persons; and there is no pre-eminence from merit, which begets pride, and which makes others too sensible of their own inferiority" (101). Filson's description of Indian society sounds like an ideal democratic republic where no citizen stands above another. Trumbull, on the other hand, offers no such salutary depictions of Indian society. Trumbull ends his account with a final paragraph that depicts a Boone who has suffered the deaths of male relatives at Indian hands:

> Two darling sons, and a brother, have I lost by savage hands, which have also taken from me 40 valuable horses and abundance of cattle. Many dark and sleepless nights have I spent, separated from the cheerful society of men, scorched by the summer's sun, and pinched by the winter's cold, an instrument ordained to settle the wilderness.—But now the scene is changed: Peace crowns the sylvan shade. (15)

The closing remarks Trumbull highlights in his Boone narrative encompass several significant points. The loss of family and property to Indians is the focus of this statement. It is not only a loss of family but the loss of males, two sons and a brother, those family members with the potential to extend the family line; the loss of family also correlates to a loss of property: horses and cattle. Boone too laments the separation from society. His purpose as settler is a lonely and difficult existence but one that has been ordained for him; Boone is but an instrument of Providence here. This picture depicts a savage existence at the hands of "savages." In this passage any happy memories of Shawnee kinship that Boone actually maintained[3] are supplanted by the turmoil and hardship of Indian cruelty and massacre of family and property. Trumbull distances Boone from the Indians.

Flint's maneuver to distance Boone from Indians furthers Trumbull's work. He argues that the settlers were not "demi-savages," as contemporary opinion has them, but "men of noble, square, erect forms, broad chests, clear, bright, truth-telling eyes, and of vigorous intellects" (107). Strengthened in their Christian communality, and not by a denial of inherited privilege as with Filson's Indians, Flint's settlers embody in their very physicality the marks of civilization, nobility, and evolution. Flint even finesses the case of Boone's historical captivity into ideological service when he qualifies Boone's adoption in its being for the sake of appearance only: "He soon became in semblance so thoroughly one of them . . . that he gained the entire confidence of the family into which he was adopted" (137). This interpretation of Boone's adoption becomes the prevalent one, and one that will be evident into the twentieth century in the comics' depictions of Boone's life. Flint articulates Boone's adoption as a taking on of Indian traits "in semblance," a superficial adaptation and not an essential conversion. Boone might seem an Indian on the outside, but his interior whiteness remains. In fact, Boone proves himself a natural superior to Indians even in their own culture. In *Indian Wars of the West* (1833), Flint relates that Boone, being "[m]ore expert at their own arts, than the Indians themselves, to fight them, and foil them, gave scope to the exulting consciousness of the exercise of his own appropriate and peculiar powers" (53). Boone's ability to become like "the Indians" does not convert him but works only to increase and strengthen the character he already possesses. Flint describes a supplementing of Boone's identity but no essential change; he keeps Indians at a distance: white settlers can be *like* them in some ways but *are not* them. The white settlers are not even "demi-savages," being much more evolved and civilized. In addition, even if a white frontiersman takes on Indian traits, he does so to strengthen himself, and to serve his nationalistic purpose (unless he allows himself to become corrupted, to become a renegade).

As can be seen, the ideological existence of Boone in these narratives navigates between white and Indian, "civilized" and "savage." Filson, Trumbull, and Flint negotiate a precariousness of frontier life, a precariousness that further suggests an overarching anxiety about the course and formation of a national identity. In the throes of settlement and westward expansion, the potential of an Anglo white nation, distinguished from European and Native cultures, performs an anxious balancing act in its attempt to maintain a seemingly stable, unchanging identity.

This ideological construction of Boone in literature and biographies finds amplification and affirmation in contemporary art. Some notable examples include Thomas Cole's painting *Daniel Boone Sitting at the Door of His Cabin on the Great Osage Lake, Kentucky* (1826); Enrico Causici's bas-relief *Conflict of Daniel Boone and the Indians, 1773* (1826–1827); Horatio Greenough's sculpture *The Rescue Group* (1837–1853); William Tylee Ranney's painting *Boone's First View of Kentucky* (1849); and George Caleb Bingham's painting *The Emigration of Daniel Boone with His Family from North Carolina to Kentucky* (1851–1852). The figure of Boone crystallizes in its various guises through the medium of these visual depictions, highlighting and extending the Boone image as constructed in written works. When one turns to visual representations of Boone, one can see the various formulations of Boone's representative status that operate to justify and abet westward expansion of the United States, specifically channeled into an Anglo white identity.

Boone's visual appearance has long possessed iconic features: the coonskin cap and buckskins might signify the generic frontiersman, but perhaps the immediate association for many is Daniel Boone (or Davy Crockett, to be fair). With these requisite visual features, the art of the nineteenth century reproduces the Boone figure, taking him through various roles: as natural man, as Indian killer, as white Indian, and as leader.

Boone as natural man is usually pictured as a loner within a larger and overwhelming landscape. Drawing from Rousseau's noble savage, this figure became prominent in Romantic circles. George Gordon Byron's reference to Boone in *Don Juan* (1821) secured Boone a place in the Romantic pantheon of heroes as natural man.[4] In US visual culture, one of the most exemplary instances of this natural man Boone occurs in Thomas Cole's *Daniel Boone Sitting at the Door of His Cabin on the Great Osage Lake, Kentucky* (1826) (Fig. 2.1). Cole's Boone is subordinated to nature; the painting's title indicates the preeminence of the setting, and the painting (much like Cole's oeuvre) emphasizes the grandiose splendor of the natural

Figure 2.1. Thomas
Cole. *Daniel Boone
Sitting at the Door of
His Cabin on the Great
Osage Lake, Kentucky.*
1826. Oil on canvas.
38 x 42 1/2 in. Mead
Art Museum, Amherst
College, Massachusetts.

environment with the frontiersman sitting in the foreground corner of a massive expanse of landscape. David Lubin argues that Cole's Boone "is a Byronic loner . . . [who] has shirked all society" (62). According to Faragher, Cole painted Boone over the drawing of an Indian (327). This composition process literally overlays an Indian with a white male, as well as confirming Boone's linkage to Indians in the natural-man incarnation. Boone as natural man represents the human being as but a smaller unit within the considerable realm of nature. The natural man interlocks with two other popular depictions: the Indian killer and the white Indian.

As Indian killer, Boone is detached from society as that brutal backwoodsman who eradicates the Indian threat to whites. Like Robert Montgomery Bird's Nathan Slaughter or the Indian hater of James Hall and Herman Melville's *The Confidence Man* (1857), Boone as Indian killer shuns society. In "The Metaphysics of Indian-Hating," Melville described this tendency: "With few companions, solitude by necessity his lengthened lot, he stands the trial—no slight one, since, next to dying, solitude rightly borne, is perhaps of fortitude the most rigorous test. . . . The sight of smoke ten miles off is provocation to one more remove from man, one step deeper into nature" (193). This statement echoes the apocryphal Boone quotation:

I fought and repelled the savages, and hoped for repose . . . was molested by interlopers from every quarter. Again I retreated to the region of the

Mississippi, but again those speculators and settlers followed me. Once more I withdrew to the licks of Missouri, and here at length I hope to find rest. But I was still pursued, for I had not been two years at the licks before a damned Yankee came and settled down within a hundred miles of me! (qtd. in Faragher 326)

Faragher rightly observes that statements such as this one that were attributed to Boone sidestepped the historical fact that he was dispossessed of his land and had to move against his will. This sidestepping demonstrates again the ideological maneuvering of Boone away from historical fact; his nomadic existence is due to his natural-man desire for freedom from society. At the same time, the Boone of this statement is an Indian killer, the warrior who hopes to find rest after his strenuous battles.

Boone as white Indian acts in a parallel fashion to the Indian killer; in fact, one might think of these two figures as two sides of the same coin. The historical Shawnee adoption of Boone generates an image of him as a white Indian. This Boone carries with it similar problems as the Indian killer for an ideological icon, as well as some problems confined to it. Both designations hinge on a perception of the white male as "savage": either through taking up Indian ways or through being the thin white line between "civilization" and "savagery." In both cases, the white male becomes "savage" in order to become Indian or to kill Indians. Both roles have some overlap with the natural man, but as a white Indian Boone's connection to nature routes through Indianness. Indian killing, like playing Indian, drives the white man further away from society and further into nature, further into "savagery." Causici's Boone is this "middle ground" frontiersman, who portrays "savage" traits while simultaneously fighting against the "savage."[5]

Causici's *Conflict of Daniel Boone and the Indians* presents an example of both the US appropriation of Italian art for the Capitol and Boone's prominence as a symbol of US white imperialism (Fig. 2.2). On the former point, this piece demonstrates the strong neoclassical style preferred in the early national period (as also discussed in chapter 1). The dependence upon Italian sculptors to decorate the Capitol, as well as the pervasive use of neoclassical style throughout the material culture of the early republic, signifies a larger cultural desire for order and containment. As some critics have argued, in neoclassical style one might detect a need to stabilize the social and political, especially following upon the combat of war and the conflict of constitutional ratification.[6] The employment of foreign, especially Italian, artists persisted until 1832, when Horatio Greenough was

Figure 2.2. Enrico Causici.
*Conflict of Daniel Boone and
the Indians.* 1826–1827.
Sandstone. US Capitol
Rotunda, above south door.

the first native-born American commissioned to sculpt for the Capitol (Castiello 67). The fascination with Italian art in the United States echoes West's encounter with the Apollo Belvedere, as well as the struggle by US white males to determine a national identity. Neoclassicism, in its rigid self-containment and modeled abstraction, offers a natural choice for white males who wish to define themselves as singular and individual yet modeled upon a central ideal of manhood. Embodying Boone in classical form moves his symbolic value toward that of civilizer and guardian of order.

Boone and the Indian stand as mirror opposites of each other, both upright, vertical pillars on each side of the frame. Boone does not touch the Indian, having a rifle in his left hand and a knife in the other. The Indian's right hand mirrors Boone's hand, both uplifted, the Indian signified as "savage" with his tomahawk; while Boone seemingly straddles that line

Figure 2.3. Horatio Greenough. *The Rescue*. 1837–1853. Marble. 141 x 122 in. Photograph taken before 1920, showing the work in situ to the right of the staircase on the east facade of the US Capitol. In storage since 1958.

using both the "civilized" rifle and the "savage" knife. The Indian's left arm stretches forward defensively, pushing Boone away. The two men's torsos, their bent legs, and the Indian's arm form a square. Though locked in conflict with the Indian, this Boone is in a position parallel to that Indian. Moreover, in this piece, Boone is admirable, somewhat uneasily perhaps, in his ability to "out-Indian" Indians. Boone's ability to appropriate the admirable skills of Indians makes him a heroic figure. The unease with this role proceeds from the risk of losing racial purity when white men play Indian. This fear not only suggests a diffusion of racialized authority but also operates as a fear of racial/national betrayal, as seen in historical figures like Simon Girty. As for the Indian killer, he is too brutal and violent, revealing an aspect of white racism that those in the East would rather not confront. Yet, although white Indians and Indian killers could not serve as appropriate models of an Anglo white identity, both were necessary to white expansion, implementing white settlement by the cross-cultural contact of white Indians and the eradication of Indian presence by Indian killers.

The potential unease that the Indian killer or white Indian might produce does not overwhelm the dominating message of the sculpture, though. It affirms Boone's symbolism as Anglo white "civilizer" and protector and guide of white expansion. Ultimately, the significance of Causici's Boone to my argument finds articulation in Susan Scheckel's reading of the sculpture. Describing the disjuncture between the event that Causici depicts (in which white settlers lost) and the artwork itself that insinuates a white victory, Scheckel argues that "it is the viewer's perception of the present and future destiny of the United States rather than the factual truth of the event recorded that provides . . . the meaning of this commemorative art" (135). In this same way, the disjuncture between the historical Boone (as Shawnee adoptee, as Spanish citizen, and as failed land speculator) and the legendary Boone (as vanguard of commerce and as a national representative) operates to provide a symbol of Anglo white identity that is more important to the nineteenth-century (and twentieth-century) consumers of Boone biographies and artwork than the actual life upon which they are based. The popular identification of Greenough's *The Rescue Group* with Boone testifies to an automatic association of the symbolic Boone with an anonymous Anglo white frontiersman.

While not intentionally a depiction of Boone, Greenough's *The Rescue Group* became associated with the frontiersman in audiences' minds (Fig. 2.3). Slotkin claims, "Without the least coaching from the sculptor, Greenough's work was popularly dubbed 'Daniel Boone Protects His Family,' testifying to the ubiquity of Boone as the archetypal American hero" (*Regeneration* 441).[7] Slotkin continues with this reading to demonstrate the symbol of Boone as rescuer and protector of civilization. Alone, *The Rescue Group* operates as a symbol of white imperialism and racism.

The sculpture presents the would-be Indian attacker as much a helpless victim as the cowering mother and child.[8] With arms outstretched in the grasp of a white male settler, the Indian is depicted in a submissive position. Greenough presents a heroic white male, a fully clothed giant to the barely dressed, smaller Indian. The tomahawk does not swing in menace but is held back by the visibly firm grip of the white male's hand around the Indian's wrist. The Indian's body bows backward in painful contortion as his left arm disappears between the bicep and chest of the white male. Here the Indian gazes upward with pleading as the white male resolutely and stoically looks down, set in his purpose. Behind the men, a mother cradles her child, her eyes watching both the action to her left and the babe in her arms. The composition of the figures is pyramidal: on bottom left, the mother–child pair, then upward to the white male's head, dominating and centering the scene, and back down to the bottom right where a dog stands, watching with anticipation. The Indian's frame is encompassed by the pioneer's frame.

In literary criticism two significant readings of *The Rescue Group* are relevant to my analysis.[9] Scheckel argues, similarly to Slotkin, that the female's and child's presence "is what motivates and justifies the violent conflict upon which the nation is built" (*Regeneration* 143, 144). Shirley Samuels differently interprets the female and child as the actual targets of the violent aggression between the two men: "In this alternate scenario, the frontiersman's threatened violence toward mother and child is inextricable from the violence directed toward the Indian who threatens them, and the Indian seems almost a surrogate victim, at once a threat to, and a substitute for, the family" (108). These differing interpretations open another avenue of interpretation for the sculpture: that the interlocking of white male and Indian, physically and through their mutual gaze, *excludes* the mother and child.[10] The white male neither protects nor attacks the representation of domesticity. Domesticity possesses marginal significance in this sculpture. What matters here is the white male's ability to overcome, in intimate, physical combat, the Indian.

As seen in the previous chapter, the Indian's body is an object of ambiguity between admiration and revulsion. While the Indian's lack of clothing serves primarily as marker of his savagery, the visible presence of his body foregrounds that "savage" body as both attractive and repulsive. This contradiction begins to emerge in Nathalia Wright's description of the Indian body:

> The treatment of the Indian, modeled with an almost Hellenistic delicacy, tends to obscure the original meaning of the work, since the figure thus seems to represent an advanced state of development. (This was Greenough's only use of the nude as other than a symbol of moral perfection, a reversal of technique which he seems not to have recognized.) (177)

Wright correctly suggests that the statue does not do what Greenough had intended. The Indian, who should represent a primitive, less advanced race, models classical beauty and form: a more suitable representation of "civility" than "savagery." The contradiction of product and intention emerges as well when considering the oppressive imagery of white domination in this statue. The relationship of white and Indian is one of subjugation and domination, but it is not wholly based on racial superiority, although that is the immediate impression. Greenough states that he "endeavoured to convey the idea of the triumph of the whites over the savage tribes, at the same time it illustrates the dangers of peopling the country" (*Letters* 221). This rings of the obvious. Yet he also describes this statue as being "a memorial of the Indian race, and an embodying of Indian character" (*Letters* 214). Greenough's intention here goes beyond simply creating a statue of racial superiority. For Greenough this difference between whites and Indians owes more to environment than inherent qualities. In "When We Speak of Man" (c. 1845–1846), he claims that "the Romans were neither braver nor better than other nations—They were only disciplined into better fighting machines" (45). With this example and others in the essay, one might understand Greenough's belief in nurture over nature, that social difference is a matter of environment, not inherent nature. Conquest occurs due to better training and learning. In *The Rescue Group*, the white frontiersman is a "better fighting machine" than the Indian is. Wright supports this reading to some extent: "His [the pioneer's] superiority is principally moral, least of all technological. It is to some degree, however, a racial superiority" (164). It is possible, then, to admire the Indian in this statue; he is not inherently inferior but the product of an environment and education that does not afford him a fighting advantage equal to the white male's. In this sense the Indian male remains an admirable object; he is a fighting machine of some regard, although ultimately falling in defeat. Of course, my argument on this point does not mean to marginalize the serious racist effect of the statue; it is better suited in storage than on the east facade of the US Capitol (from where it was removed in 1958). Yet Greenough's intention to embody Indian character as a classical body lends credence to a more nuanced understanding of the statue that takes into account the paradoxical white perception of Indians that oscillates between admiration and repulsion.

In the final two examples, paintings by Ranney and Bingham depict a Boone as scout and leader (see Figs. 2.4 and 2.5). In these paintings his symbolic status becomes that of the patriarch or leader. When Bingham first mentions the composition of *Emigration of Boone* to James Rollins in 1851, he claims, "The subject is a popular one in the West, and one which has never yet been painted" ("Letters" 21). At first glance, this seems a puzzling statement, since William Ranney's *Boone's First View of Kentucky* (1849) had appeared just two years before, but as Nancy Rash rightly demonstrates, Bingham's treatment of Boone is innovative in that

Figure 2.4. William Tylee Ranney. *Boone's First View of Kentucky.* 1849. Oil on canvas, 36 x 53 1/2 in. Gilcrease Museum, Tulsa, Oklahoma.

the frontiersman is no longer alone, fighting Indians, or in the company of men only: he is accompanied by his family in the transportation of white domesticity into the West. Before entering fully into the discussion of Bingham's painting in this regard, it would be appropriate to briefly examine Ranney's painting, for it offers a stark contrast to the domesticated Boone: Ranney's painting presents the fraternal Boone ensconced in male companionship on the frontier. Ranney's *Boone's First View of Kentucky* offers a vision of the white settler and his male comrades as commanders of the landscape, situated upon an overlook. While the Moses/Promised Land imagery of this painting (a theme shared with Bingham's painting) is obvious, what is most remarkable for my analysis is the depiction of male camaraderie. Dawn Glanz sheds light on this aspect in seeing this painting as an egalitarian scene in which Boone is not singled out from the group (18).[11] This particular interpretation depends upon seeing Boone not as the figure pointing to the landscape, but as the figure in center.[12] Even if this particular identification does not hold, Ranney does not single out this Boone with any significant marks; he is one of the men in a portrait of fraternal equality.

Unlike Ranney's painting and other preceding artistic depictions of Boone, Bingham's *Emigration of Boone* brings domesticity into the spotlight as a significant factor in white expansion.[13] Traditionally, this painting

Figure 2.5. George Caleb Bingham. *The Emigration of Daniel Boone*. 1851–1852. Oil on canvas, 36 1/2 x 50 1/4 in. Mildred Lane Kemper Art Museum, Washington University, St. Louis, Missouri.

has been read as a moment of manifest destiny, depicting the movement of white settlers westward variously as the Israelites to the Promised Land or the flight into Egypt with Boone as paternal guide. In this painting Boone is the guiding leader, right hand grasping the bridle of the white horse that carries Rebecca. He is the patriarch of the group, all other men diminished in size in comparison. The order of this painting draws attention most for my purposes here. Boone and his companions center the painting, and upon them the light falls. As Nancy Rash observes, "Contrasting with the horrific Salvatoran setting, the figures embodied a classical calm" (61).[14] What differentiates Bingham's painting from previous Boone visuals is the focused inclusion of women and children. As Rash argues, this painting depicts western settlement as dependent upon the presence of wives and children. Without them, expansion would be impossible. Rash specifically locates this belief in Bingham's Whig politics, viewing settlement as expansion of commerce that necessitated wives and children to build homes and, then, towns: "The painting of *Daniel Boone* then was a paean to the beginnings of familial settlement" (64). While Causici, Greenough, and Ranney offer more ambiguous depictions of Boone's status (his wrestling with Indians and appearance straddle the line between white "civility" and

Indian "savagery"), Bingham firmly places Boone as an Anglo white protector of domesticity (and therefore commerce and the market).[15]

This rooting of Boone in domesticity, too, poses him as the patriarch;
a status that the neoclassical style of the painting works to reinforce as a
republican paternal order based upon rational consensus. Various guide-
book descriptions of Causici's *Boone* lend credence to his image as calm
emblem of order.[16] Scheckel cites commentary from Jonathan Elliott (1830),
who remarks upon Boone's "cool intrepidity," and Robert Mills (1834), who
describes the "cool resolution and self possession" of Boone (qtd. 137). The
white male's self-containment and control stand in marked contrast to the
"ferocity and recklessness of the savage" (Mills) and "the frantic face and
vigorous frame of the savage" (Elliott). This gesture toward rational thought
as guide to governance and social order becomes especially important
in Boone's role as Indian killer. Lubin suggests this importance when he
argues, "The Boone of Flint and Greenough kills Indians not out of hate
but responsibility, and the Boone of Bingham does not kill at all, merely
guides. . . . This is the Daniel Boone of liberal consensus . . . a man driven to
do what he has to do not by ugly, primitive hate, but by a shining impulse
toward liberty for all (of his own race)" (83). The gesture toward "cool"
rational order and consensus exists not only in Boone's actions in these
works but also in the neoclassical style itself. For Bingham in particular,
his classicism, as Angela Miller argues, "served as a semantic code through
which to negotiate the competing claims of local and universal truth" (113).
This classicized Boone operates as a vision of the white male as patriarch.

As these various texts demonstrate, the Boone figure possesses much
symbolic potential that becomes expressed in a variety of ways: as natural
man, as Indian fighter, as white Indian, and as leader. Significant here is
that these various roles do not always reconcile with each other and thus
can produce dissonance in viewing the Boone mythos. Cooper's Hawkeye
might represent a more ideologically controlled construction of the Boone
mythos, more clearly drawn as the ideal white frontiersman, especially in
purging the historical particularities that accompany Boone. Hawkeye
embodies a version of the white frontiersman that draws from the Boone
mythos while articulating a masculine identity detached from the domestic
that safeguards and patrols the frontier border. This is the white frontiersman that will take on staying rhetorical and ideological power.

Hawkeye's character has drawn much critical attention because of his
playing Indian and his modeling of isolated manhood or the natural man.
Leslie Fiedler views Hawkeye as rejecting the domestic world and, fitting

the overarching argument of *Love and Death in the American Novel*, representing the man who escapes "civilization" (192–95). Slotkin adds the racial dimension of Hawkeye's character, identifying "Leatherstocking's obsession with the question of racial loyalties" (*Regeneration* 493). Janet Dean brings together these two strains of Cooper criticism in her essay on the exchange of women in the novel, specifically Cora, and how it "reproduces and intensifies anxieties over control of the frontier itself" (47–48). More important to my argument is her characterization of Hawkeye. For Dean, Hawkeye is "a frontier border guard who restricts racial interaction" (54). She evidences this function in Hawkeye's refusal to translate Munro's assurance of an egalitarian afterlife to the Indian girls who have sung for Cora's funeral. This point anchors this chapter's understanding of Hawkeye. As a racial "border guard," Hawkeye exerts a controlling and ordering influence in the novel, a function that illustrates another significant aspect of the white frontiersman.

In Cooper's novel Hawkeye represents an ideal man: his vigor and courage arise from his frontier experience and knowledge of Indian ways. He is, as he states a myriad of times, "a man without a cross." His blood is not mixed, but he owes no racial allegiance to whites either and so has no lasting bonds with his race. In the novel's end, Cooper describes Hawkeye as "[d]eserted by all of his color" (413). This racial disconnection compounds upon Hawkeye's detachment from family. Hawkeye states to Chingachgook: "I have no kin, and I may also say, like you, no people" (414). These words conflate a domestic family attachment with a racial attachment. A man without kin is a man without a people (race); therefore, he is truly "a man without a cross," whether it be a "cross" (mixing) of blood or a "cross" (to bear) of allegiance.

While his status as a white Indian has received much critical scrutiny, I want to draw this analysis to focus on Hawkeye's vehement antidomestic stance, which defines his status as frontiersman. For Hawkeye the accoutrements of civilization (mainly embodied in literacy and formal education) are emasculating and weakening. In a conversation with Chingachgook, Hawkeye launches one of his first salvos against literacy. He describes to his Indian companion the tradition of writing as opposed to oral tradition. He goes on to claim, "In consequence of this bad fashion, a man who is too conscientious to misspend his days among the women, in learning the names of black marks, may never hear of the deeds of his fathers, nor feel a pride in striving to outdo them" (35). According to Hawkeye, reading is the province of women that takes the male away from a competitive tradition in which he seeks to outdo his father. Reading interferes with the rightful passage of manhood from father to son and distracts a man from fulfilling his masculine role. Lora Romero expertly articulates this point when she argues, "For Cooper, to read in the book of nature is to be educated through the paternal apprenticeship rather than the maternal representational system [of books]" (47). This passage foregrounds Hawkeye's initial hostile encounters with David Gamut, who embodies the acculturated man that Hawkeye denigrates.

The antidomestic rhetoric arises most prominently in Hawkeye's encounters with Gamut, the obvious symbol of white civility and the home in his combining of education and religion in his job as a psalmody teacher. Initially, Hawkeye mocks Gamut's profession, calling it "a strange calling . . . to go through life, like a catbird, mocking all the ups and downs that may happen to come out of other men's throats" (67). The main indictment here is that Gamut is merely an imitator. But Hawkeye's words are quickly lost in the following scene in which the sisters sing, and even the scout's manly facade softens "as [he] gradually suffered his rigid features to relax until . . . he felt his iron nature subdued" (68). He then recollects back to his boyhood life in the settlements and even weeps. Therefore, while Hawkeye may be consciously antidomestic, Cooper demonstrates in this scene a belief in the power of domestic ties: the sisters' singing of a hymn reminds the frontiersman of his ties to civilization and domesticity. As a side note, the Indians listen with similarly rapt attention, but their attitude does not soften; instead they "listened with an attention that seemed to turn them into stone" (68). They do not feel a stirring of inner feeling; or if they do, they do not express it. From what Cooper shows, Chingachgook and Uncas are more attuned to listening than to feeling the song. Their "natur'" disconnects them from the domestic sympathy in which the whites can fully participate.

While Hawkeye betrays the capacity for sentimental feeling, this does not alter his general view of literacy. In his debate with Gamut on predestination, Hawkeye attacks reading, again as a feminine pursuit. When Gamut questions Hawkeye for support of his doctrine, Hawkeye replies "with singular and ill-concealed disdain":

Book! . . . Do you take me for a whimpering boy at the apron string of one of your old gals; and this good rifle on my knee for the feather of a goose's wing, my ox's horn for a bottle of ink, and my leathern pouch for a cross-

barred handkercher to carry my dinner? Book! What have such as I, who
am a warrior of the wilderness, though a man without a cross, to do with
books? (137–38)

The connection of manhood and wilderness living is antithetical to a domestic education. This line of argument continues in a later passage:

> The Lord never intended that the man should place all his endeavors in his
> throat, to the neglect of other and better gifts! But he has fallen into the
> hand of some silly woman, when he should have been gathering his educa-
> tion under a blue sky, among the beauties of the forest. (265)

Hawkeye opposes a "natural" education to the "artificial" under the tutelage
of "some silly woman." As has been seen in previous examples, Hawkeye
draws a connection between femininity, literacy, and domesticity. Men who
fall into the hands of women will lose their manhood and pursue endeavors
that waste more valuable and practical gifts, such as hunting, tracking, and
warriorship. Under this paradigm of thinking, becoming a man requires
performing the "manly" actions of woodsmanship commonly associated
with "Indians." Hawkeye preserves his manliness by shunning the trappings
of the settlements and maintaining his vigor and vitality in the company of
Chingachgook and Uncas. For Hawkeye, his antidomesticity and frontier
proximity strengthen his character as a man.

Hawkeye resonates as an important figure in this study, as well, in his
negotiation of Indianness and whiteness. As explored above with Boone,
the white frontiersman must perform a precarious balancing act of assimi-
lating those skills necessary to survival in the wilderness (an assimilation
characterized as Indianization) with policing and maintaining his whiteness, persevering in the marginal world of the frontier as a white man
connected to the "civilized" order in which he enjoys his racial privilege
and power. If he is unable or unwilling to maintain that balance, he will
become a renegade or a white Indian. The former category is one met with
much revulsion, while the latter can attain an admirable status, although
still faced with suspicion. Hawkeye vehemently defends his whiteness,
as also seen with Boone's hagiographers who defend and emphasize his
loyalty to a white American cause. What happens, though, if the white
frontiersman does not properly police his racial or national identity, if the
white frontiersman does not maintain his proper allegiances? Hawkeye's

and Boone's interlocutors carefully maintain the frontiersman's white-ness, yet other white frontiersmen have demonstrated the frailty of such maintenance.

Simon Girty is the perennial American villain, notorious as the prototypi-cal white renegade. He occupies the same frontier stage as Boone, ever the nemesis to the loyal and brave frontier hero in various historical and fictional narratives. Girty represents treason, turning his back not only on his country but also on his race. Slotkin positions Girty as an "antitype" of Boone (*Regeneration* 291), a characterization that Emerson Bennett expresses in *The Renegade: A Historical Romance of Border Life* (1848) in describing Boone as being "contra-distinguished from Girty in every way" (iii–iv). Slotkin frames Girty's villainous status within a myth of the fall; Simon Girty, and others like him, have "succumb[ed] to the evil tempta-tion of the wilderness" (*Regeneration* 286). The wilderness experience has "degraded" them so that "[t]hey embody all the negative, evil possibilities inherent in the emigration to the wilderness" (291). Faragher addresses Girty in relationship to fears of loyalty on the frontier: "On the Upper Ohio that spring [1778] a number of prominent frontiersmen went over to the British side, most notably Simon Girty, his brothers James and George, and Alexander McKee, all of whom became notorious Tory agents among the Indians. Boone had Loyalist kin, and his disappearance was interpreted by some in the context of considerable anxiety about frontier loyalties" (167). In *Simon Girty: The White Savage*, one of the few biographies of Girty, Thomas Boyd verifies Girty's despised status: "Of all the men remembered from those years Simon Girty, who has been called the anomaly of western history, was perhaps the most widely and deeply hated" (4). A set of often-quoted lines of poetry on Girty describes him thus,

> The outlawed white man, by Ohio's flood,
> Whose vengeance shamed the Indian's thirst for blood;
> Whose hellish arts surpassed the red man far;
> Whose hate enkindled many a border war . . . (qtd. in Boyd 5)

While Boyd attempts to paint a more sympathetic portrait of Girty, the biographer concedes the hatred that Girty inspires. Boyd draws at-tention to incidents in which Girty acts humanely, as when he intercedes for Simon Kenton, saving him from execution twice, or when Girty saves another, Henry Baker, from execution by Indian captors. In the popular imagination, though, such moments of kindness do not ameliorate Girty's perceived treason or his behavior in the execution of Colonel Crawford. Bakeless, in his Boone biography, observes, "The incident became famous, both because Simon Girty, the 'white Indian,' sat by to enjoy the fun and also because it was better reported than most such tragedies" (264). Boyd describes the rhetorical power of the incident but provides a contextual reminder: "His burning is a scene which warms the blood of every patriotic American, yes, and blinds the eye. For he had no right to expect to live; and if the Delawares had spared him they would have shown themselves so much more humane than the average borderer of that day that the contrast would even now be painful" (166).

An early appearance of Girty happens to be in the first significant biography of Boone in Filson's *Kentucke* (1784). Filson describes the increasing attacks from neighboring Indians in 1782, attacks spurred on by Girty and McKee (57). Girty appears here as he will in succeeding depictions: leading the Indians against the white settlers. On this point, Girty's speech preceding the attacks on Bryan Station and at the Blue Licks is often repeated. Bakeless cites it in full (273–74). Faragher also cites this speech (216). In it Girty incites his Indian audience to strike at the white settlers who "have destroyed the cane, trodden down the clover, killed the deer and the buffalo, the bear and the raccoon." Citing the white encroachment on natural resources, Girty presents this ultimatum: "Unless you rise in the majesty of your might and exterminate their whole race, you may bid adieu to the hunting grounds of your fathers." Perhaps this speech is what Filson is thinking of when he states, "Their savage minds were inflamed to mischief by two abandoned men, Captains McKee and Girty" (57).

Emerson Bennet's novel *The Renegade* features Girty as a main character. This novel follows the frontier-genteel paradigm as seen in the Leatherstocking Tales and in Bird's *Nick of the Woods*. Boone is the rough frontiersman, his status marked by his dialect, in contrast to Algernon Reynolds, the genteel Easterner. Smith discusses the role of class distinction and the genteel hero. Dialect is often a marker of the rougher frontiersman in contrast with the genteel Easterner. In fact, a dialect could preclude a hero from being considered appropriate for a "sentimental courtship" (98). Sometimes the dialect disguises the fact that the frontier hero is actually genteel. For my purposes, Smith identifies an area of tension between the frontier and the domestic.[17] Bennett conveys Reynolds's gentility through his proper dialect and his physical appearance: "His features . . . were mostly of the Grecian cast" (10–11). Boone's features are also admirable—"His forehead was high, full and noble"—but do not obtain to the level of Reynolds's: "good, regular, though not strictly speaking, handsome features" (13).

Most telling of how Bennett constructs the character types of the novel is his description of the main characters' fates in the end of the story, as seen in these three excerpts:

> Shortly after their marriage, Algernon and Ella bid farewell to their friends in the west, and returned to the east, where a long and happy career awaited them; and where they lived to recount to their children and grandchildren the thrilling narratives of their captivity, and their wild and romantic adventures while pioneers on the borders of Kentucky.

. . .

> Boone continued a resident of Kentucky, until he fancied it too populous for his comfort, when he removed with his family to Missouri, where he spent much of his time in fishing and hunting, and where he finally died at an advanced age.

. . .

> Girty, notwithstanding his outrageous crimes against humanity, continued to live among the Indians for a great number of years, the inveterate and barbarous foe of his race. In the celebrated battle of the Thames, a desperate white man led on a band of savages, who fought with great fury, but were at length overpowered and their leader cut to pieces by Colonel Johnson's mounted men. The mangled corse of this leader was afterwards recognized as the notorious and once dreaded Simon Girty—The Renegade. (137, 138)

Bennett delivers these three fates for these main characters. Algernon Reynolds is a young Easterner who retreats to Kentucky believing he has killed his cousin. The novel resolves his flight of conscience by revealing in the end that the cousin did not die by Algernon's hand. The cousin's totally unrelated death results in Algernon inheriting that cousin's wealth, thus allowing Algernon to marry his love, Ella, and return east. Algernon takes his frontier experience and integrates it into his domestic life. Boone plays the part of the "Indian-hater" in this novel, and his removal farther west, beyond the reach of "civilization," is in keeping with this image. The rest of his life spent "fishing and hunting" conforms to that figure of Boone who resists integration into domestic society. His importance in the novel, though, rests most significantly, for the discussion here, upon his being a foil to the main villain: Simon Girty, "The Renegade."

While Bennett's novel follows a typical narrative of white novices in the wilderness who face captivity and are rescued by their more experienced frontier counterparts, its main objective, as the title demonstrates, is to depict the character of Simon Girty and demonstrate his race betrayal. The last lines of the novel drive this point home: Girty is "the inveterate and barbarous foe of his race" who meets his death at the Battle of Thames. Usually, the Battle of Thames is more significant in US history as marking the death of Tecumseh, with Colonel Johnson's name attached to the Indian leader's demise. In Bennett's story, Girty appears to take Tecumseh's place. Girty is a more vicious and dangerous enemy than Indians. His being a white man turned Indian constitutes part of his heightened threat; the possibility that a white man can become Indian attacks notions of racial purity and essential identity.

Beyond that racial amalgamation, Girty as "renegade" is a threat in his power to rouse Indian aggression and lead Indians into hostility against whites. Simon Girty's power as a leader presents him as a much more dangerous icon than simply his "playing Indian." In his introduction, Bennett reports that Girty had become among the Senecas "a chief . . . of no little distinction" (iii). Bennett also demonstrates Girty's ability to arouse the passions of Indians. Girty delivers a speech, much like Magua in *Last of the Mohicans*, demanding the death of the white captives and calling for "a speedy and bloody retaliation upon the pioneers of Kentucky":

> As Girty concluded his speech, which was listened to in breathless silence, there was a great sensation in the house, and an almost unanimous grunt of approval from the chiefs and braves there assembled. It needed but this, to arouse their vindictive passions against the white invader to the extreme, and they bent upon the unfortunate prisoners, eyes which seemed inflamed with rage and revenge. Girty perceived, at a glance, that he had succeeded to the full of his heart's desire; and with a devilish smile of satisfaction on his features, he drew back among the warriors, to listen to the harangues of the others. (96)

Girty's speech finds "an almost unanimous grunt of approval" and arouses "vindictive passions." Girty's leadership operates not through the rational deliberation of consensus but plays to the passions of the mob. The Indians' "unanimous grunt" depicts the "savage" quality of their collective agreement. Girty does not bring about rational consensus but collective passion. John McClung (1832), whom Bennett echoes as a likely source,[18] describes those "few renegade white men [who] were mingled with them [Indians], and inflamed their wild passions. . . . Among them the most remarkable was *Simon Girty*" (66). Bennett provides this same language of arousing passion to initiate a collective action against whites. "The Renegade" appears as a double threat in its deadly combination of white male authority with "savage" passions. The white man playing Indian is dangerous not only in terms of the potential for betrayal and treason but also in its potential to detach from or oppose domesticity.

Some sense of the antebellum attitude toward the relationship between the frontier and the domestic establishment is evident in an essay that appears in an 1836 issue of the *American Monthly Magazine*. Albert Pike's "Life in Arkansas: The Philosophy of Deer Hunting" spends its better part extolling the romantic aspects of the outdoors life.[19] In the concluding paragraphs, Pike reminds his audience that though a life beyond the home has its intrinsic value, a man must return to "his own humble sphere," where he "owes his duty to the society in which he lives" (159). It is in the domestic sphere that a man finds its riches: "That man is most happy . . . who is thoroughly convinced that at his own calm fireside, with one there to love him for himself alone, there is more to live for than in the proudest honors and the most gorgeous wealth which ambition can crave or avarice desire" (159). A man may range beyond the borders of his domestic space, but he must return to know that it is there, "at his own calm fireside," that he finds his true worth and contentment. As discussed above, Hawkeye sets himself apart from civilization and domesticity yet maintains his connection: he protects the women, he is affected by the hymn, and so his allegiance to civilization (though he refuses to join it) stays strong. His frontier allegiance has not pulled him away from his obligations to his race (though he may claim no such obligations). On the other hand, in *Nick of the Woods*, Abel Doe, the renegade, has forsaken that warm fire and loving (white) spouse of "civilized" domesticity.

Abel Doe has been, as the novel calls it, "Injunized." In addition, it is through this "Injunization" that Richard Braxley, the main villain, performs his machinations in his attempt to rob Roland Forrester of his inheritance and marry Edith Forrester. This question of inheritance encompasses Telie Doe, too, who has no rightful inheritance, since her supposed father has gone Indian. Bird accentuates the instability of the line between "white" and "Indian" when Telie and the Forresters have been captured and she attempts to persuade her father of his whiteness: "[Y]ou are a white man, father, and not an Indian; yes, father, you are *no* Indian: and you promised no harm should be done,—you did, father, you *did* promise!" (226). This instability of racial allegiance presents one threat to a unified national identity. Furthermore, the "renegade parent" here is, perhaps, an even greater threat. His promises cannot be trusted. He proves false. Moreover, the father who proves false is a danger to maintaining a stable white male authority.

The novel emphasizes the importance of honesty and integrity for the white male in the scene where Abel offers Roland freedom in exchange for marrying Telie. Bird invokes "the mighty fathers of the republic," whom Roland turns to in faith and spirit, "not [to] stoop to the meanness of falsehood and deception even in that moment of peril and fear" (379), the moment when Abel Doe offers to free Roland if he will marry Telie, Abel's supposed daughter. Marrying Telie, then, would mean escape for Roland. His refusal to do so rests upon the "mighty fathers of the republic," who are cloaked in honesty, integrity, and uprightness. Bird invokes the "mighty fathers" as the guides and guardians of liberty and democracy. If they are corrupted, so too will be the nation. The "Injunized father" is a corrupted father and therefore is a direct threat to the nation's course.

The corrupted father as Indian represents what a white male US citizen could become. This novel engages in a doubleness in which the white characters cross the line between "civilized white" and "red savage": threats of marriage with "Injunized" whites, captivity, and resorts to violence all walk the line between civilization and savagery. This distinction of identities parallels a demarcation of family relations between the white fathers and Indian brothers.

Such marking of familial categories works from a distinguishing between "proper" family alignment that descends from a father and an "improper" family alignment in equality with siblings. By the novel's rules, the proper transmission of rights and privileges proceeds from the father, while the improper transmission proceeds from the brother. This division marks a contrast between vertical and horizontal relations. In the novel, both types of relations contest each other, but in the end the vertical, top-down structure prevails. Roland's invocation of "the mighty fathers of the republic" is a prime example of the paternalist vision of society. The recovery at novel's end of the vertically transmitted inheritance affirms the hierarchical structure that composes such a paternalist structure. The novel finds stability and security through a paternal transmission of rights. The white Indian operates outside of this paternalist structure, though, and so is a threat to white domesticity and male authority.

The racial value system of *Nick* determines that a white who turns Indian commits apostasy. Colonel Bruce refers to Abel Doe as one of the "apostatized villains" who has become Indian, likening him to "Girty, Elliot, and the rest of them refugee scoundrels" (41). Abel Doe's status betrays Telie's full acceptance into heteronormative domesticity, for Bruce states, "A bad thing for her, to have an Injunized father; for if it war'nt for him, I reckon my son Tom, the brute, would take to her, and marry her" (41). Telie herself feels sympathy for her "father" (who is really not her father, but one John Atkinson; Telie turns out to be the long-lost cousin of the Forresters), rationalizing his living among the Indians as protecting the white settlers from attacks: "[Y]es, I know it well enough, though they won't believe it,—that he keeps the Indians from hurting them" (67). Yet, as she reveals shortly after, Telie knows that she must remove to where no one knows that she is "the white Indian's daughter." Such is the recourse for a daughter whose father has gone Indian, an act whose severity becomes clearly evident in the narrator's description of white Indians as "those apostate white men, renegades from the States, traitors to their country and to civilization, who were, at that day, in so many instances, found uniting their fortunes with the Indians, following, and even leading them, in their bloody incursions upon the frontiers" (306–7). To become "Injunized" is an automatic rejection of Anglo white racial and national identity. Loyalty to nation goes hand in hand with loyalty to "civilization." In one instance, Nathan sees proof of one white man's "apostasy" "in the appearance of some half a dozen naked children, of fairer hue than the savages, yet not so pale as those of his own race" (307). This intermixed offspring stands as undeniable proof of this particular renegade's renunciation of whiteness and its supposed linkage to "civilization."

The enmity against white Indians is particularly vivid in one of the final scenes of the novel, in which the regulators begin to attack Abel Doe crying, "No quarter for turn-coats and traitors! no mercy for white Injuns!" (392). This frenzied crowd is subdued, though, by Roland's intervention, followed by Colonel Bruce's; he stops the men by invoking the father–daughter bond between Telie and Abel: "Off, you perditioned brutes! Would you kill the man before the eyes of his own natteral-born daughter? Kill Injuns, you brutes,—thar's the meat for you!" (392–93). Bruce reroutes the crowd's anger toward Indians by placing before them the domestic relationship of father and daughter. Abel sees some measure of redemption in the final pages when he turns over the final will that properly reinstates the Forresters to their inheritance. Abel's death and the razing of the Indian village clear from the novel's landscape any nonwhite presence. The deaths of both the Indian enemies *and* the white Indians clear the way for the whites to regain their proper lives either on the frontier (as with the Bruces and Telie) or back East (as with the Forresters).

Abel Doe, then, presents, along with Simon Girty, a particular fear of the potential for playing Indian to seduce white men from their perceived proper allegiances and obligations. The white frontiersman stands upon a tightrope of racial identification. While appropriation of Indianness is allowable to a certain degree, and even viewed as admirable, one must be careful not to fall fully into the Indian's way of life. The line between Boone and Girty is a tenuous one. It is a negotiation of identity that bears analogy to the admiration dynamic found in the treatment of Indian males discussed in chapter 1. Flirtations with Indianness must not become romances.

These two opening chapters demonstrate early incarnations of playing Indian and the Indian male that carry on into the twentieth century. The concerns found in these nineteenth-century treatments of Indianness, about manhood, nationhood, and racial identity, remain in the later texts under examination in this study, although the historical and cultural contexts change. With this understanding of the nineteenth-century precedents in place, this book now turns toward the twentieth century to examine how the frontier and playing Indian operate in comics.

CHAPTER THREE

# FROM THE NINETEENTH TO THE TWENTIETH CENTURY

*The Frontier Mythos in Comics Adaptations*

AS EVIDENCED IN THE PREVIOUS CHAPTERS, THE INDIAN MALE AND THE white frontiersman operated as powerful, though sometimes ambiguous, symbols of physical strength and masculine fortitude during the nineteenth century. These figures embodied the ideal male through a complex of imagery, written and visual, that found a foothold during the nineteenth century and, as this chapter will show, was transmitted into the twentieth century via a lineage of the frontier mythos from nineteenth-century art and literature to dime novels around the turn of the century to popular media of the twentieth century such as film, TV shows, and, the focus for the rest of this study, comic books. Perhaps one of the earliest studies to describe the lineage of the frontier mythos is Henry Nash Smith's *Virgin Land*. Smith illustrates such a lineage in the nineteenth century originating with Daniel Boone, descending to the Leatherstocking stories, then to dime novels. John Cawelti expands upon and further develops this lineage in *The Six-Gun Mystique* and *Adventure, Mystery, and Romance*, surveying the development of the Western in the twentieth century with works like Owen Wister's *The Virginian* and the rise of the cinematic Western. Slotkin's *Gunfighter Nation* follows suit in examining how the ideology of the frontier continued to possess symbolic and ideological power in American culture in the twentieth century. Following Slotkin's line of argument, Theodore Roosevelt qualifies as an exemplar of the transitioning of the frontier myth of the nineteenth century into the twentieth. Roosevelt admired the writings of Cooper and Parkman and cofounded the Boone and Crockett Club in 1887 (*Gunfighter* 33, 37). Roosevelt's example illustrates the perpetuation of the ideology of the rugged frontier life as remedy to the enervation of urban life. On this point, Slotkin posits that Roosevelt "felt he had acquired, through immersion in the wilderness, a capacity for 'strenuous' life and achievement that set him above the selfishness and sloth of the leisured and moneyed classes whose political impotence he accused" (*Gunfighter* 37). The importance of Parkman as a source of this ideology cannot be overlooked. Kim Townshend confirms Parkman's influence on American men into the twentieth century: "Representative among them are Teddy Roosevelt, other admirers (and illustrators) of Parkman like Owen Wister and Frederic Remington, Ernest Hemingway, John F. Kennedy, Ronald Reagan, assorted huntsmen, gunslingers, and detectives" (112). Along with Parkman, Boone and Hawkeye also possess lasting influence into twentieth-century American culture in their embodying the mythology of the frontier and heroic masculinity. Matthew Costello identifies a particular strain of this rhetoric of the frontier and its lineage: "The persistent power of the individual in American culture is represented in the American vision of heroism, ranging from Daniel Boone and Natty Bumpo through the cowboy on the frontier and the private detective in urban America to the superhero in comic books" (42). Robert C. Harvey also traces the lineage of the frontier mythos from Boone to Cooper to dime novels, then connects the Western hero to the superhero: "[T]he superhero, after all, is but the Western heroic persona elevated to near omnipotence" (63–64, 65). Furthermore, film at the turn of the century takes up the Western genre, thus transmitting the themes, imagery, and character types popular in the nineteenth century. L. G. Moses confirms this point: "The movies drew upon the novels of James Fenimore Cooper, dime novels, and Wild West shows for their themes" (225). As the above scholarship demonstrates, and as this study reiterates, the line of the frontier mythos and the Western exists unbroken from the late-eighteenth-century imaginings of Boone to the films and television shows of the twentieth century. One area that the bulk of this scholarship does not address is comics, and so the following pages seek to illustrate how the comics of the twentieth century echo and modify their cultural and artistic precedents and companions in the depiction of the frontier and of playing Indian.

The defining qualities of the frontier and playing Indian that exist in the mid-twentieth century comics owe a debt to the prevalent shorthand of Western and frontier imagery that descended from the nineteenth century. Cooper's, Parkman's, and Boone's mythologies are major sources of the frontier iconography and imagery that would inform the standard popular perception of the frontier. In the late nineteenth century, this popular perception of the frontier was highly influenced by the likes of Frederick Jackson Turner's frontier thesis, Buffalo Bill's Wild West shows, and dime novel Westerns. Richard White argues that "the very ubiquity of frontier icons allowed Turner and Buffalo Bill to deliver powerful messages with incredible economy and resonance" ("Frederick Jackson Turner" 11). These two major voices in shaping American popular understanding of the frontier at the turn of the century relied upon a standard set of images that allowed them to reference economically well known shorthand of image and symbol. The dime novel Westerns also partook of this "cultural short-hand," as Bill Brown calls it, "legible thanks to the popularity of Cooper and his imitators" (33). Daryl Jones also identifies Cooper's influence, argu-ing that "[i]n setting their novels on the frontier . . . dime novelists were merely following the trail that Cooper had blazed a generation earlier" (23). Harvey describes this lineage as well, tracing the Western mythos from Boone to Cooper to dime novels to Buffalo Bill to Teddy Roosevelt (63–64). Turner, Buffalo Bill, and the dime Westerns provide a bridge transmitting the popular imagery of the frontier into the twentieth century, a transmis-sion that would continue most pervasively by film and then, in parallel, by comics after World War II.

Furthermore, the development of mass production must be noted in fueling the ubiquity of the frontier imagery. M. Thomas Inge argues that figures like Boone and Buffalo Bill "achieved national prominence not because of the persistence of folktales and oral traditions but because their exploits entered the pages of books, dime novels, almanacs, news-paper columns, and sheet music" (141). Michael Kammen views Buffalo Bill's Wild West as an example of popular culture, as he distinguishes it from mass culture, in the show's visitation of communities and creation of participatory experience (78). Following Kammen's model, Buffalo Bill provides a striking example of that movement from popular culture to proto–mass culture; his shows operated on the local and immediate level, but the merchandising spread beyond those local encounters, a point cor-roborated by Joy S. Kasson: "Millions of people saw Buffalo Bill's Wild West during its heyday, but many millions more saw the posters plastered over every surface when the show came to town, and souvenir books, programs, and photographs became part of the spectators' imaginative life" (196). Kasson's observation also emphasizes the visual nature of Buffalo Bill's dissemination, a significant factor as this study turns to comics. Bill Brown speaks more specifically to the relationship between mass production and the dime novel: "The material facts of the dime novel's production and distribution help us to appreciate the Western as a rationalization of the West that synchronized the realm of leisure in the rhythms of work and industry" (30). On this point, Michael Denning thoroughly examines the relationship between dime novel reading and the patterns of working-class life. Denning's description of dime novel production warrants citation here, too: the industry's marketing and trademark of characters detached from authorial ownership (20) predicates a similar model in the comics industry. The production of dime novels also anticipates the production of comic books. Daryl Jones describes the working conditions of the dime novelist that sound much like the working conditions of the comics creator in the early shops: "working in the comparative anonymity of a large publishing house, meeting rigid deadlines, and looking to sales as the sole measure of artistry" (4). In this way dime novels anticipate the comic book's mass production and distribution and its role in consumer culture as well as transmitting from the nineteenth century many conventions and themes of the Western.

Likewise, Buffalo Bill's Wild West anticipates that distribution of frontier imagery to popular culture. Slotkin states that between 1885 and 1905 the Wild West "was the most important commercial vehicle for the fabrication and transmission of the Myth of the Frontier" (*Gunfighter* 87). Important in this transmission is its reductive quality, its refiguring of history into that "cultural shorthand" that typifies the Western genre in American culture. Slotkin notes such "reductions of complex events into 'typical scenes' based on the formulas of popular literary mythology [drawn from Cooper and dime novels]" (*Gunfighter* 69). This reduction and shorthand are significant for my study in that they demonstrate an important aspect of playing Indian: the performance of Indianness. In the Wild West shows, this performance becomes codified into a set of visual conventions. Furthermore, the performance itself is valorized: the actual act of playing Indian is a central component of these shows, even so much that actual Native persons play Indian, that is, perform a role popularly understood to be "Indian." Philip Deloria articulates the problematic nature of "native people playing Indian": "Although they might alter Indian stereotypes, native people playing Indian might also reaffirm them for a stubborn white audience, making Indianness an even more powerful construct and creating a circular, reinforcing catch-22 of meaning that would prove difficult to circumvent" (126). Indianness becomes an identity that even actual Native persons must perform in order to be viewed as "Indian." White illustrates the complicated mimesis and performativity of these shows (35). Kasson identifies the tension between authenticity and fiction in these performances, a tension of which, to a certain extent, both the Native performers and the audience were aware (211, 221). The Buffalo Bill show, and others like it, put the spotlight on the performance of Indianness, and with that is an integral influence in the development of a visual rhetoric of playing Indian. The theatricality of the Wild West entertainment detaches the symbolic from the historical, disconnects the imitation from the original, to isolate and hyperbolize key visual elements as the imagined essence of the Indian, the very embodiment of an imagined Indian.

Buffalo Bill's Wild West provides a crucial link between the nineteenth century and the twentieth century in the depiction and perception of the frontier and of the Indian. Its appropriation of Cooper and dime novel conventions also performed an adaptation of those conventions to a twentieth-century environment of mass production and popular entertainment. The merchandising that accompanied Cody's shows anticipates a consumerist culture that would emerge more fully in the twentieth century. The Wild West sold a myth, sold an atmosphere that presented nostalgia for an imagined Indian and affirmed the rightness of the American myth of progress. The millions who witnessed the shows, and the millions more who saw the images or read the newspaper articles about the show, participated in a neatly packaged commodity representation of the frontier, one that excised the actuality of conflict, and the messy ethical qualms of "manifest destiny," to provide entertaining flirtations with danger and exoticism, while standardizing a set of characteristics that define "true" Indianness. Kasson argues for "[u]nderstanding the Wild West as a site of memory" (222), and much of what this chapter seeks to understand is how the manufactured memory of "the frontier" remains in the American cultural consciousness via comic book adaptations. These comic book adaptations, along with their cultural counterparts in the Western genre, keep alive the rhetoric of the heroic Indian and the heroic frontiersman (along with their negative counterparts, the savage and the renegade).

A title that will frequently arise in this chapter's examination of adaptations is Gilberton's *Classics Illustrated*. Founded by Albert Lewis Kanter, the line aimed to introduce "great literature" to children via the comics medium. One telling example of Gilberton's perception of its series as transcending comics and occupying the company of "high" culture was its refusal to join the Comics Magazine Association of America and adopt the Comics Code. Gilberton argued this position on the grounds of its own self-regulation, the association of the series with "the classics," the quality of the content, and the series' educational mission (Nyberg 117; William B. Jones 168; Beaty 162). These points also reveal the positioning of *Classics Illustrated* as a conduit of "official" culture, and with that, "official" American culture, especially in consideration of the adaptations and historic chronicles that this chapter examines. Such a charge to express Americanness is evident in the supplemental material included alongside the literature adaptations. Michael Sawyer describes the "fillers which contained informative and educational articles 'stressing Americana and democracy at work'" (4). This type of filler (along with, according to Sawyer, "opera librettos, biographies, and history") also served to legitimate the *Classics Illustrated* texts, a concern that informs the transition to painted covers in 1951. Sawyer provides background on this move: "The new image was supposed to render the Classics as a cultured comic that more closely reflected the original works on which they were based" (10). As Rocco Versaci aptly observes, Gilberton's line produced a tense conflict between utilizing the comics medium and aspiring to a perceived legitimacy free of the supposed immaturity of comics. Versaci argues, "The result is that both comic book and 'literature' get short-changed: the comic book is denied full expression of its signifying capabilities, and 'literature' loses its stylistic diversity as the unique features of each writer are downplayed in favor of consistency" (192). In this regard, *Classics Illustrated* participates in the transmission of American ideology, picking up in its depictions of Parkman or Cooper and Daniel Boone, for instance, the mythos of the frontier as it has been handed down from the nineteenth century. *The Oregon Trail* and *The Last of the Mohicans* are two *Classics* titles that this chapter examines. In addition, the *Classics* adaptation of the John Bakeless Boone biography reveals how *Classics Illustrated* functions as the predominant vehicle of adaptations in twentieth-century comics and thus is a central player below.

*The Oregon Trail* finds its comics rebirth in the *Classics Illustrated* series in issue 72 (June 1950), with writing by John O'Rourke and art by Henry Carl Kiefer. This issue saw eleven printings, and, with most comic books in the *Classics Illustrated* line, it was reprinted with two different covers (a line-drawing cover and a painted cover, as William B. Jones distinguishes them). These two covers represent the paradoxical perception of the Indian as either noble or savage. As is readily evident, these two covers depict the savage and the noble, the Indian as attacker and threat to the white settler and the Indian as companion and guide. The first cover plays out a typical "cowboys and Indians" scene; the war-bonneted Indian in the foreground and the furious action of the cover convey adventure and excitement (Fig. 3.1). The second cover's Indian shares some similar visual style with the attacker, yet this one appears fully clothed, perhaps

Figure 3.1. First cover of *Classics Illustrated* #72: *The Oregon Trail* (June 1950). Gilberton Company.

a signal to his being more amenable to white civilization in juxtaposition to the bare-chested fighters (Fig. 3.2). The white man on the painted cover wears an outfit that aligns him with the frontiersman figure, or possibly the popular image of Boone.

These contrasting images echo those produced by Buffalo Bill's Wild West. *On the Stage Coach* is a poster (Fig. 3.3) that depicts a band of Indians on horseback attacking the Deadwood coach in a composition that the first *Classics Illustrated* cover echoes. While there may not be a direct or conscious connection between these two images, separated by over fifty years, the reliance upon this type of scene for the comic book demonstrates its staying power in American culture, especially when the story within the comic book does not feature such a scene. The second cover is more

Figure 3.2. Second cover
of *Classics Illustrated*
*#72: The Oregon Trail*
(June 1950). Gilberton
Company.

faithful to the contents of Parkman's narrative, but one can also recognize
in it the echoes of composition and imagery found in Buffalo Bill visuals.
Specifically, this cover echoes an 1885 William Notman photograph of
Sitting Bull and Buffalo Bill (Fig. 3.4) that was, according to Kasson, "the
most widely distributed one" of a group of pictures of the two men (178).
In this photograph, Buffalo Bill stands on the right, pointing off camera,
as Sitting Bull looks in the same direction. The second *Classics Illustrated*
cover reverses this composition, placing the Indian on the right in a dominant position, standing, and so taller than the white frontiersman, who
crouches and stares off to where the Indian points. This comparison of
these two sets of images does not imply that a direct relationship of influence exists between the Buffalo Bill visuals and the *Classics Illustrated*

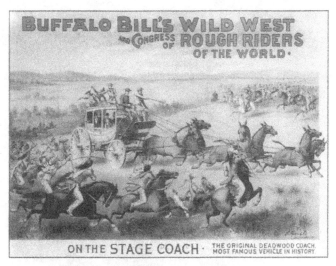

Figure 3.3. *On the Stage Coach.* 1887. Color lithograph, poster.

covers. This comparison, at the least, demonstrates how these opposing images of the Indian—as either violent attacker or peaceful guide—possess staying power in American culture.

As for the adaptation itself, William B. Jones points out how this issue uses no dialogue balloons, a move that Jones connects back to the Hal Foster style in *Tarzan* and *Prince Valiant*, as well as indicating "the degree to which the artist saw himself as employed in the illustration of books rather than the drawing of comics" (73, 75). For the purposes of this analysis, it is notable as to how O'Rourke chooses to focus Parkman's narrative, in this case highlighting the warlike nature of the Indian characters. The opening page introduces the major characters of the narrative: Parkman, who is "joining a band of war-like Dacotah Indians"; the Whirlwind, who is "conducting war against the tribe of Snake Indians who had ambushed and slain his son"; Colonel Kearney, who is "maintaining peace on the western frontier"; and the Panther, who is "free from the jealousy and cunning of his people." While such characterization of the Indians is not absent in Parkman's original narrative, the comic book's ability to heighten and condense selective aspects of the original narrative calls greater attention to this warlike depiction of the Indian characters. Significant as well is that the comic characterizes Colonel Kearney, the representative of official US governance, as a peacekeeper, a force of order reining in the chaos of the frontier, and not an aggressor. The second page's narration

Figure 3.4. *Buffalo Bill and Sitting Bull*. 1885. Photograph by W. Notman.

continues this emphasis on the state of war, stating that "[t]he summer of 1846 was a season of warlike excitement among all the western bands of the Dacotah." This text accompanies a page-wide panel showing a group of nondescript Indians, some sitting, some standing, and a couple on horse-back, most with arms raised and holding bows, spear, and tomahawks. The bottom three-quarters of the page contains three panels: on the left, a vertical single panel with an Indian on horseback, arm raised, wearing a full headdress, the caption reading: "Many war parties had been sent out . . ." On this panel's right are two smaller panels, the top one depicting a skirmish between the Snakes and Dacotah, and the bottom one showing the death of Whirlwind's son. This initial sequence concludes with Whirl-wind gaining his vengeance for the death of his son. For some perspective here, in Parkman's original text this particular story does not appear until chapter 10. Granted, Parkman's opening exposition and journey to Dakota territory may not make for what would be perceived to be gripping comic book material, yet the effect here is to cast the Indians as primarily warlike aggressors with this opening sequence devoted to such actions.

At the same time, this opening sequence runs counter to the promise of the original cover in its depiction of "cowboys vs. Indians." The comic adaptation mostly depicts relations between Indians and whites as peaceful. Parkman lives among them, and the narrative communicates an experience more in line with the second cover. The threat of violence against white settlers does emerge later in the comic book, though. Parkman converses with one settler who explains how he keeps the Indians at peace by offering them free access to his cornfield. Parkman then meets with a wagon train that had been attacked (although this action is not shown). Then he and his companions come across an Arapaho village, where they give out presents, an act that they perceive will ensure their safety. After this encounter, the narration explains, "In the evening, we could see the wolves running about the prairie within a few rods of our camp fire. However, I felt more at ease with these wolves than the human wolves nearby." O'Rourke paraphrases Parkman's original language, but "human wolves" remains the same in both texts (see page 401 in Parkman's text). Earlier in the original narrative, Parkman paints a similar fear of Indians, speaking of the Indian hospitality within their towns that would be hostility on the plain: "[B]ut doubtless one half at least of our kind hosts, had they met us alone and unarmed on the prairie, would have robbed us of our horses, and perchance bestowed an arrow upon us beside. Trust not an Indian" (201). Yet preceding this dire warning, Parkman seems to admire also the warring nature (or "the gift and natur' of the Indian," as Hawkeye would say) of these Indians:

> This fierce and evil spirit awakens their most eager aspirations, and calls forth their greatest energies. It is chiefly this that saves them from lethargy and utter abasement. Without its powerful stimulus they would be like the unwarlike tribes beyond the mountains. . . . These latter have little of humanity except form; but the proud and ambitious Dahcotah warrior can sometimes boast of heroic virtues. (200)

While the violent tendencies of these Indians are something to fear, these same tendencies invigorate them, make them energetic and vital, and distinguish them in a positive way from the "unwarlike tribes." Whether Parkman implies that such a warlike nature can be a model for the white male is arguable. If Parkman views the "nature" of the Indian as warlike, then when he does not exercise that nature, he does not fulfill the potential of his race, and thus falls short of his "gifts." The white man, on the other hand, is not a warlike "savage" and so would not necessarily be expected to practice war as a means to achieving "heroic virtues." Such categorization does not preclude the white man from experiencing the invigoration of battle, though, and a powerful current in the comic and the book is the potential of the frontier, with its dangers and its exotic peoples, to reenergize the visiting white male, a point also evident in this book's first chapter's analysis of Parkman's depiction of Indian male bodies.

The comic book concludes with the rhetoric of the vanishing Indian and the inevitable victory of the settlers: "The days of the Indian and buffalo as rulers of the west are numbered," and "The Oregon Trail was being broadened to a great wide highway by the thousands of pioneers who would not be conquered by savages or the privations of their desperate journey." Parkman's own writing engages in a similar elegiac tone. He speaks of the "great changes" in store as white settlers move into the west: "[T]he buffalo will dwindle away, and the large wandering communities who depend on them for support must be broken and scattered. The Indians will soon be corrupted by the example of the whites, abased by whiskey and overawed by military posts" (252). With this the settler will be able to travel in safety through what were once Indian lands, yet Parkman seems saddened by this development: "Its [Indian country's] danger and its charm will have disappeared altogether" (252). The charm of the country lies in its danger. In addition, in that danger seems to be the promise of vital and strong manhood.

Largely, this adaptation of *The Oregon Trail* is typical of the *Classics Illustrated* line. In terms of this analysis, this *Classics* adaptation performs that work of isolating the frontier as the proving grounds of the American spirit and of American manhood. *The Last of the Mohicans*, too, dramatizes the frontier similarly, and so its comics adaptations (of which there are quite a few) will provide an even more vivid illustration of the patterns and ideologies at work in the transmission of frontier mythos and playing Indian in comic books.

*The Last of the Mohicans* probably is one of the most-adapted American novels in American popular culture. Jeffrey Walker posits that Cooper's novel "has probably generated more attention from Hollywood filmmakers than virtually any other American novel." Walker estimates that in the twentieth century "more than a dozen interpretations of the novel have appeared in various forms" (n.pag.). A television series, *Hawkeye and the Last of the Mohicans*, included Lon Chaney, Jr., as Chingachgook and was adapted as a comic book series. Martin Barker and Roger Sabin identify eight American comic book adaptations, with the earliest being produced in the 1940s. The influence of *Mohicans* in comic art and American Western comics has even been documented as spreading to Japan in the 1950s. Ryan Holmberg delivers an enlightening analysis of Shigeru Sugiura's *The Last of the Mohicans* (1953, remade in 1974) and its debt to the visual styles of Western-genre comics such as *Indians* #3 and *Tomahawk* (146–49). As Holmberg states, "If Cooper's novel provided the basic story and characters, guidelines for how to visualize them—and the directions in which to digress—came instead from titles like Fred Ray's *Tomahawk* and Alex Toth's *Johnny Thunder*, and to a lesser extent from Jesse Marsh's *Tarzan*" (121). One might extract from this statement a more general truth underlying this chapter as to the role of comic books in defining and originating the visuals of playing Indian and the frontier in American culture while perpetuating and/or challenging the ideologies of race and culture being transmitted from previous works and texts.

Probably the earliest comics adaptation, as Barker and Sabin show, appears as a ten-part series in *Target Comics* v. 2 #12, v. 3 #1–9 (Feb. 1942–Nov. 1942),[1] with art by Harold DeLay and text mainly from Cooper, with occasional paraphrasing or additional narrative exposition. During the same year, the 1942 *Classic Comics* title (which would become *Classics Illustrated* in 1947) appeared. *Classics Illustrated* would regularly reprint its stories, and these reprints are identified by the "Highest Reorder Number" (HRN) that appears either on the inside cover or the back. *Mohicans* was the fourth story in the series, with a publication date of August 1942.[2] Jack Davis produced a six-page adaptation in 1954 that appears in *Two-Fisted Tales* #40 (Dec. 1954–Jan. 1955). *Classics Illustrated* produced a revamped adaptation in 1959 with pencils by John Severin and inks by Stephen Addeo. In 1976 Marvel's first adaptation was released under its Classics Comics series. This adaptation was written by Doug Moench, best known for his work on Marvel's *The Master of Kung Fu* and DC's Batman, especially the "Knightfall" storyline. Dark Horse published its adaptation in 1992 with Jack Jackson's script and art. Jackson's work before this adaptation includes *Los Tejanos* and *Comanche Moon*, graphic novels that demonstrate his attention to historical detail. Marvel revived its comic book adaptations with the Marvel Illustrated series, releasing *Last of the Mohicans* in a six-issue series in 2007 (the graphic novel following in 2008). This adaptation was written by Roy Thomas, known for his work on *Conan the Barbarian*, as well as various major Marvel heroes, and his work as editor-in-chief of Marvel in the early seventies.

Each adaptation follows the same basic plot points, including such significant moments as the standoff at the waterfall hideout, the two captures and rescues of the Munro daughters, the massacre at Fort William Henry, and the final fight between Uncas and Magua resulting in their deaths and Cora's. In contrast to the film adaptations, which Walker charges with consistently altering and distorting Cooper's original characterizations, the comic adaptations stay true to the original roles of the characters. Uncas emerges as a central character in the post–*Classics Illustrated* versions, while Hawkeye is typically secondary. The romance between Uncas and Cora is present, although in keeping with the subtle implication of the novel. Like the films, the comics tend to rely heavily on the adventure plot of the novel rather than developing its themes of European–Native relations, the nature of conquest and settlement, or the character of American identity. Jackson's adaptation is an exception in this regard in raising the problems of European settlement and its effects on the indigenous peoples.

The *Target Comics* serial adheres closely to the original storyline and includes details that are not found in other versions, especially concerning the violence found in the novel. For example, in part 4, a half-page panel depicts Chingachgook about to scalp a fallen Huron after the first rescue, his act occurring in the background while the other men gather around Alice and Cora. The text does not refer to his action. The opening panel of part 5 shows Chingachgook with tomahawk raised to attack the French soldier, previewing the action to be depicted later. When the narrative reaches this scene, the comic devotes seven panels to the sequence in which the travelers encounter the French soldier and get past him, yet Chingachgook goes back to kill the soldier. When the elder Mohican returns to the group, the comic describes him doing so "with a satisfied grin." This characterization of his mood seems an interpretation of Cooper's description of Chingachgook as having "the air of a man who believed he had done a deed of merit" (162). Hawkeye's remark on Chingachgook's actions is paraphrased from the original text: "It would have been cruel for a white man, but it's natural for an Indian!" Part 6 depicts the Fort William Henry massacre in relatively greater detail than some of the succeeding adaptations, discussed in more detail below.

In the first *Classics Illustrated* version (1942), the narrative makes a steady course in following the original plot but has little feel of narrative action or tension; it proceeds more like a checklist of major events of the novel than an autonomous narrative that runs upon its own energy and conflict. Jack Davis's 1954 adaptation streamlines the story with a focus on the most potent action sequences. The story is framed as a conflict between the Mohicans and the Huron. Chingachgook, Uncas, and Hawkeye are the protagonists, with Magua as the villain, and the rest of the characters marginally present, except for Cora in the end (who is also blonde). Such a compression of the story obviously excludes many details. This version emphasizes the scenes of combat. The fight at William Henry is conflated with the final battle between the Uncas-led Delaware and Magua and the Huron. The William Henry battle (not really a massacre in this version) occupies a page-wide panel and depicts a flurry of bodies entangled in conflict. Uncas fights to rescue Cora, but his motivation for doing so is not present in this comic. A comprehensive adaptation is not the goal, anyway, as the comic's preface explains: "These six pages attempt only to give a tantalizing glimpse into that great classic" (1).

The 1959 *Classics* revamp shortens the first *Classics* version by about fourteen pages, and thus the narrative is more compact and moves quicker, and it proceeds more smoothly, too. Barker and Sabin judge it an improvement over its predecessor, especially in its fairer treatment of the Native characters and customs (165–68). The 1959 version also seems more at home in being a comic book, a quality that the 1976 version more strongly embraces. Moench's 1976 narrative draws out of Cooper's novel the key points of action, organizing the narrative around the major scenes of conflict, structuring the story upon these sensational moments of action and violence. Jackson's 1992 adaptation follows many of the same plot points as the 1976 version. Jackson places less emphasis on the fight scenes, often recounted in narration rather than shown. Two examples that show this are the fight at the waterfall and the massacre at the fort. In the latter instance, Jackson includes the detail about the woman's infant being murdered by one of the Huron, a detail not included in the previous versions. Roy Thomas in 2007 is able to tell the story over six issues, resulting in over 130 pages for his adaptation, and thus is able to develop in more depth key scenes and to add in others (such as the ceremonial preparation of Uncas before attacking Magua in the final sequence).

The point in looking at these adaptations is not so much to tie them to any specific cultural contexts for the comic books themselves but to show how the comics medium is used and understood in its transmission of Cooper's story. These different adaptations reveal different emphases and priorities in retelling the story in comic book form. This analysis reveals, then, not only the persistence of Cooper's story and its conventions in

American culture but also the changing perception of comics as an art form. *Classics Illustrated* subordinates the form to the content. Marvel's 1976 version adheres to the conventions of the superhero comic book in its narrative action and its art. Jack Jackson's adaptation, drawn in black and white, centers the narrative upon the interactions among the characters and raises some of the ethical issues found in the story. His version connects the story to history. Thomas's version might be viewed as an expansion of the first Marvel adaptation; he achieves greater character depth than *Classics Illustrated*, for sure, but does not fully address the historical themes found in Jackson. In other words, *Classics Illustrated* is interested only in conveying the work as a literary classic, the 1976 adaptation is interested in conveying the work as a comic book action story, the 1992 adaptation is interested in the historical and human implications of the narrative, and the 2007 adaptation seeks to retell the original story while utilizing the comics medium to its potential.

Two aspects of these adaptations provide illustrative points of comparison: 1) the characterizations of Uncas and Cora and their relationship and 2) the art and style of the various comics as exemplified by the depiction of the massacre at Fort William Henry in each of these adaptations.

The characterization of Uncas, especially concerning the tension between his "nobility" and "savagery," the addressing or not of Cora's mixed-blood status, and the relationship between these two characters, receive varied depictions in these adaptations. *Target Comics* makes no concrete reference to the possible romance between Uncas and Cora. For example, the end does not mention any of the sentiments of Uncas and Cora joining in the afterlife, as found in the novel. *Classics Illustrated* (1942) accentuates the "noble" side of Uncas. This version also makes no mention of Cora's bloodline, while leaving the relationship between her and Uncas barely visible. The 1959 version also holds to a subdued depiction of Uncas's affection for Cora. His attending to the sisters at Glenn's Falls (a moment that Cooper uses to identify a potential interest of Uncas in Cora) is absent. This version includes Uncas's initial refusal to abandon the women at Glenn's Falls, but, as in the novel, Cora persuades him to join his father and Hawkeye. One other subtle hint of Uncas's affection for Cora surfaces in this version: his watching her as Magua takes her away, as described in the comic: "He kept his eyes on Cora until she was out of sight" (42). Cora's racial lineage also receives no mention.

Marvel's 1976 adaptation centers the narrative upon Uncas as the dominant character; he is the hero, and with his prominence, this adaptation poses the romance between him and Cora more concretely and obviously. In Jackson's version the romantic connection between Cora and Uncas is more implied, in keeping with the original, although in the end it is addressed explicitly in their burial: "Although life never permitted them an expression of their love, Cora and Uncas were united in death according to Delaware custom." Cora's mixed blood is a detail that Jackson includes, in contrast to preceding adaptations; Thomas's version also includes this part. Barker and Sabin observe the exclusion of Cora's mixed race from most of the adaptations, along with the killing of Gamut's colt, a move that they attribute to "the same protective sensibilities that led to much the same exclusions in most book abridgments" (153). Like Jackson, Thomas also leaves the Uncas–Cora attachment more inferred than explicit. One key panel conveys a connection between the two; when Cora bids her friends and family farewell before being taken by Magua, one horizontal panel is devoted to Cora and Uncas exchanging an intense gaze in silence: the implication is that they feel something for each other, but they do not verbalize it. As in the novel, Thomas includes Uncas watching Cora as she leaves with Magua: "Uncas kept his eyes upon the form of Cora . . . until the colors of her dress . . . were blended with the foliage of the forest." These pieces of narration extend over three panels that provide a notable departure from the typical layout of the graphic novel. Cora's departure proceeds over the course of three panels, descending from the top of the page. In the first panel, a full horizontal length across the page, Cora's face is shown in close-up as she looks back over her shoulder. The second panel is a smaller horizontal, framed, and is a medium shot with both Magua and Cora in view. The third panel is slightly shorter, but wider than the previous one and is a wider shot: Cora and Magua are becoming shadows in the forest as in the middle distance and foreground Delaware men watch the departure. These top three panels overlay a nearly full-page, depth-of-field shot that reverses the previous perspective to show Uncas in the right foregrounded as the dominant figure of the composition, with Hawkeye, Heyward, and Alice also watching as Cora leaves. The visual composition of these panels and the lingering of the pace upon Uncas's sorrow in losing Cora bespeak his romantic feeling for her.

Unlike the 1942, 1959, and 1976 versions, Jackson's includes details that might lessen the perception of Uncas's heroic status: his killing of Gamut's horse and his scalping of an Oneida, whose tribe was an ally to the British. This latter incident gives cause to illustrate the disruption of natural alliances that the war has produced. Hawkeye explains, "He should have been friend, yet he was foe. It is to be expected, when nature's order is thrown into disarray." Thomas's adaptation includes the incident in which Chingachgook kills and scalps a French soldier leading to the oft-noted words of Hawkeye, which follow the original almost exactly: "'Twould have been a cruel and an inhuman act for a whiteskin . . . but 'tis the gift and nature of an Indian . . . and I suppose it could not be denied."

How these adaptations choose to end the story provides insight into their respective treatments of Cora and Uncas's romance. *Classics Illustrated*'s 1942 version ends the story before the burial of Uncas and Cora, which in the novel is occasion for expressing romantic sentiments ascribed to the couple. Unlike its predecessor, the 1959 version includes the assurance at Cora's funeral that Uncas would accompany and protect her on her death's journey. The 1976 and 1992 versions include the burial but not Hawkeye's objection in the novel to the idea that Cora and Uncas will reside in the same afterlife together. The 2007 adaptation recounts their burial but makes no explicit mention in the text of their being side by side, although the final panel shows their grave mounds beside each other; further, there is no mention of the two departed reuniting in the afterlife (and thus no objection from Hawkeye on that point).

The depictions of Uncas and Cora and their relationship provide insight into the cultural expectations shaping these adaptations. The adaptations generally dampen or omit Uncas's violent behavior as found in the novel, while variously emphasizing his romantic attachment to Cora. The degree of emphasis placed on the violence of Uncas or his love for Cora might reflect broader expectations for depicting the "Indian" or for miscegenation. In the same way, the omission or inclusion of Cora's racial lineage might also reflect contemporary expectations about race. In all, the choices made in these adaptations are telling in reflecting their cultural context. On this note, the art and style of the adaptations provide a sense of how comic art changes during the twentieth century as well as the comics' reaction to standards of taste and propriety in presenting the content.

*Classics Illustrated* offers an initial example of differences in art and style in the two different covers that appear for *Mohicans*. The early one, drawn by Ray Ramsey, possesses standard comic style and depicts Magua and Uncas in their final fight with Hawkeye in the background. The second cover, which is unattributed, is a painted close-up of, presumably, Chingachgook, since the portrait follows very closely Cooper's description of the Mohican upon his introduction in the story: "His closely shaven head, on which no other hair than the well-known and chivalrous scalping

Figure 3.5. First cover. *Classic Comics* #4 (Aug. 1942). Gilberton Company.

tuft was preserved, was without ornament of any kind, with the exception of a solitary eagle's plume that crossed his crown and depended over the left shoulder" (32). With the exception of the feather being on the right instead of the left, this cover follows Cooper's description exactly.

The first cover conveys action and excitement, as well as violence (Fig. 3.5). The distinction between Uncas, in his fringed shirt, and Magua, in just a loincloth, conveys their respective nobility and savagery. The second cover offers a more humanized portrait of the Mohican, his eyes making full contact with the viewer; yet his lack of clothing, hairstyle, feather, and facial features mark him as other, as Indian (Fig. 3.6). This change of cover might also indicate an attempt to convey a more serious tone for the adaptation, an attempt to distance the comic from the visuals and style commonly

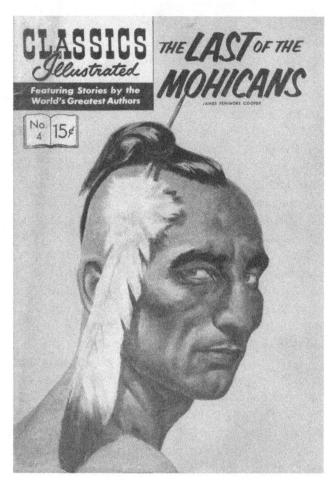

Figure 3.6. Second cover. *Classics Illustrated* #4 (Nov. 1959). Gilberton Company.

associated with comic books (a difference also visible in the covers for *The Oregon Trail* discussed above). Rocco Versaci reads this change to painted covers, after 1951, as a sign of *Classics Illustrated*'s posture as "serious" literature (186). The first cover's scene, though, is the one that will be echoed by succeeding adaptations.[3] The fight between Magua and Uncas is also used for the covers of the 1976 and 1992 versions. The 2007 series departs from that convention in presenting Hawkeye battling an Indian, with the faces of Uncas and Chingachgook inset in the upper left; this cover is also used for the graphic novel's cover. This choice may well have been influenced by Michael Mann's 1992 film and its positioning of Hawkeye as the main protagonist, a possibility supported by the similarity in features of Marvel's 2007 Hawkeye to Daniel Day-Lewis's Hawkeye in the Mann film.

The art by Ray Ramsey in *Classics Illustrated* is stilted and basic, but that is to be expected in a series in which the art is subordinate to the story. As Joseph Witek remarks in examining the *Classics Illustrated* depiction of the fall of Fort Sumter, "[t]his narrative's characteristic strategies demonstrate an attempt to produce a comic book as little like a typical comic book as possible while still exploiting the form's storytelling potential" (35). The simplicity of the art keeps the focus on the text and the story itself. Even the text possesses a stilted quality. Versaci provides insight on this point: "One of the trademarks of the *Classics Illustrated* style is this 'mechanical' lettering style that conveys a stiffness in all of the elements requiring text: narration, dialogue, and thoughts" (190). The most remarkable visual features of the comic lie in the distinction between Uncas and Magua. In keeping with Cooper's juxtaposition of the noble Uncas to the savage Magua, the latter is drawn with exaggerated hooknose, gaunt face, and beady eyes. Uncas's face is more symmetrical, with smoother features, and bears close resemblance to the white characters (although his skin is of a darker hue and he wears the Mohican hairstyle). Overall, as with the other comics in the *Classics Illustrated* line, this adaptation of *The Last of the Mohicans* suffers from drab style and standardized art, by which, as Versaci argues, "the comic book is denied full expression of its signifying capabilities" (192). Artistically, the 1959 version demonstrates a noticeable improvement.

Marvel's 1976 adaptation, on the other hand, exercises the comic book form in a more evident and accomplished manner. The art style, composition, and narrative structure exhibit those conventions that by the 1970s would be standard in comics, a fact that becomes evident in comparison to the earlier *Classics Illustrated* versions. Versaci notes the departure of Marvel's line from *Classics Illustrated*: "[T]hese newer versions embraced a looser, more dynamic visual style that employed devices such as erratically shaped word balloons, sound effects, and a far less 'gridlike' layout style; in short, the *Classics Comics* were not afraid to look like comic books" (192–93). The male characters, especially the Indians, are drawn with pronounced muscularity. They exhibit the form of the superhero with exaggerated muscle definition. The females exude sexuality and pronounced feminine features (although not to the buxom degree of typical female comic book characters). *Classics Illustrated* presents the human form in general as flat and vaguely defined. Skin color in these two versions marks another contrast. In Marvel's 1976 adaptation, the difference of hue between the whites and the Indians is present, but barely so, while in *Classics Illustrated* the Indians possess a much darker hue than the whites do. Action scenes in the 1976 version possess energy and kinetic movement: fights depicted with raised arms and swinging tomahawks, faces snarling in angry grimace, along with the sound effects and motion lines that indicate action. Such composition is in stark contrast to the fight scenes in *Classics Illustrated* that are static and staid in comparison, eschewing the sound effects and action lines common to comics visuals.

The opening splash page of the 1976 adaptation further affirms this adaptation's emphasis on action and physicality of the characters. The novel's full cast appears in disproportionate sizes on this page. In the lower left, Uncas and Cora are together. Cora strikes a seductive pose in a red dress with legs fully revealed, as behind her Uncas is situated. From behind this pair, the much larger form of Magua emerges, his mouth open in an angry scream, his left arm extended and cutting across the whole page, a knife pointed downward gripped in his hand. Moving diagonally up and to the right, Chingachgook stands in the center of the page, his legs and arms spread, a tomahawk in his right hand and spear in the other. Like Magua, he is frozen in mid-scream. Both Magua and Chingachgook exhibit well-defined musculature, with the latter clothed in a loincloth, thus revealing his physique. Beside Chingachgook and facing page right, Hawkeye stands with his rifle at the ready. Moving finally into the upper right, Alice and Heyward are present. Alice's blonde hair floats over to the left, her tresses a background to Chingachgook and Hawkeye. Alice is a dominant figure in terms of the size given to her face; her striking beauty contrasts sharply to the unrestrained anger exhibited by Magua and Chingachgook. Behind her, only half-visible, Heyward occupies a subordinate position. This title page greets the reader with a sensationalized portrait of the characters, composed in pairs: Uncas–Cora, Chingachgook–Hawkeye, and Alice–Heyward, with Magua unpaired. This page places obvious emphasis on the physical features of the characters, the Indian males' muscled bodies and the attractiveness of the sisters.

In the 1992 adaptation, Jackson's black-and-white art and its roughly hewn lines focus the text upon the story and the characters. Jackson's underground comix pedigree and his historically anchored work in graphic novels like *Comanche Moon* and *Los Tejanos* bring to his adaptation a clearer sense of the context and the human implications of the story. His art and style mark his adaptation as clearly distinct from the others, as well as aligning his version with a tradition in comic art associated with artistic integrity, individual expression, and resistance to the status quo. In contrast, Thomas's 2007 version adheres more closely to the typical comic book style. Its panel layout distinguishes it from the previous adaptations, though. The standard layout in this adaptation consists of four to five panels to a page, stretching horizontally across, with bleed to the page edge. Characters often break out of the panel frame, and variations to the layout function to accentuate shifts in action and focus. These varying artistic styles in these adaptations can be more vividly demonstrated through an examination of the depictions of one of the novel's central incidents: the massacre at Fort William Henry.

Since this scene is present in every adaptation, and since it is a central incident of the narrative (even occurring at the midway point of the novel), it stands as an exemplary moment to compare the differing stylistic choices of the artist for each of these adaptations. How the massacre is initiated, how it is depicted, and choices between visualizing or narrating the events are key points of comparison here. The *Target Comics* adaptation depicts the massacre in some detail in the opening panel. The scene is foreshadowed in the first panel that shows in the foreground Magua capturing Alice, and in the background the battle raging. In the near-center is the infamous encounter between the Huron and the mother: the Huron holds the infant upside down by a leg while the mother kneels before him with arms outstretched, her back to the reader. In the body of the comic, the massacre is depicted only with Magua's signal and the rush of the Huron onto the surrendering group of English.

In the 1942 *Classics Illustrated* version, a Huron takes a shawl, and then the attack begins. The narration explains, "The scene that follows is too horrible to describe." The scene of the massacre is shown from the distance, with trees framing the fight and creating containment of the scene. The 1959 adaptation devotes one panel to depict the Huron beginning their attack at Magua's command, with no mention of women and children among the group departing from William Henry or the encounter that spurs the fight. In the 1976 adaptation Magua initiates the attack. Perspective is in the midst of the battle; from the left upper corner, a Huron's head and arms are shown, his right hand at the throat of a British shoulder and left hand with knife raised to strike down. The two figures emerge horizontally from the left side of the panel. The Huron's knife leads the eye to the center of the panel, where the bulk of the action occurs: a mass of bare-chested Huron and red-coated British, the Huron with the upper hand as they stab and murder the soldiers. From this point in the panel, the eye is then caught by the handle of a hatchet as it angles down to the bottom right corner, where the face of a screaming white man is shown, with a small portion of the tomahawk's blade visible, while the rest is buried, unseen, in the man's neck. The Huron's knife on the left and hatchet on the right balance each other in their opposite corners of the panel and emphasize the violence of the massacre. Unlike the 1942 version, the scene is uncontained, this panel implying unseen action beyond its frame. This scene owes much to the Kirby style of rendering intense and varied action within the space of the panel. Following Charles Hatfield's breakdown of a typical Kirby scene (*Alternative Comics* 54–55), one can see how this scene of the massacre portrays "synchronic images" that depict a flurry of events occurring in an extended sequence seeming to happen at once.

The difference between these depictions of the same scene is remarkable and demonstrates the evolution of comic art within the span of three decades. *Classics Illustrated* places the scene in the distance; the reader is detached from the action not only by distance but also by the framing of the panel. Trees border the action, creating boundaries and containment of the violence. Such discrete framing places the reader outside the story. William Moebius, concerning picture books, observes, "Framed, the illustration provides a limited glimpse 'into' a world. Unframed, the illustration constitutes a total experience, the view from 'within'" (141). *Classics Illustrated*, then, creates a limited view of the scene from without, while Marvel's 1976 version, following Kirby's style, depicts the same scene as unframed and thus places the reader within the action. As mentioned above, this difference signals a shift in style and art in comics in which the distance between the reader and the action, and violence, of the story is drastically reduced. Kirby's influence is definitely in effect in terms of the development of comic art on this point. Furthermore, this difference of style and composition not only points to a maturation of comic art but also reveals differing attitudes toward the depiction of violence. *Classics Illustrated*, in its gestures toward legitimacy in conveying "classic" literature in the comic form, would be expected to shy away from intense engagement of the reader in a scene of violence. Sawyer confirms this point when describing Kanter and Gilberton's 1951 changes: "The violence was toned down and an effort was made to have these comics become attractive to everyone, not just youngsters" (10).

In the 1992 version Jackson spends little time on the massacre itself. As in the novel, a Huron takes an infant as ransom for a desired shawl. Jackson explains, "We shall not dwell on all the horrors that succeeded . . ." Huron warriors are shown running from the woods to attack the British, and that is all. Jackson's forgoing of actually depicting the massacre may stem from narrative emphasis: his story is not concerned with the adventure aspect of the narrative, as is usually the case. By deemphasizing the actual fight, but emphasizing the consequences of it, Jackson ties the story into its overarching theme of the disruption of balance and human relations that European actions have created. Jackson's leaving the battle scene offstage is not the censorious action of *Classics Illustrated*, but a narrative choice to highlight elements of the story beyond the sensational.

In the Thomas adaptation, the massacre scene returns to a place of prominence in the narrative. In this version the massacre occupies near- ly four pages from the initial action of the shawl and infant to Magua's absconding with the daughters. As in previous adaptations, and in the original, a Huron takes a woman's shawl, then her child. Included in this later adaptation are more details about the deaths of the mother and her child. The child's and mother's murders are described as Cora and Alice are shown witnessing the horrible events. The next panel, and last on the page, presents a close-up of the mother's face on the ground, her eyes open and lifeless, and from the right side the child's hand extends, its forefinger pointing in death to the mother. The horror of these deaths is illustrated in their aftermath. Turning the page reveals the massacre beginning in full. Four horizontal panels of similar size depict the main action of the massacre. The top panel is a close-up of Magua's face as he whoops out the signal to attack. The second panel shows a group of Huron directly facing and approaching the reader, their faces twisted in anger and mouths open in screams. The reader stands in the position of the British soldiers, women, and children in this panel. The third panel presents a side view of the attack; the only victims shown are soldiers. This panel is bookended by a Huron, whose head and left arm are seen emerging from the left, with knife drawn, as he targets a cowering British man on the panel's right side. Between these two figures the battle rages as British soldiers fall under the blows of the attacking Huron. The final panel on this page moves the perspective to an aerial view in which the men are distinguishable only by the red uniforms of the British and the tawny forms of the Indians. The next page brings the focus to Cora, Alice, and Gamut. After Magua kidnaps the sisters, the narrative shifts to the aftermath of the massacre. A half-page panel shows the Huron pillaging the dead soldiers, trying on their uniforms and caps, as bloodied bodies lie upon the ground. In the foreground, in the bottom right corner, a Huron holds his arm up hori- zontally, knife aiming downward, his victim unseen off-panel, except for a raised hand. This sequence fully depicts the massacre, involving the reader much more intimately in the events than in the previous versions.

This selection of adaptations demonstrates on one count the development of comics art and differing approaches that various writers and artists take in adapting *The Last of the Mohicans*. One can readily see the fashion in which conventional comics arts have progressed from the 1940s to the early 2000s by even a quick survey of these comic books. Furthermore, the constant return of comic book artists and writers to this particular story is perhaps in itself a testament to the appeal and power of Cooper's story. As is a defining thread of this study, these comics adaptations attest to the persistence of the frontier mythos in American culture, a persistence also detectable in the propagation of the Boone legend in the twentieth century.

Given the rich history of Boone's symbolism, examined in chapter 2, the comics that arrive during the mid-twentieth century are able to convey easily a figure of frontier bravery and leadership who represents the ideals and victories of America. In the context of a postwar world in which the United States finds itself battling the perceived menace of communism both home and abroad, Boone's heroic figure must certainly take on additional symbolic dimensions. This section examines some of the 1940s and 1950s comic book series featuring Boone.

Boone's popularity in American culture finds its way from the nineteenth century into the twentieth through one major vein: dime novels. Daryl Jones argues that Boone represents one important character type of the dime novels: the backwoodsman (34). A number of dime novels featuring Boone were published during the dime novel period, such as Percy St. John's *Queen of the Woods; or, The Shawnee Captive* (1868), Joseph E. Badger's *The Wood King; or, Daniel Boone's Last Trail* (1873), John Sherman's *Daniel Boone's Best Shot; or, The Perils of Kentucky* (1892), and Paul Braddon's *Daniel Boone, the Hero of Kentucky* (1893) (Jones 34–35, 179). Jones typifies the Boone backwoodsman: "Shrewd but spiritually unblemished, he personifies the Romantic, primitivistic notion that Nature is the handiwork of God" (27).

*Classics Illustrated* #96 (June 1952) is an adaptation of John Bakeless's 1939 biography, *Daniel Boone: Master of the Wilderness*. Between 1953 and 1965, at least seven comic book series devoted to Daniel Boone were published: *Fighting Daniel Boone* (Avon, 1953), *Exploits of Daniel Boone* (Quality, 1955), *Legends of Daniel Boone* (DC, 1955), *Dan'l Boone: Greatest Frontiersman of All* (Magazine Enterprises, 1955), *Frontier Scout Dan'l Boone* (Charlton, 1956), *Fighting Daniel Boone* (I. W. Publishing, 1958), and

*Daniel Boone* (Western, 1965, based on the Fess Parker television show). Boone made appearances in other comic book titles devoted to frontier or Western tales, such as *Wild Frontier* (1955) and *Heroes of the Wild Frontier* (1956). While these series were usually short-lived, their appearance marks a popularity of the frontiersman during this time period, a popularity that perhaps sees its fullest fruition in the Fess Parker television series that ran from 1964 to 1970. Another comic book that deserves mention here is *Tomahawk* (1947–1972); while not explicitly linked to Boone, Tomahawk's origin story, dress, and setting make for a clear resemblance. Chapter 4 discusses *Tomahawk* in more detail.

A correlation between the state of the comic book industry from 1952 to 1954 and the surge of Boone comics from 1952 to 1958 is worth exploring. Jean-Paul Gabilliet describes the sharp decline of comic book releases during this period, placing the "collapse in the annual number of comic book releases" as occurring in 1953 (46). Gabilliet demonstrates that the collapse occurred before the institution of the Comics Code Authority, and he thus counters the popular perception of the Code's supposed devastating effect on the comic book industry's production (one can still argue for a devastating effect in terms of censorship and artistic freedom). Gabilliet states, "The 'crisis,' in the economic sense of the term, debuted in 1953, when the declining number of new releases combined with a precipitous collapse of circulation figures" (47).

Although the number of Boone releases is but a small portion of the total number of releases occurring during those years (declining from 2,880 in 1953 and stabilizing around the 1,500 mark in 1959 [Gabilliet 46]), their production by a variety of publishers (including Gilberton and DC, as well as smaller presses) argues for a definite interest in the figure and perception of his economic potential as a comic book character. This interest in Boone might owe to a variety of factors: the need for a "safe" comic book in light of public disapproval of the medium, and a political shift in the United States toward conservative ideology. Gabilliet identifies this latter point as an aspect of 1953's political and ideological environment that is relevant to that year's decline of the industry (47). More specifically, Daniel Boone represents an ideal American; his wilderness cunning and masculine virtues construct him as a potent symbol of the perceived ideals of US strength and values. One important note must be kept in mind when considering this spate of Boone comics in the 1950s: the Fess Parker television show did not air until 1964. It might be easy to conflate the TV show with these releases, but the chronology shows that the comic books predated the show by a decade. On this point, though, Disney released its feature film *Davy Crockett: King of the Wild Frontier* in 1955, a film compiled from the television episodes that appeared in 1954 and 1955. Not to conflate Crockett and Boone, but the Crockett film indicates an interest in the frontier mythos that the Boone comics are certainly parties to in their production.

The Daniel Boone comics of the 1950s generally were highly conventional and staid products. Artistically, little distinguishes them. Thematically, their invocations of the heroic Boone and his embodiment of the frontier spirit, of the ideal American, merit attention in this study. The titles examined here include *Classics Illustrated*'s adaptation of the John Bakeless Boone biography, *Exploits of Daniel Boone, Dan'l Boone: Greatest Frontiersman of All*, and *Frontier Scout Dan'l Boone*. This section also examines Boone's appearance in the *Tomahawk* series. This focus, though, provides a substantial representation of the popular depiction of Boone that these comics are maintaining.

*Classics Illustrated* #96 was an adaptation of John Bakeless's *Daniel Boone: Master of the Wilderness*. While Bakeless provides a fairly nuanced and comprehensive survey of Boone's life, the comic adaptation must be selective in the incidents and moments it presents. On this point one can easily understand the particular incidents that the adaptation emphasizes. As in the typical Boone timeline, *Classics* details the kidnapping and rescue of Boone's daughter and the Callaway girls, Boone's capture and adoption, his court-martial, the Blue Licks defeat, and Boone's move to St. Louis due to legalities of land ownership.

The rescue of the Boone and Callaway daughters receives six pages. The resonance with *The Last of the Mohicans* is obvious here: the capture of Cora and Alice in Cooper is thought to be based on this incident from Boone's life. Appearing here in *Classics Illustrated*, there is something of an echo chamber effect. A reader might be coming to this comic having read *The Last of the Mohicans* (or maybe even the *Classics* adaptation). The association between these separate stories of Indian capture and rescue by a white frontier hero solidifies an image of white heroism in the face of Indian aggression. In fact, this adaptation hews closely to the conventional treatment of Indians as aggressors and the frontier as a constant battle between whites and Indians.

Little understanding or sympathy for Indians exists in the *Classics* version of Boone's life. They are typically described as a "horde of savages," such as at the battle of Boonesborough. This depiction of the Indian as enemy holds true during Boone's capture and adoption, too. His adoption in this version follows the line of his aiming to deceive his captors in order to escape and warn Boonesborough. The narration explicitly makes this point: "Boone completely fooled the Shawnees, who thought he really had become one of them. Unfortunately, his own men misunderstood." This wording keeps with Bakeless, who writes, "Having been accepted as a friend, Boone was eager to keep up the pose. He joked and made friends with the warriors, and there may have been some surly and suspicious glances from the other whites at a leader who had first made them surrender to the redskins and now seemed to be on the best of terms with his savage captors" (168). Yet Bakeless also observes that Boone enjoyed the way of life among the Indians. Quoting Lyman C. Draper, Boone was "apparently so contented among the parcel of dirty Indians" (178). Bakeless amplifies this observation, remarking, "He was, in fact, living the life he loved best" (178).

After Boone's return the court-martial occurs, and *Classics* devotes five panels to this incident, allowing Boone to voice his defense, and presenting his exoneration and promotion in quick measure. The court-martial moment within the frame of Boone's image and legend possesses deeper significance in its airing of the concerns and fears about loyalty and treason. Bakeless addresses such concerns directly, observing, "There was a good deal of changing sides about this time" (204), and "Things were all very mixed-up out there in the backwoods, where the hard task of survival was the main problem" (205). There is almost a sense of understanding for why a settler might "go Indian."

The "white Indian," though, does not receive sympathy in Bakeless and in the *Classics* adaptation. Bakeless describes Boone seeing the brothers of Simon Girty at the Shawnee camp: "With the warriors about the fire were several white men, hardly distinguishable from redskins in their rough woods dress. Worse and worse. White brains were directing red savagery. . . . Worst of all, here were the 'white Indians,' George and James Girty, brothers of the notorious Simon whose mere name spread terror along the American frontier" (161). These lines deliver a biting indictment of white collusion with Indian forces. Bakeless presents the image of a white man directing or instigating Indian aggression against whites as a deplorable one. Simon Girty appears in Bakeless as cruel, watching Colonel William Crawford burned at the stake: "Simon Girty, the 'white Indian,' sat by to enjoy the fun" (264).

Additionally, in the comic, Girty appears, making his famous speech at Old Chillicothe as the Shawnee prepared to attack Bryan's Station. His words in the comic are an abridged version of what appears in Bakeless. In the comic he appears in Indian dress, wearing a headband (which contrasts with other comics depictions that usually show him dressed as a white). He speaks to the gathered council: "Brothers, the long knives have overrun your country and usurped your hunting grounds. Unless you rise and exterminate their whole race, you may bid goodbye to the hunting grounds." These two sentences are transferred almost verbatim from Bakeless's version (the comic substitutes "goodbye" for "adieu"). Girty, then, is not only a traitor, but also an advocate for the genocide of the whites. Yet this speech is most likely a fabrication. Consul Willshire Butterfield, in his *History of the Girtys* (1890), notes, "It is hardly necessary to inform the reader that this speech is fictitious. It bears upon its face its own refutation" (191 note).[4] According to Butterfield, Girty lacked the literacy and education to make such a speech, and even if he had, it would have been in a Native language. The source for the speech for Bakeless (and referred to by Faragher, although he omits the extermination language) is John Bradford's *Notes on Kentucky* (1826–1829). Bakeless believes the speech to be accurate, at least in content: "The florid tone is an unhappy mingling of aboriginal eloquence and eighteenth-century translation, but the content is probably reported with fair accuracy" (455 n.273.4). From Bradford, Butterfield quotes this depiction of Girty, along with Alexander McKee, as "two renegade white men, unprincipled in disposition, and stained with the blood of innocent women and children—their lives were assimilated to the customs and habits of the Indians" (372 appendix O). This estimation of the white Indian finds expression in the *Classics* comic via Bakeless. While the actuality of the speech may be in question, its power to demonize Girty, and therefore the white renegade, persists with force in this comic, and in other comics depicting Girty, even into the twentieth century. Whatever the actual language of Girty's speech, the image that *Classics* portrays of Girty and, by extension, the white Indian is one of cruelty and brutality: a white man who would incite Indians to "exterminate." Moreover, this image of the renegade white stands in stark contrast to the heroic Boone.

Following from Bakeless, *Classics Illustrated* presents the typical heroic legend of Boone's life. He is depicted as a hunter and an Indian fighter in keeping with the depictions found in other comic books on Boone of the time. For example, the cover of the first issue of *Exploits of Daniel Boone* presents a notable rhetorical positioning of Boone and his status in American history. Naming him the "greatest American frontier hero," the cover text goes on to speak of "the sturdy pioneers who built our nation and defended it with their lives," then lists a standard catalog of famous names like Kit Carson and Davy Crockett. This text goes on to proclaim that Daniel Boone "stands head and shoulders above the rest . . . his daring deeds overshadow by far those of any other frontier hero." The title plus text occupies the left top corner of the cover. Beneath these words, Daniel Boone is shown completing a punch at an Indian, who falls backward toward the viewer. In the background other Indians run at Boone from behind, and arrows land around him. The cover then lists at its bottom Boone's résumé, as it were: "Pioneer Trapper Indian Fighter Guide Explorer Scout Trail Blazer Soldier Hunter Woodsman Patriot." As discussed in chapter 2, Boone as symbolic figure has been utilized to represent numerous roles, and this cover names most, if not all, of them. His fulfillment of these various roles is also visible in the other comic series.

These comic series share a consistent mixture of fact and fiction. Some of the stories are drawn somewhat faithfully from actual history, while others are purely fictional accounts. In addition, sometimes a mixture of fact and fiction exists within the same story. The first story in *Exploits* #1, "Doom at the Stake," revolves around Boone's capture by the Shawnee and his adoption. The next two stories, "Raid on the Scioto" and "Assault on Boonesborough," detail Boone's return from captivity and defense of his settlement. "Sell-Out" from *Dan'l Boone* focuses upon the capture of Boone and his men at the salt lick. "Daniel Boone in the Shawnee Ambush" in *Heroes of the Wild Frontier* #2 details his capture, adoption, and escape. Other stories depict the capture of Boone's daughter and two other girls from the settlement ("Rescue from the Redskins" in *Exploits* #3 and "Daniel Boone in the Shawnee Ambush"). This rescue plot, with echoes of Cooper, exists in fictional stories, too: *Frontier Scout*'s "The Wild River" presents his saving a woman from "redskins" and escorting her to the safety of the settlement. "Born to the Frontier" in *Dan'l Boone* shows him tracking an Indian party to rescue settlers' daughters who had been captured. "Spirit of the Frontier," in *Dan'l Boone*, follows Boone and another character, Barlow, as they rescue a mother and daughter from capture, a rescue that prompts the mother's conversion to comprehending the value of frontier living: "Seeing you two in action just now . . . your courage and quick-thinking . . . showed me how blinded I'd been by soft Virginia living and the scared talk of city-bred relatives. . . . There's nothing finer than the frontier spirit . . . nor anybody better for Polly to marry than a frontiersman" (6). These words enact a harmonizing of the domestic and the frontier spheres often posed as irreconcilable.

A consistent theme throughout these Boone comics, and in frontier comics in general, is the value and power of the "frontier spirit." Boone embodies this spirit of courage and self-reliance, a hard living that strengthens and vitalizes. "The Pilgrims from Pennsylvania" from *Exploits* delivers this point in the contrast of the soft eastern folk who arrive on the frontier deceived by false stories of good roads and teeming cities. Boone encounters these city folk as one of them, Lucius Bascom, is singing, Gamut-like. Boone informs Bascom that he is "in the midst of a Shawanese war party after scalps, mister! If they heard you, you're in a tight fix!" Boone helps the settlers fend off the attack. In the closing panel, Boone tells Bascom and the settlers, "You've got courage and sense, Bascom! You're welcome and wanted! Good land is free to decent people out here!" (ignoring the fact that the land was not actually "free," since it was already inhabited by Native peoples). The settlers reply, "Hooray! We'll all stay and learn to farm! Maybe we'll make that land agent's lies come true some day!" The soft eastern folk have begun their transformation into hard and hardy settlers, and the promise and idealism of American civilization resounds in their words.

Daniel Boone also appears in the *Tomahawk* series in "Daniel Boone—King of the Hunters!" (*Star Spangled Comics* #88: Jan. 1949). Tomahawk, DC's frontier hero and an obvious copy of Boone, runs into Boone while hunting an Indian renegade named Black Deer. Their meeting testifies to the two frontiersmen's equal tracking skills. While each one attempts to find the other, they back into each other. Shaking hands, Boone says, "No wonder I couldn't get too close! It was you I was tryin' to track! The cagiest woodsman alive!" To which Tomahawk responds, "An' no wonder I couldn't corner you! No one—not even the smartest Injun—ever tricked Dan'l Boone!" Boone's legend as being even superior to an Indian in tracking and woodcraft is evident here, and Tomahawk, as a fictional version of Boone, echoes that legend. While the two men appear as nearly exact duplicates of each other, the signifying distinction between them is that Boone uses a rifle, and Tomahawk uses, well, a tomahawk.

The two join forces to subdue Black Deer before he causes conflict between the Indians and the settlers. This plot then proceeds based on a comparison between the relative merits of Boone's rifle and Tom's tomahawk. Tomahawk tells Boone that a rifle is too noisy; Boone prefers his rifle anyway. As Boone and Tomahawk make their way from one incident to another, the tomahawk proves a handier tool. Then, faced with a bear, and Boone's rifle broken, they use gunpowder to project the tomahawk at the bear with enough force to kill it (7). At the end of the story, after capturing Black Deer, Boone decrees that both weapons are equally effective: "We both found out that a tomahawk's as good as a rifle out here—an' a rifle's as good as a tomahawk" (8). This story, then, presents that dichotomy between the "civilized" rifle and the "savage" tomahawk (a version of which can be seen in Causici's *Conflict of Daniel Boone and the Indians*, for example). Boone's insistence on using the rifle is in keeping with marking him as on the side of civilization though he is skilled and schooled in Indian ways. Tomahawk's use of his namesake weapon, at least symbolically, would place him on the "savage" side. This story, though, finds equivalence between the two weapons: Boone's skepticism is refuted, and Tomahawk's weapon becomes whitewashed, perhaps. Any symbolic resonance of the tomahawk's perceived primitivism becomes muted by its technological marriage with gunpowder and its proven utility in Tomahawk's hands.

While this particular story serves as yet another illustration of Boone's recurring presence in mid-century comic books, as well as his persistence as a potent American hero into the twentieth century, it also participates in that powerful imagery of the tomahawk as a marker of Indianness. In addition, in that regard Tom Hawk's use of the tomahawk conveys the hero's ability to appropriate successfully Indian ways while maintaining his whiteness. In a way, then, Boone works to anchor the character of Tomahawk on the side of whiteness.

Boone says, "Good land is free to decent people out here!" Boone's mission, then, in these comics, is to assure that this promise stays true. Not everyone on the frontier is a decent person, though. While the Indians in these comics are variously villainous and peaceful, one of the recurring villain-types that deserves greater focus at this point is the white renegade. The white renegade represents a subversion of the playing Indian ideal. White renegades side with or conspire with the Indians to the detriment of the white settlers. This villain is an ideal one for Boone to complement his status as national hero, but also draw into question the unease that crossing racial boundaries can produce.

The second issue of *Exploits* includes a story about a renegade, "The Web of the White Savage." The opening narration spares no kindness for the renegade: "Renegade . . . the vilest word in the English language! The renegade was a white man who had taken to living in the wilderness as a savage . . . more cruel and brutal . . . more despicable than the lowest red torturer!" In this story Marcus Sanger is "the terrible turncoat" who lures Daniel Boone and his sidekick Sam into an Indian ambush. In the story's end, after Daniel has turned the renegade over to the settlement, he remarks, "A renegade on the loose is more dangerous than a lobo wolf!" The renegade is painted as the worst kind of villain. In the mid-1950s climate of Cold War paranoia about communist traitors and spies, the description above must have resonated deeply. In this vein, Boone as the backwoodsman stands as the moral balance to the renegade. While both men have spent time with Indians, the renegade is dastardly and treasonous, while Boone, obviously, is not.

A later issue of *Exploits* also treats the renegade theme. In "Menace of the Renegades," supply trains to the settlement are being raided by white men who are framing Indians for the theft. *Dan'l Boone* features the white renegade, too. "Peril Shadows the Forest Trail" (Dec. 1955) features as the main villain Dr. Mortell, who is revealed to be assisting the Indians in attacking the settlements. At one point Mortell speaks to his Indian conspirators: "We're in these raids together—you for vengeance because your land's being taken . . . I for the money you steal while raiding!" (5). The white renegade's motives in these comics are usually financial. Of course, Boone uncovers Mortell's treachery and sets things right. In the same issue, another story treats the renegade theme. "Renegade on the River" centers around Big Mike Trent, a flatboat captain on the Ohio River. He allows Indians to raid his boat, capture the crew, and take the supplies. The narration explains how afterward he "is left alone—to reflect on the profits a man can make by betraying his fellows" (3). Boone enters the scene when he is captured and brought to the same camp as the betrayed rivermen. Boone and the rivermen escape and return home, and then Boone finds Trent's boat and warns the new crew about their captain. Boone fights Trent but is knocked out by one of the crew loyal to Trent. Regaining consciousness, Boone steers the boat into the rapids, causing the Indians to become seasick and then easily overcome by the crew. Mike Trent is tied up, and his renegade days are done. *Dan'l Boone* #7 includes a prose piece entitled "The Real Renegade." In this story Jim Kirby and Tad Jones are waiting to ambush a suspected renegade, Fred Morgan. Kirby tells Tad to "cool down" while they wait for Morgan. Tad thinks, "There was no need that he could see to bottle up anger that was aimed at a man so low enough to sell out his own people to the Indians!" The story reveals, though, that Morgan is not a renegade but has been manipulated by the "real renegade," Bart Wilcox. This turn of events demonstrates how deceitful and dangerous the renegade can be. These renegades typify the disloyalty of the white settler who would trade profits for the defense and stability of the white settlements.

Perhaps the most famous (or infamous) white renegade is Simon Girty, and he appears in the *Dan'l Boone* series, as well. The story's title, "Simon Girty Worst of the Renegades," fairly sums up the judgment of Girty. Unlike the majority of the art in this series, this story utilizes figurative imagery. The opening panel presents a giant Simon Girty towering over a mass of fleeing settlers as if he were Godzilla. The lead-in narration sets up Girty's villainy: "He loomed like an evil giant over the perilous frontier! The mere mention of his name was enough to strike fear into settlers' hearts! Only Dan'l Boone was a match for 'Simon Girty Worst of the Renegades'" (1). If such characterization is not effective in conveying Girty's nature, he is also described as being "crueller than the cruellest savage." Some backstory explains how Girty was captured by the Seneca and becomes their fiercest warrior: "But he was a man apart . . . neither Indian nor settler!" (2). Girty's in-between status is expressed in another figurative image. Shown holding dolls of a white man and an Indian, Girty mimics their voices. The white man: "I'm better than you because I'm so much smarter." The Indian: "You can't hold a candle to me when it comes to fighting and woodlore . . . and you're a snivelling soft-hearted fool, ever yearning for peace!" (2). Girty's hatred for the settler rests upon a perceived elitism, while his alignment with the Indian rests upon a perceived fighting spirit. Unlike Mortell and Trent, Girty is not depicted so much as a renegade for financial gain, but as a rejection of white culture and "civilized" living. Girty leads raids on the settlements, which are successful in Boone's absence, but when he returns, Girty's success falters, and so he focuses on Boone as his adversary (3). Girty gains entry into the fort in disguise; he and Boone face off: "They were giants, both of them, when it came to strength and fighting skill" (5). The story closes with Girty subdued but the ending somewhat open as the closing narration describes Girty's confidence that he will be able to escape (5).

These stories depict white renegades as traitors and pose Boone as the ideal balance and defense against such traitors. Boone's character in these particular stories is defined by what he is not and what he opposes: the white renegade. At the same time, these comics must also contend with Boone's historical adoption by the Shawnee and what that fact might portend for assessing Boone's loyalty. Boone's proximity to Indianness is often depicted as an admirable quality. He is able to track and rescue white victims. He can predict how Indians are going to fight and counter their actions. "Born to the Frontier" in *Dan'l Boone* details Boone's early life. He learns from Indians: "Young Daniel spent a heap of time with them," and "From those friendly Indians, Daniel learned so much about red man's ways" (3). In this story, after Boone has assisted in the rescue of captured settler girls, one of the men asks how he was able to track so well. Boone replies, "Been close to Indians ever since I was a young'un. So close that folks say I 'think Indian'" (3). To "think Indian" but not "be Indian" seems a crucial distinction. *Exploits* depicts his captivity in "Doom at the Stake." The narrative details Boone's captivity and adoption, although there is emphasis on his remaining loyal to the American side. For instance, Dan'l agrees to Chief Blackfish's adoption: "Tell the chief that to be the son of such a great and famous warrior would be a mighty honor! We are happy to be here!" In the following panel, sidekick Sam questions Boone:

SAM: Are you crazy, Dan'l? We ain't no sich ting!
DAN'L: We've got to make them think we are! Until they believe us, we'll never escape to Boonsborough!

The question of Boone's loyalty comes into view in a later exchange between him and Blackfish after learning of the intended attack upon Boonesborough:

DAN'L: But . . . but those are *my* people in Boonesborough! That is my settlement . . . my own family . . .
BLACKFISH: Your people are here! All white blood was washed from you! We are your family, Sheltowee! If not you are our enemy . . .

Needless to say, Dan'l doesn't see things Blackfish's way, so he and Sam escape and return home to warn of the attack.

"Sell-Out" from *Dan'l Boone* addresses concerns over Boone's loyalty even more directly. The opening narration exclaims: "No blacker night had ever clamped down on the wilderness than when the settlers saw Dan'l Boone siding with the Shawnees against his own people! Even those who had stood up for Dan'l were convinced at last! This was a sell-out!" (1). This story derives from the capture of Boone and his men at the salt lick. The historical event produced some unease among some contemporaries in that it seemed that Boone too easily surrendered to the Shawnee. His subsequent adoption did not provide assurance for suspicious minds on that count either (Boone's court-martial was based on his actions at the salt lick, although he was exonerated and even promoted). This story develops this unease, voiced by Boone's fellow captives at the Shawnee camp. In one sequence the men tie up Boone and attempt to ransom him to Blackfish for their release. Boone escapes and attacks the men, as one of them exclaims, "Ye're a demon, Boone—turnin' against your own people again and again as ye've done" (6). Boone eventually effects their escape, and he explains to the men how he was pretending to side with the Shawnee. Boone's apparent disloyalty was merely an act to help them escape, thus sustaining his status as a national hero.

In these comics Boone's role as national hero finds expression in different ways. Generally, he is the trailblazer, striking out into the wilderness to make the way for the advancing American nation. He protects the settlements and defends the weak and innocent on the frontier. Like the standard comic book hero, Boone consistently shows up where his help is needed. The setting of these stories emphasizes Boone's relevance to national identity. *Exploits* sets its stories during the Revolution and positions Boone in opposition to the British and their Indian allies. *Frontier Scout* and *Dan'l Boone* set stories, when the time period is explicitly mentioned, during the French and Indian War. Boone's proximity to the Revolution perhaps makes him appear more "American," a device that will be seen later in this study in *White Indian* and *Tomahawk*.

These adaptations of novels like *The Last of the Mohicans* and continuing mythmaking of figures like Daniel Boone demonstrate a clear connection between the frontier mythos of the nineteenth century and the priorities and values of American culture in the twentieth century. A definite transmission of American values occurs via the lineage of the frontier and the white Indian as inherited by the comics of postwar America. As popular culture shifts from novels to dime novels to comic books, to identify one particular strain of transmission, the themes and values remain consistent, although transplanted to different contexts and perhaps perceived through a different lens (such as viewing Boone's nationalism in terms of anticommunist Americanism). Policing racial lines, ascertaining national or racial loyalty, and identifying traitors circulate throughout these mid-century comics as they adapt and modify the myths and figures of the previous century. This line of transmission from one century to the next becomes further amplified in the comics centered upon the white Indian or playing Indian. These comics participate in the playing Indian trope while at times corroborating the ideologies or values as passed down via the American frontier myth but also challenging or questioning assumptions held by such ideologies.

CHAPTER FOUR

# "WHITE BLOOD TURNS RED"

## *Playing Indian in US Comics*

*Tubby:* Hey, looket me, Lulu! I'm a full-blooded Cherokee!

*Lulu:* What have you got on your face?

*Tubby:* Sssh! Let's go outside . . . you can't trust these palefaces—
they're always givin' us fire water an'—

*Lulu:* But what have you got on your face?

*Tubby:* Iodine! Looks good, eh?

*Lulu:* Yes . . . you sure look like an Indian.

WITH THIS EXCHANGE, LITTLE LULU AND TUBBY COMMENCE THEIR
adventure in "Indian Uprising" (*Four Color* #120: Oct. 1946). Later in the
story, Lulu's mother asks what Lulu and her friends are doing, and she
explains, "Well, we're playing Indian. . . ." This story illustrates the apparent banality of this game of playing Indian. The nonchalance and ease
with which Lulu, Tubby, and Alvin masquerade as Indians demonstrate
how acceptable and ordinary this practice seems. Furthermore, this comic
depicts playing Indian through the usual props: tomahawks, headbands,
and feathers. The adorable scamps even stain their skin with iodine to
become "red." This image of Lulu and Tubby provides a vivid example of
playing Indian, a provocative image suggesting the belief that anyone can
play Indian through superficial and visual dress or staining of the skin.[1]
As this chapter shows, Little Lulu was not the only comic book character
participating in this racial masquerade.

   Among the wide variety of genres found in comic books of the mid-
twentieth century, the Western and frontier genres possess a prominent
place in American culture, given the continual fascination with frontier
life in the United State. According to Maurice Horn, Western comic strips
began appearing in the 1900s, with an increase in number in the 1920s

(18–23). Comics parallel the popularity of the genre in cinema and television. Slotkin provides specific numbers attesting to the Western's popularity in cinema and television, demarcating the years between 1947 and 1972 as a period that witnessed a notably high production of features and shows in the genre (*Gunfighter* 347–49). Randy Duncan and Matthew J. Smith observe that the Western was a popular genre across multiple media from the early twentieth century onward, with two titles in 1937 tying as the first comic book Westerns published: *Western Picture Stories* and *Star Ranger* (199). A cursory glance at titles from the 1940s and 1950s reveals an abundance of Western comic books with such titles as *Six-Gun Heroes*, *Cheyenne Kid*, *Gene Autry Comics*, and *Red Ryder Comics*, just to name a few. Michelle Nolan estimates that by 1959 at least 3,478 Western comics were published, with that number later reaching upward toward 5,000 (23). Western comic books had both financial and cultural power. William W. Savage notes, "The figures are obscure, at best, but evidently there was money to be made from cowboy comic books, probably because of the tie-in factor involving television and other media" (133 n.2). Savage also argues, "The heroic cowboy was a staple of American popular culture in the 1950s" (66). Many of these series were short-lived, but the preponderance of titles illustrates the popularity of the genre. The Western comic books are also home to a prevalent trope in American culture: playing Indian and the white Indian.

Perhaps one of the earliest examples of the white Indian trope in comics appears in Garrett Price's *White Boy*.[2] Price's newspaper strip was published weekly from 1933 to 1936 (preceding the first Western comic books), with a title change in 1935 to *White Boy in Skull Valley*. In this strip, the protagonist is a white teenager whose family has fallen victim to the Sioux. A rival tribe then adopts him and gives him the name "Whiteboy." Ron Goulart deems the strip "[o]ne of the best drawn, and unquestionably most unusual, of Western comics" and places Price's inventiveness and originality alongside George Herriman and Frank King (135). Goulart also argues that Price's strip precedes Milton Caniff's work "in the imaginative use of color to create not only a sense of place but to convey mood" (135). Maurice Horn states, "The main appeal of the strip . . . was Price's incredibly evocative artwork" (27). On artistic merit alone, *White Boy* deserves recognition for its place in comic strip history.

Also delivered by the art is a story that is quite familiar now by this point in this study: "Whiteboy," as he is known in the comic until the *Skull Valley* change, where he becomes "Bob White," is a white teenager adopted into the fictional Rainbow tribe. The first two strips, from October 1 and 8, 1933, present Whiteboy's introduction and adoption. A Rainbow tribe raiding party attacks the Sioux and brings back Whiteboy. The second strip presents his adoption: the chief speaks to the captive, "White boy, your race has invaded our lands. We should kill you—but—your life is spared—you shall be the son of the widow Broken-Wing, whose son died of a white man's bullet."

Over the course of the next few months of the strip, Whiteboy tries to escape, but Starlight, a female Indian his age, retrieves him. The two escape a wildfire and, when they face kidnapping by the Sioux, are saved by a group of warriors from the Rainbow tribe. Later, a raiding party retrieves horses stolen by Sioux, one of which is Whiteboy's horse, Bunny. They also meet a white trader, Dan Brown, who remains, often encouraging Whiteboy to leave. As the strip progresses, Whiteboy and his peers from the tribe engage in various adventures. The comic maintains a relatively evenhanded treatment of the Native-based characters, although the use of "redskin" is problematic, but overall Price treats his subjects with humanity and an effort toward realism (especially more so than other depictions of Native peoples in popular culture).

Price engages with the question of Whiteboy's assimilation, too. Dan Brown voices the concern about "going Native": "See here son, you listen to Old Dan—I know these redskins, buck and squaw—one white man is worth a whole tribe of them! Don't mix with 'em—don't grow up to be a squaw man!" (Dec. 24, 1933). The following month, Whiteboy is shown considering leaving with Brown: "[M]aybe I will leave these redskins and go away with him" (Jan. 28, 1934). Judging from the initial thirty-two comics, Price appears to be developing a thematic thread regarding Whiteboy's place and his assimilation in the tribe. In fact, Whiteboy remains with the tribe until the sudden editorial change of the comic in April 1935, when, as Goulart describes, the strip "takes place in the present West and has acquired the trappings of a more conventional cowboy comic strip" (probably due to a decision by Captain Joseph M. Patterson, head of the syndicate) (136). Whatever the reason for the change might have been, the result is that the comic strip transforms from being about a white Indian to being about a cowboy.

Worth noting, too, concerning Whiteboy's assimilation, is that he does not adopt the dress of the tribe. He wears a white shirt and blue pants, sometimes with a coonskin hat. Whiteboy does not display the visual signs of Indianness. His dress maintains his distinction from the other members of the tribe. If the visual signs are any indication, then, Whiteboy does not fully assimilate, does not fully "go Indian." His name attests to this fact, too. On this point he differs from the white Indians that would follow in comics. Perhaps one of the attractions to playing Indian in comics is the thrill of the visuals, the dressing up in headdress and war paint. This superficial transformation is one that carries much power in a medium largely based on the impressiveness of costume and display. Price does not engage in such sensational display in his strip, though.

During and after World War II, a number of comic book series focus on the white hero playing Indian. The playing Indian trope exists in *Golden Arrow* (1940–1953 in *Whiz Comics* and a solo series from 1942 to 1947). While the blonde Golden Arrow is not an adopted Indian and neither dresses nor looks "Indian," his origin story depicts him as growing up in the wilderness and gaining near-superhuman abilities through his attunement with nature. Both *White Boy* and *Golden Arrow* feature a significant convention that recurs often in white Indian comics: the death of parents as initiation into the wilderness or into becoming Indian. The death of the white family (and, as we will see below in *White Indian*, death of the love interest) represents a disconnection from white civilization, a disconnection that is necessary to becoming attuned to wilderness living. More importantly, within the iconography of playing Indian, Golden Arrow's use of the bow and arrow while fighting injustice on the frontier marks him as a hybrid of white and Indian that later comic books would more fully develop in the late 1940s and early 1950s, a period that produces the bulk of playing Indian comic books.

*Blazing West* (1948–1951) features Injun Jones, a white man raised by Indians. Marvel introduced *The Apache Kid* in 1950, with the hero a white orphan who was raised by the Apache and in adulthood poses as a white soldier while changing into Indian disguise to fight crime. The anthology series *Indians* (1950–1953) includes Manzar the White Indian, a white man adopted as a child by the Sioux, who operates under the name Bright Arrow. Manzar is credited to John Starr, who also is mainly responsible for Firehair, a female hero who is adopted by the Dakota. First appearing in *Ranger Comics* in 1945 and remaining in print until 1952, Firehair's stories pose a gender switch in this usually male-dominated genre. *White Indian* appeared from 1949 to 1952 in *The Durango Kid* and is remembered mainly for its artwork by Frank Frazetta. Between 1953 and 1954, these Frazetta-drawn stories were reprinted in three issues under the title *White Indian*; two more issues followed in 1954 and 1955 featuring new stories. Crossing over from radio, *Straight Arrow* appeared from 1950 to 1956 and reverses the white Indian trope, with the protagonist a Comanche who plays white in order to conceal his heroic Indian identity. The longest-running series connected to this trope is *Tomahawk*. Tomahawk's premiere is in *Star Spangled Comics* #69 (June 1947), and the self-standing comic series ran for 140 issues from 1950 to 1972. After 1969 *Tomahawk* would also include another Firehair, this one a white male adopted by Indians. This Firehair was created by Joe Kubert and first appears in *Showcase* #85–87 (1969), then returns on a regular basis starting with *Tomahawk* #132 (Jan.–Feb. 1971). *White Chief of the Pawnee Indians* (1951) and *Pawnee Bill* (1951) both tell the story of Pawnee Bill (Gordon William Lillie, a proprietor of and performer in a Wild West show from the 1880s to 1900s), who in the latter comic is billed as being "cleverer than his fellow white men and craftier than the Indians among whom he lived" ("Trail of the Ambush Killers"). Golden Warrior, a white man adopted by the Cheyenne, appears as well in *Pawnee Bill* #3. Another adoptee of the Cheyenne was *Cheyenne Kid* (1957–1973); with his parents killed in a Cheyenne raid, he is adopted and raised as an Indian but leaves the tribe to become an army scout. Even superheroes during this period had their turn at playing Indian, including Plastic Man, Captain Marvel, Superman, and Batman (more on them in chapter 5). With the Western's popularity in decline into the 1970s, the white Indian becomes less frequent a character, although in the late 1970s Scalphunter makes his first appearance in *Weird Western Tales* #39 (Mar.–Apr. 1977).

These stories depict, in various ways, the white hero playing Indian, a depiction that implements specific recurring characteristics: adoption by Indians, the white hero with Indian clothing or weapons, Indianness as strength and valor, the Indianized hero as upholder of justice on the frontier, and, in some cases, echoes of superhero conventions in a secret identity or sidekick. This chapter examines this topic on four points: 1) an overview of the conventions that distinguish the playing Indian comic books, 2) a focus on the construction and performance of gender, 3) an examination of nationalism and loyalty, and 4) the construction of race and difference.

The comic books examined in this chapter reveal the potency of playing Indian as imagery and symbol in comic art. A multifaceted system of metaphor revolves around the popular imagining of Indianness that, when channeled through comic art, emphasizes in playing Indian physical strength and martial power. The protagonists of these comic books, then, in their Indian masquerade, project an image that utilizes imagined

Indianness as a means to an end, a vehicle for white men (and, in one instance, a woman) to transform from weakness to strength, from man to superman. This construction of the heroic white Indian also connects explicitly to fighting for what is "right": whether that is for the American way or for the execution of justice on the frontier.

A recurring set of conventions exists in most, if not all, of the comic books under consideration here, many of which overlap with superhero conventions. Perhaps the most important shared feature of these conventions, and obviously foundational to the concept of the white Indian, is the adoption by an Indian tribe or parent. Sometimes this adoption occurs when the protagonist is a child, sometimes when he is an adult. With this adoption, the hero usually excels at his Indian training, many times besting his Indian peers in hunting, shooting, and tracking.

Dress and weapons play an important role in marking and distinguishing the hero's Indianness from his whiteness; visual markers clearly illustrate the white man's switching from white to Indian. The sometimes seen combination of "white" dress with "Indian" acts as a sign of the character's cultural and racial intermixture. This utilization of visual and material markers also gravitates around a conventional set of items, such as the headdress and buckskins for clothes and the tomahawk and bow and arrow for weapons.

These comic books also typically associate bravery and strength with Indianness, and sometimes weakness, passivity, or villainy with whiteness. In some examples the transformation into an Indian provides the white hero with strength and fortitude that he did not or could not have had before that metamorphosis. These preceding two qualities play quite neatly into a superhero paradigm.

For some of these heroes, their everyday white identity serves to conceal their heroic Indian identity. Like Clark Kent or Bruce Wayne, the white Indian hero will change into his Indian costume and, in that sartorial change, be able to openly practice his strength and power. While not all of these comic books present the secret-identity aspect of the superhero, all of them do present the hero as protector of innocents (whether white or Indian) and upholder of justice. The white Indian protagonists participate in the heroic vigilantism that is the core of the superhero story.

As for those villains who threaten innocents and are the purveyors of injustice, the stock adversary is many times a white bandit or swindler, victimizing either honest settlers or innocent Indians. Along with this convention of the white villain, usually if an Indian or tribe participates in treachery, they do so under the direction or deceit of a white character. Indian characters in these comic books are mostly presented as sympathetic and respectable, though primitive and easily fooled. This convention is in keeping with the paternalistic relationship of white protagonists to nonwhite characters presented in comics of this era, especially in the jungle comics (Savage 76–77; Wright 73–75).

While not every one of these comic books may participate in every one of these themes, these conventions are found with a high degree of frequency throughout these stories (as well as being inherited from a preceding body of literature, art, and media in the United States). The rest of this section examines these recurring traits more concretely in a few selections of white-Indian comic books.

"Golden Warrior and the Raiders of Terror Canyon" (*Pawnee Bill* #3: July 1951), while a brief bit of comics ephemera, provides a handy and concise example of many of the traits listed above. The opening narration of the story offers this exposition:

> A white man trained to think and act like an Indian, but live like a white man! Such is the strange destiny of Golden Warrior, raised from childhood, as the son of Chief Mountain Thunder of the Cheyenne, when murderous outlaws slew the boy's parents, when David Brown, the child, reached manhood, his mission was to stamp out evil from the territory. (1)

This text contains important elements for the white Indian trope in comic books: adoption, cross-cultural existence, and the mission to fight evil. Later in the story, Brown "grows into the tribe's keenest archer"; he excels at Indian skills, which checks off another important convention.

As the story progresses, Brown enters adulthood and his adoptive father initiates him into his life's purpose. Chief Thunder presents his adopted son with an outfit—gold loincloth, headband, and mask, along with a bow and arrow—and a mission: "Now you must give your life to stamp out all evil, whether it be Indian or white" (2). Brown in his guise as Golden Warrior maintains his whiteness through biological traits like his skin color and blonde hair, while marking his Indianness with material items: the loincloth, headband, and bow and arrows (Fig. 4.1). These visual cues suggest his whiteness as essential and permanent, and his Indianness as adoptable and temporary.

Setting out on his new life, Brown takes up residence with a rancher and his daughter. After defeating the story's villains as Golden Warrior,

Figure 4.1. Golden Warrior.
Lou Cameron (art), "Golden
Warrior and the Raiders of Terror
Canyon." *Pawnee Bill* #3 (July
1951). Story Comics.

the next morning he talks to the rancher he had helped. Faking having
slept through the night, he asks about the night before, to which Iris, the
daughter, replies, "You mean you slept through it all, the attack—and didn't
see him, the Golden Warrior—he was wonderful." The story ends with the
hero's words: "A golden Indian? I'd like to meet him myself!" These closing
panels exhibit the secret identity trope with dialogue that would have been
right at home in an exchange between Lois Lane and Clark Kent.

These superhero conventions are also present in *Indians* and *Straight
Arrow*. *Indians* features Manzar the White Indian, or the Bright Arrow.
To his friends and neighbors, he is Dan Carter, a trader, but when trouble
arises, he becomes Manzar the Bright Arrow. *Straight Arrow* shares much
with the Manzar stories thematically and plotwise. In this series the protagonist is Steve Adams, a rancher who transforms into Straight Arrow.

Like the preceding comic books, *Tomahawk* features a white male hero
who adopts Indian skills and props, and the series' longevity might attest
to the power of the playing Indian trope in comics. "Flames along the
Frontier" (*Star Spangled Comics* #69: June 1947) introduces Tom Hawk and

shows how he became Tomahawk. Through the course of the story, Tom Hawk learns the Indian ways, meets his sidekick, Dan Hunter, and fights white renegades on the frontier. Many of the hallmarks of the white Indian comic are here: adoption, strength through Indianization, and white renegades as villains. The association to Daniel Boone is readily apparent, as this story is set in Kentucky, while Tom Hawk's capture by Indians echoes Boone's captivity as well. During Tom Hawk's capture, he rescues one of the captors, Black Thunder, from a rampaging moose and is then offered freedom but is advised to stay and learn from the Indians. Tom does so, is "called Tomahawk by his Indian brothers," and "becomes skilled in Indian ways," earning Black Thunder's praise: "Your eye is keener, your hand steadier, than any brave's in the tribe!" *Tomahawk* is especially notable for Frederick Ray's attention to authentic detail, as Harvey points out, and with Ray's dedicated and lengthy tenure as artist for the comic, Harvey also notes that "the artwork of the books is stylistically unified, which in turn imparts to the series and the character a distinctive flavor" (51).

As has been suggested in this discussion so far, the power of playing Indian is fueled in part by its fantasy of male empowerment. By becoming Indian, a white male becomes stronger, faster, and braver. He becomes a hero. The next section explores more fully the gender dimension of playing Indian: how empowered masculinity is performed and how that performance is routed through a gender switch to present a fantasy of female empowerment through playing Indian.

Concerns about the strength and integrity of masculinity in the Unites States were in heavy circulation during the mid-century period. K. A. Cuordileone offers a comprehensive examination of this "crisis in American masculinity," showing that there was "an excessive preoccupation with—and anxiety about—masculinity in Cold War American politics" (516). This preoccupation produced "a political culture that put a new premium on hard masculine toughness and rendered anything less than that soft and feminine and, as such, a real or potential threat to the security of the nation," and "an exaggerated cult of masculine toughness and virility surfaced in American political culture" (516).[3] Cuordileone argues that militarization and the threat of nuclear war also fueled anxieties about manhood, and anxiety in general (527). Affluence, conformity, and the role of women drew much of the speculation as sources for the much-discussed masculine anxiety. In *The Vital Center* (1950), Arthur Schlesinger, Jr., argues, "Our industrial organization overpowers man, unnerves him, demoralizes him. The problem remains of ordering society so that it will subdue the tendencies of industrial organization, produce a wide amount of basic satisfaction and preserve a substantial degree of individual freedom" (171). While Schlesinger uses "man" in the universal sense here, the effects of organization on manhood were front and center as urgent concerns. He would more directly grapple with manhood in "The Crisis of American Masculinity" (1958), associating the uncertainty about manhood being registered during the 1950s with the loss of identity and individualism; in the submission to the group, the male loses grasp of his manhood (242–43). Schlesinger goes on to recommend: "For men to become men again, in short, their first task is to recover a sense of individual spontaneity. And to do this a man must visualize himself as an individual apart from the group" (244). For Philip Wylie, in *Generation of Vipers* (1942), increasing abundance was a cause of enervation and complacency. Men had become beholden to routine, conformity, and commodities: "The exalted common man is slave of instinct, slave of the herd, slave of superstition, slave of magical gadgets" (114). David Riesman's *The Lonely Crowd* (1950) distinguished between the "other-directed" person as a product of mid-century life in America, from the "inner-directed" person of the past, with the latter being associated with hardness and masculinity. In addition, William F. Whyte's *The Organization Man* (1956) poses that men were subordinated to the organization, and thus their individuality and initiative were sacrificed to becoming a team player.[4]

If these developments of affluence, conformity, the apocalyptic potential of the bomb, and the perceived advance of female domination are indeed sources of a masculine anxiety, would not the stories of the Old West and the frontier be attractive in that regard? Schlesinger, in passing, points to the frontier as home to a stable sense of masculinity: "The frontiersmen of James Fenimore Cooper . . . never had any concern about masculinity; they were men, and it did not occur to them to think twice about it" (237). On the frontier the male hero asserts a greater degree of control over those forces that would do harm. The frontiersman, the cowboy, and the white Indian are all of the same cloth in their ability to control their environment and not be subject to technological and foreign threats to their safety and security. On the frontier, women are secondary actors, if present at all. The cowboy and the frontiersman are rugged individuals. In addition, the white Indian is perhaps the ideal nonconformist, willing to turn his back on the accoutrements of white civilization and embrace his primitive nature. The men on the frontier are certainly not "other-directed." They are certainly not "soft."

Given the heightened rhetoric of masculinity and hardness/softness delineated as value markers of a citizen's nationalist integrity and patriotism, the attachment of masculine reinvigoration to playing Indian finds vivid expression in such a context. Playing Indian in these mid-century comics echoes that masculine rhetoric of the nineteenth-century white Indians, yet in the Cold War context, a more urgent anxiety about national security and loyalty is voiced. This section focuses on the rhetoric of manhood in playing Indian comics, with *White Indian* as the representative example. Firehair will then be examined in its regendering of the playing Indian trope through a female protagonist.

*White Indian* centers upon a narrative of white male rebirth and reinvigoration through playing Indian. Many of the *White Indian* stories are set during the Revolution and involve Dan Brand[5] aiding the American forces, while usually facing off against a traitor to the American side. The first story, "White Indian," appearing in *The Durango Kid* #1 (Oct.—Nov. 1949), features the origin of the titular hero and encompasses the theme of urbanized masculine weakness purged through frontier experience. Dan Brand, the protagonist, escapes urban flaccidity to obtain rugged strength through playing Indian. This first episode opens with Dan Brand about to marry Lucy Wharton. Their wedding is interrupted by a rival for Lucy's hand, Peter Bradford, who attempts to shoot Brand. Lucy jumps in front of the bullet and dies.[6] Brand swears vengeance upon Bradford, following him west; yet Brand's city background proves him unfit for the wilderness.

This plot point illustrates a key thematic element in this kind of story: the white male must leave behind the domesticated life of the city in order to become a man. The story exhibits a clear juxtaposition between life in the city versus life in the wilderness: "Only an iron will for vengeance kept him going—for his *town-bred muscles and tea-party ways were puny weapons* against the might of the elements and the trackless vastness of the wilderness" (emphasis added). Brand's "civilized" ways prove detrimental to him as he travels into the wilderness. He possesses "puny weapons." Those "town-bred muscles and tea-party ways" provide little strength to survive in the wilderness. Furthermore, "tea-party ways" emphasizes the feminized state of urban life. Brand is immersed in social circles that provide no development or exercise of his physical strength, and thus no preservation or nurturing of his masculinity. Although his thirst for vengeance helps him to persevere in spirit, his physical self suffers from the limitations incurred by city living.

Immediately following this piece of narration is a bear attack that will set the stage for Brand's rebirth. While preceding narration pitted Brand against the tough conditions of the wilderness, in this scene the hero confronts an actual embodiment of the savage violence that exists beyond the city. A bear or cougar attack is a recurring event in the white Indian comic books, too, and demonstrates the hero's physical strength (something that will also be present in the Firehair comic books discussed below). In fact, the animal attack is a common trope in frontier and Western stories. Kent Ladd Steckmesser observes, "There is a complete American bestiary in frontier narratives, and hand-to-claw combats with buffaloes, bears, and mountain lions are a standard fixture" (244). Steckmesser adds that "[s]uch tales are a recognized badge of prowess" (244). Although the bear mauls and pins Brand, he is able to kill the bear, though near death himself. Brand passes out. In the next panel, he awakens to the sight of an Indian chief flanked by his son and wife. The chief is Great Deer of the Catawbas, who has cared for and nursed Brand from the brink of death. From this moment forward, the reader witnesses Brand's passage from citified weakness to wilderness strength, a passage obtained through his Indianization. Although Brand immediately wants to continue his hunt for Bradford, Great Deer urges him to slow down and learn "the ways of the forest, the Indian lore" that will allow him to survive the wilderness and defeat his enemy (similar to Tomahawk's being advised to stay and learn from the Indians). In this turn of events, the Dan Brand of tea parties and city living has died figuratively in order for the Dan Brand of the wilderness to be born. This rebirth occurs through Indianization, a transformation illustrated in the succeeding panels: he is dressed in leggings only, hunts deer, wrestles with his new Indian acquaintances (and wins), and after a year's time has been fully reborn as a white Indian, fully versed in the ways of the wilderness.

His newfound strength receives its first test in the form of an attack by Chippewas, enraged by "firewater" that they have received from (not surprisingly) Peter Bradford. Brand and his adopted tribe fight off the attackers, but in their retreat Bradford shoots and kills Great Deer. This development further binds Brand to his new Indian family, and he finds himself on a mission to avenge not only his departed fiancée but also the death of his adoptive father. The panels featuring Brand exacting his revenge against Bradford follow this progression: Brand punches Bradford, bending him backward from the blow, saying, "That's for Great Deer!" The

Figure 4.2. Closing panels of first story of *White Indian*. Frank Frazetta (art), as reprinted in *White Indian* #11 (1953). Vanguard Productions.

succeeding panel moves the viewpoint farther out, showing Bradford falling over a cliff edge as Brand completes another swing, adding, "And this is for Lucy!" Brand has gained his vengeance, but his story has just begun (and perhaps Bradford's fatal fall from the cliff ledge is an echo of Magua's fate in *The Last of the Mohicans*).

The final panels of this episode affirm Brand's separation from civilization and his fraternity with Tipi, Great Deer's biological son, who pledges to remain with Brand. Brand replies, "I have no one either, Tipi—no one to love! I think I have found my home and my future here—in the wilds!" (Fig. 4.2). Thus, Dan Brand's origin story ends, with boy sidekick in tow, and his adventures as "White Indian" begin. Notable in this piece of dialogue between the two is that both males view themselves as unattached from familial or domestic attachments: they have "no one to love." One might further surmise that if Brand had married, had remained in the city with his beloved Lucy, he would never have shed his "town-bred muscles and tea-party ways." While Brand's self-enforced exile from his home appears to be a curse (he has lost the woman he loves), within a framework of masculine ideology, his evolution turns out to be a blessing: he is freed from the effeminizing or enervating forces of city and civilization and has become a "real" man. Dan Brand's rebirth as white Indian reveals a reinvigorated masculinity; the death of his wife-to-be spurs him on toward a reawakening of manhood typified by physical strength, violent superiority, and wilderness savvy adorned with Indian props.

A later story, "Brothers of the Wilderness," directly presents Dan with the question of returning to "civilized life" when a settler asks, "Why do you spend your life in the wilderness like this? You ought to settle down on the soil with us—raise a family—help start a great city!" (34). Dan responds, "[M]y life in the wilds with Tipi is dearer to me than anything else. You see, we have a mission together—and Tipi is closer than a brother!" (35). On one level this response might read as a choice for the fraternal over the paternal; Dan chooses to be a brother rather than a father. Attendant upon that choice is the homosocial nature of his relationship with Tipi that speaks to the perception of freedom being found in the detachment from heteronormative and domestic relationships. Dan rejects raising a family and founding a city for roaming the wilderness with his blood brother. Dan also justifies his decision by invoking the mission: his work is to protect the innocent and battle villains on the frontier, a mission that he would not be able to accomplish if he were tied down at home with a wife and children.

Dan Brand's story is a typical one within the playing Indian narrative, as well as within the frontier mythos in general. By leaving the city and becoming Indian, he is able to regain his masculine strength and assert his physical prowess in the wilderness, unattached from domestic or familial restraints. While these stories conventionally revolve around a male protagonist, one series performs a gender switch, placing a female in the role of the hero and the white Indian.

The Firehair comic books feature a female hero who has become Indian (a rare thing indeed in comic books).[7] Firehair, variously called the Queen of the Sagebrush Frontier, White Queen of the Indians, Warrior-Maid of the Wild Dakotas, and White Daughter of the Sioux, first appears in Fiction House's *Rangers Comics* #21 (Feb. 1945), then gets her own title, *Firehair Comics* in 1948 (which initially featured reprints from the *Rangers* series), becoming *Pioneer West Romances* with the third issue. In *Rangers Comics* she becomes the cover star with issue 40 (Apr. 1948), a status she retains for the next twenty-five issues of the series (with her last appearance dated June 1952). Between *Rangers Comics* and her own series, Firehair's stories were in circulation from 1945 to 1952. Similar to her male counterparts examined above, Firehair transforms from weak city girl to strong Indianized warrior in her origin story. Her first cover appearance (Fig. 4.3) shows her as a fierce fighter, squaring off in hand-to-hand combat with ferocious beasts. The cover of *Pioneer West Romances* #7 (Fig. 4.4) also depicts her as a warrior: she is on horseback, spear in hand, thundering forward.

*Rangers Comics* #21 presents Firehair's origin story. Princess, soon renamed Lynn Cabot, accompanies her father to the western frontier, leaving behind their home in Boston. Princess is dainty and feminine, her hopes centered on finding her "Prince Charming." Princess and her father join a wagon train, where talk of "redskins" circulates among the travelers. Meanwhile, the villain of the story, Fingers, a white man, masquerades along with his accomplices as an Indian raiding party. They attack the wagon train, killing most of the settlers, and ignore an unconscious Princess, thinking that she has died. After the bandits depart, a lone Indian, named Little Ax, rescues Princess and takes her back to his village. She recovers but has lost her memory and so is given a home with the tribe.

In the following *Rangers* issue, Firehair has been assimilated into the tribe. The opening of this second story presents her with bow and arrow, outshooting her female competitors, and then ably fighting a jealous female rival. Firehair is recognized as a fierce and brave warrior, and her skills are constantly demonstrated throughout each story. For instance, Firehair and Little Ax capture a horse; then a bear attacks Little Ax, but Firehair and Little Ax are able to fight off the bear. This story culminates in a plot by Fingers to raid the Indian village while the men are away. When Fingers and his bandits try to steal the tribe's horses, Firehair pursues them, throwing a tomahawk at one of the men, who exclaims, "A squaw—aa-agh!" as the weapon hits him in the head. She replies, "A squaw, horse-thief, but *a better man* than you" (*Rangers Comics* #22, emphasis added). Firehair has outmanned the horse thief in her ability to fight, exhibiting a strength that casts her in a masculine role. This strength is also demonstrated through multiple instances in which she kills an attacking animal. For example, the cover of *Ranger Comics* #42 (Fig. 4.5) shows Firehair fighting off a lynx while Little Ax cowers behind her. In a sequence from *Pioneer West Romances* #6 (Fig. 4.6), Firehair saves Little Ax and another man from a panther attack. She plays the hero while these men are the "damsels in

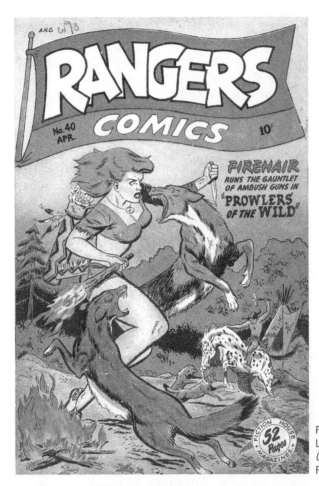

Figure 4.3. Cover. Bob Lubbers (art), *Rangers Comics* #40 (Apr. 1948). Fiction House Magazines.

distress." Her strength and bravery are also explicitly expressed in *Pioneer West Romances* #3: "Some remember Firehair for her kindness . . . others for her courage . . . still others recall her wisdom, strength, beauty . . . *and* deadly Dakota weapons—ever poised to strike in the cause of justice" ("Heartbreak Range").

Many of the same themes seen in the comic books featuring white males as Indian are found in the Firehair stories: she finds strength and courage in her adoption by the Indians, and she proves herself an able warrior, outdoing even her Indian companions. Her stories revolve around fighting for justice, rescuing those in danger, and protecting her tribe from unjust accusations or swindlers. She also navigates independent of romantic attachments. While the occasional romantic longing arises—as in one

Figure 4.4. Cover. *Pioneer West Romances* #7 (Spring 1951). Fiction House Magazines.

instance in "Siren of the Silver Sage" she thinks, "Love . . . strange! It comes to everyone sooner or later . . . what must it be like? Thirst? Hunger? I wonder if the Great Spirit will ever see that Firehair too is lonely!" (*Pioneer West Romances* #3)—for the most part, she shares much with her male counterparts, consistently presented as an independent and self-reliant character, her characterization eschewing the damsel-in-distress trope.

Given these common conventions, Firehair's gender makes her an exception to the rule for white Indian comics, but viewed within the context of the comic books of the time, her character may not appear so exceptional after all. While the playing Indian aspect of Firehair distinguishes her series, her primitivism aligns her with the "jungle queen" comics, thus placing her in Fiction House's heavily marketed genre of the jungle comics.

Figures 4.5. Firehair saves men from wild-cats. Bob Lubbers (art), *Rangers Comics* #42 (Aug. 1948). Fiction House Magazines.

Firehair shares company with other Fiction House jungle queens such as Sheena, Queen of the Jungle, or Kazanda (who also appeared in *Rangers Comics*), a fact made clear in advertising found within the Firehair comic books. Given this particular context, Firehair appears to be a modification of the jungle queen, transplanted from the jungle to the western plains. This jungle-queen dimension of Firehair's character reveals two important aspects of her comic within the context of this study: 1) the paternalist attitude of these comic books and 2) the exploitative nature of these comics. Like her counterparts in the jungle queen stories, Firehair functions in a paternalistic role. Savage's characterization of jungle comics is relevant on this point: "The status of blacks as items of fauna underscored the imperialist, colonialist, paternalistic, and racist thrust of the jungle comics"

Figures 4.6. Firehair saves men from wildcats. Bob Webb (pencils) and David Heames (inks), *Pioneer West Romances* #6 (1950). Fiction House Magazines.

(Savage 76). Swap "blacks" with "Indians," and "jungle" with "Western," and this quote would accurately describe the Firehair comics. In addition, one cannot ignore the exploitative nature of the Firehair comics. As with her jungle queen peers, these comic books were quite adept at placing Firehair in various states of undress and revealing, provocative poses. The exploitative aspects of these comics are also readily evident when viewing the covers for Firehair's appearances in *Rangers Comics* before she became the cover star. These covers often presented a woman in torn clothing, in bondage (disturbingly so at times), and at the mercy of a villain while a male hero swoops in for the rescue. Such images especially undercut any implications of female empowerment that Firehair might possess. Granted, as the comic books moved into the 1950s, a detectable toning down of these images occurred, probably in response to the increasing public scrutiny of comic books at that time. Even so, there still exists the tension between presenting Firehair as a sexual object and presenting her as a strong female hero (not to imply that a strong female hero cannot be sexual). Given the context and creative forces at play in this comic, the tension, or even contradiction, between agency and objectness is more pronounced in this instance.

One significant aspect of this Indianization illustrated in this section is its representation of the white hero's metamorphosis from weak to strong. The logic of this transformation depends upon the perception that so-called civilized living weakens a person or does not allow him or her to exercise fully his or her strength. Playing Indian offers a way to regain that lost power or fully exercise that strength. On this point playing Indian also serves to affirm and strengthen masculinity as physically strong, morally upright, and courageous. Even if a woman plays this role, the values and traits are still gendered as masculine (see Firehair's "better man than you" above). While viewing playing Indian as a source for male empowerment is the dominant interpretation of this trope, this comic offers an exception, that in the case of the Firehair comics, female empowerment is drawn from playing Indian. Playing Indian, then, can stand as a general route to reinvigoration and strength for the white hero regardless of gender. While that may be true in the general sense, it does not negate the fact that the solid majority of these comic books narrate the revitalization and empowerment of male heroes. With this line of argument, one observes a powerful attraction to playing Indian for comic book creators and readers.

This antidomestic strain of masculine rhetoric does not exist alone, though. While this rhetoric casts the family and home life as a threat to masculine autonomy and individuality, such thinking ultimately concedes to the perception of family as foundation and anchor for society's morality and integrity. The desire to "go West" and assert one's manhood must be anchored by solid footing in the family. For instance, in 1781 Crèvecoeur anchors the decision of his "American farmer," James, to move to the frontier in the rhetoric of family integrity and his paternal role: maintaining their ties to civilization through proper instruction of his children in farming and religion (219–20, 224). The importance of the family to the male also finds expression in the postwar period. Elaine Tyler May shows that a segment of men viewed family as satisfying and a foundation for success and motivation (33). One husband in 1955 describes how marriage "increased my horizons, defined my goals and purposes in life, strengthened my convictions" (qtd. in May 33). The perception of home as a source of security was also prevalent during this period; the family provided a sense of comfort and defense in a world where nuclear devastation seemed imminent (26).

The family was an important component of defining and defending the integrity of American society and of manhood. Family had to be controlled, though, through the proper practice of gender roles. One particular phenomenon perceived as detrimental in this aspect was the perceived problem of "Momism": overindulgent mothers doting on their children while neglecting their husbands. Such mothers could prove detrimental to the moral integrity of their sons (May 93). This threat was considered harmful not only on the personal level but on a broader social and political plane, too. May contends that the "sources of popular and official ideology insisted that male power was as necessary in the home as in the political realm, for the two were connected" (94). By this logic, men weakened by women (as either the doting mother or the seductive tramp) were unable to resist communism; they would be unable "to prevent the destruction of the nation's moral fiber and its inevitable result: communist takeover from inside as well as outside the country" (May 94). One can see, then, the relationship being deployed between the maintenance of manhood and the defense of the American way. This connection raises the importance of nationalism and patriotic loyalty, a theme also found in these comic books.

Many of these comics were published before the stranglehold of McCarthy and the House Un-American Activities Committee, but their appearance during Truman's second term connects them to an atmosphere of increasing anxiety and paranoia about loyalty (especially exemplified by the case of Alger Hiss). Such an atmosphere made for fertile fantasy for mid-twentieth-century American audiences. J. Fred MacDonald demonstrates the role that Westerns played in Cold War America. Although he focuses on the television Western, his analysis bears relevant implications for the genre as it appeared in comics, too. MacDonald argues, "In a Cold War society where there were threats to existence and where similar toughness seemed necessary, Western heroes offered role models in resolve and courage. Their weekly exploits demonstrated a protective mentality suited to the popular perception of Cold War realities: basically law-abiding, but capable of great force in defense of civilization" (134–35). Important, too, to my analysis is MacDonald's attribution of the Western's success in its appeal to citizens "whose external enemies seemed perpetually poised for attack and whose internal politics generated fear of subversion and disloyalty" (139–40). Slotkin also argues for an ideological correlation between the Western and the Cold War: "The rise and fall of the Western mirrors the development of the Cold War and its sustaining ideological consensus" (*Gunfighter* 347). A question that bears upon the analysis of playing Indian in comics of the postwar period is how evident are the ideological concerns and anxieties of Cold War culture in these comic books. One particular anxiety regarding the traitor and treason emerges in these comics: an anxiety especially exacerbated by the potential of the frontiersman or white Indian to cross the racial line, and the threat of the white renegade. Although that fear of disloyalty exists on the frontier, this space also provides the opportunity to exercise strength and manliness. On the other hand, such realization of manhood also threatens the stability of the domestic. In all, then, these comic books deliver a dynamic of playing Indian that seeks to resolve anxieties of loyalty and masculinity while further perpetuating an antidomestic stance.

*White Indian*'s plots often revolve around traitors and spies; Dan Brand works to weed out the disloyal villains and preserve the cause of the American Revolution. The main enemy in these comics is the British. Even more threatening, though, are the traitors to the American cause. While the British stand as the overall nemesis, Brand's actual face-to-face battles are more commonly with Americans who have joined the British side. Given the Cold War context of the comic, which appeared alongside comics depicting heroic American soldiers in Korea, an implication here is that the greatest danger for the United States is its citizens who would sympathize with the enemy, whether it be the British during the 1770s or the communists in the 1950s.[8] As with the recurring plot in many early Captain America stories, the more dangerous enemy in *White Indian* is the fifth column. The stories of *White Indian* consistently emphasize Brand's loyalty to the American side and his ongoing battle against those who would betray the cause of America's independence.

Along with the fear of communist infiltrators and spies, there is an anxiety about the softening of national fortitude due to American abundance and affluence, a concern not isolated to the mid-twentieth century. Rupert Wilkinson quotes John Adams in 1819 questioning the potential negative effect of luxury upon American toughness and mettle: "Will you tell me how to prevent riches from producing luxury? Will you tell me how to prevent luxury from producing effeminacy, intoxication, extravagance, vice and folly?" (80). John F. Kennedy echoed this sentiment during his presidential campaign (76). Abundance has, according to Kennedy, "weaned and wooed us from the tough condition in which, heretofore, we have approached whatever it is we have had to do. . . . A nation, replete with goods and services, confident that 'there's more where that came from,' may feel less ardor for questing" (qtd. in Wilkinson 76). Wilkinson links this "fear of winding down," as he names it, to a constellation of anxieties during the postwar, Cold War period: fears of lost vitality, of apathetic conformity, of enervation, and of distraction from the national covenant.

The turn to frontier comics, and playing Indian, in the late forties offers an alternative to and assurance against these fears. Frontier heroes like Daniel Boone (as discussed in chapters 2 and 3) embody a national strength and fortitude capable of overcoming adversaries to the American way. Playing Indian operates in the same ideological vein. Playing Indian offers the performance of strength and virility so desired for the white American male. The virtues and superlatives of the imagined Indian compensate for the perceived softness of affluence. At the same time, playing Indian requires a crossing of racial boundary; the white male takes on, at least superficially, Indian characteristics, and thus he must ably demonstrate his racial loyalty, which is intertwined with national loyalty.

Another complication in playing Indian as an element of nationalist rhetoric is its antidomestic stance. As discussed above in relation to the affirmation of masculinity in playing Indian, the hero gains his strength and power in part through his separation from the home and the family. Unburdened by domestic attachments, the hero is able to fulfill his manly potential. While this works for a rhetoric of masculinity, it is problematic for a nationalist rhetoric, especially within the Cold War context. To understand better this point, Matthew Costello's concise summary of research on the family's role in the Cold War is most useful: "The rhetoric of the government and anticommunist experts—that the family was the bulwark of American values and thus the greatest weapon against the communists—linked the popular fear of communists to fears about the breakdown of the family" (51). If the family provides the foundation of American values and strengthens the nation against the assault of enemies, then what value is there in the lone male on the frontier? The isolated manhood of the white Indian or frontiersman possesses significant rhetorical power on one hand but proves detrimental in supporting a domestic base for an American establishment. This tension highlights the importance of depicting the white Indian or frontiersman heroes as stable proponents of American ideals and values.

While there is usually an implicit nationalism in most of the playing Indian comics, *White Indian* and *Tomahawk* stand out because of their being set during the American Revolution. These heroes explicitly serve the cause of American independence, and thus the founding of the nation. *White Indian's* depiction of city life as weakening and softening accords with notions of national character being weakened by affluence and abundance. Dan Brand's initiation into the wilderness and his playing Indian make him a formidable warrior for the American cause, a fact most evident in his participation in the American Revolution. Likewise with Tomahawk: like Boone, he is versed in Indian ways and, with his Rangers, fights the good fight for independence. The rest of this section explores more closely how each of these characters promotes nationalism in playing Indian.

The imperative to identify clearly Dan Brand's national loyalty appears in the instance of the 1953 reprint of Dan Brand's first story. This reprint adds an introduction:

> Way back, when our country was young . . . and the truly great pioneers were the intrepid pioneers of the backwoods . . . the greatest of the backwoodsmen was Dan Brand . . . and his little Indian friend, Tipi, who blazed new trails of adventure for others to follow, pushing civilization and justice across the continent of the 'new' world! Here was white American and brown American fighting common deadly enemies side by side!

This language frames Brand's story more securely within an American nationalist context. Such rhetoric was not absent in the original stories, though.

The opening exposition of "The Battle of the Dungeons" explains, "When the American Revolution exploded its shot heard 'round the world men of the frontier, fed up with the tyranny of the king and his governors, rallied to the cause. Fighters like Dan Brand and his Indian friend, Tipi, were important leaders in the guerilla warfare of the wilds" (59). This story, set in 1773, features an American traitor, Bleeker, who leads British soldiers to the cabin of "frontier rebels" preparing for revolution. The American rebels are arrested and jailed at the governor's home. Dan and Tipi infiltrate the governor's home, with its scenes of luxury and decadence, to rescue the captured rebels. After the successful rescue, one of the men thanks Dan, suggesting that he'd "make a brilliant general." As usual, Dan opts to remain in the wilderness: "But I'm not looking for a gold braid! I prefer to fight it out right here in the woods!" (65). "Tory Treachery" repeats the traitor motif in its opening exposition: "Not all Americans supported the Revolution in 1776. No, there were some traitors like D'Arcy—rich, powerful, and treacherous—who hated the people and were loyal only to the king" (75). As with the British governor above, the American traitor is wealthy, and the need for wealth is the central conflict of the story. George Washington tells Dan that they need funds for supplies and ammunition, so the hero returns to his home and to his circle of upper-class acquaintances to raise money for the war effort. Dan meets with D'Arcy, who is astonished by Dan's new way of life: "Mercy, Dan—such rush and secrecy! And what an outlandish costume you're wearing—a frontiersman, by Jove! And what is this? I swear—an Indian, a savage [referring to Tipi]!" (77). D'Arcy's snobbery, and implied treachery, is illustrated when he slaps Tipi for spilling drink on D'Arcy's clothes. When Dan makes his request to a group of wealthy citizens, only one agrees to help, thus marking him as a target of the traitorous D'Arcy, who ends up stealing the money intended for the American cause. The story resolves in Dan attacking the traitors and retrieving the funds; the traitors are defeated, and the revolutionary cause can stay on track.

As the example of D'Arcy shows, prejudice toward Tipi functions as a sign of disloyalty to the American cause. "The Blood of Valley Forge" demonstrates this motif, too. The opening panels present a group of men conspiring against Dan as he gives a recruitment speech. One of these men, Hutchins, trips Tipi, who then protests. Hutchins responds with a slap and this admonishment: "This will teach you to open your mouth to your superiors, you red savage!" Dan comes to Tipi's defense: "Our colonial army is teaching England a lesson in equality, Hutchins—but it looks as though I'll have to give *you* a special lesson in that! Put up your fists!" (94). The Loyalist betrays not only the fight for liberty but also the ideal of equality. The traitor motif is also found in "The Trail of the Traitor," in which Dan and Tipi must retrieve stolen battle plans for Washington. "River Gauntlet" presents a scout who had worked for Washington but has switched to the British side because, as he explains, "I'm employin' my talents where they gits paid the most!" (102). Dan Brand and Tipi's pursuit of turncoats marks them as staunchly loyal Americans, a fact also demonstrated in their assistance to key historical figures like George Washington.

Dan Brand helps Washington in "Massacre" (with Al Williamson, *The Durango Kid* #8, Dec.–Jan. 1951).[9] Dan Brand and Tipi are assisting the British Colonial Army against Huron and Iroquois who have been spurred on by the French to attack the English settlers. The story depicts a younger George Washington (who is still a colonel) as a student of Brand's military strategy. A stark contrast is evident between British and Indian military tactics. The British, "in perfect step, ranks straight as rulers, colors flying, drums rolling, bugles blowing" (70), are no match for the guerilla ambush of the enemy Indians. Earlier, Dan Brand had tried to convince General Braddock of this fact. When Washington agrees with Brand, Braddock responds, "When those deuced savages see our disciplined formations and hear our bugles, they'll run like the cowards they are! Imagine—primitive savages beating His Majesty's troops! Impossible!" (69) As one might predict, the British army is scattered and sent running. Of course, Brand saves the day, having brought in Chippewa, Catawba, and Mohawk allies. This narrative bolsters the "savage" methods of fighting over the "civilized." However, this contrast does not so much praise actual indigenous methods as appropriate the guerilla style of fighting as a foreshadowing for the upcoming American colonists' fight against the British.

Washington figures as a significant side character in this episode: when the British army retreats, Washington attempts to stand his ground but must relent and accompany his fleeing army. Upon meeting Brand, Washington stays with the white Indian, stating, "I'm going to stay here and fight with you, Dan—to learn how it's done!" (71). Most tellingly, in the episode's final panel, Washington, with hand concealing his mouth, states to Brand, "It's not just the way to fight Indians, Dan—it may also be the way to fight the British, some day—understand?" Brand responds with the story's last words, "I do, Colonel! Some day we'll want our independence—and at that time, sir, I'm sure it'll be General Washington!" (73). This narrative works in an ironic way: the audience knows what will come, although the characters do not (at least not precisely). Given the reader's knowledge of who Washington will become and the war for independence that will occur, Brand's actions here inject into this bit of national mythmaking the presence and necessity of Indianness. The British "civilized" military are no match for the "savage" Indian tactics. Moreover, the implication here is that the British will again be no match for the "savage" American revolutionaries.

"Savagery," then, becomes a marker for effective fighting, a key to military victory in America. Important, though, is that Dan Brand, a white male, acts as the vehicle to introduce the Indian way of fighting to the Americans. In the opening pages, the text highlights the savagery of the attacking Iroquois and Huron: they are a "bloodthirsty army," and their attack is described as a "massacre." In a wide panel on the bottom of the second page, a battle scene between the Indians and settlers is depicted. A voice from a faceless mob of attacking Indians proclaims, "Kill! Kill! Kill! We shall line our wigwams with the scalps of the white men!" (68). This panel also features a rhetorical element of depicting Indians as a chaotic mass; the attacking Indians form a single entity, smashed together into an indeterminate mass of red and black, arms raised with tomahawks, faces barely discernible, while on the right, one Indian carries away a screaming white woman. It seems, then, the episode works to metamorphose the violent savagery of the Indian attacks (depicted as villainous in the opening) into an appropriate form of battle for future white Americans to gain independence. Yet a possible contradiction exists here: the Iroquois and Huron state their motive for attacking as "revenge against the settler who takes away our hunting lands!" (68). Is one to view these Indians as fighting for their land, fighting for their own autonomy? This motive is somewhat undercut by the French bribery of using rifles and alcohol in the preceding panel, yet one might observe here two analogous motives in fighting against a perceived invader: the Indians against the settlers and the Americans against the British. The comic's ending ties together the Indians and the white Americans through implementing similar guerilla-style combat; yet divergent value judgments are implied about these groups' respective motives: when the Indians fight back, it is "massacre," and when the Americans fight back, it is "independence."

This contradiction illustrates the complexity of trying to have your cake and eat it too, as Deloria describes playing Indian. If the narrative's logic asserts that the way the colonial Americans will gain their independence is through adopting Indian methods of warfare, then the narrative must contend with the fact that it has also depicted those methods as brutally violent and savage. This logical conundrum is where Dan Brand comes in. As an intermediary between Indians and whites, Brand filters out the "savagery" and "villainy" of the Indian methods, transmitting them to George Washington, who will use these whitewashed military strategies. Worth noting here, too, is that Brand rarely resolves his violent conflicts with the villains with murder. Brand is willing and capable of fighting, but he always chooses to spare his adversary's life: in a duel, he shoots his pistol in the air, and in another fight, for example, he opts to use his fists rather than a knife. One might read this avoidance of murder not only as a matter of content restriction but also as a sign that Brand has retained his civility; he has not become a "bloodthirsty savage" even though he has taken on the ways of the Indian. This general characteristic of Dan Brand throughout the series further supports viewing him as a filter of Indian "savagery," separating the needed capacity for violent force from the so-called savage.

*Tomahawk* echoes many of the patriotic themes of *White Indian*: Tomahawk takes part in the Revolution, assisting the American cause. During the *Star Spangled Comics* run, Tomahawk's adventures would vary from frontier plots before the Revolution to stories set during the war, often with the hero assisting Washington. During these Revolution stories, Indians would still be present but were not typically the actual enemy.

Generally, the Indians of *Tomahawk* were not inherently evil. In most cases, Indian aggression against Americans and settlers sprang from British incitement, renegade whites, or outlaw Indians (usually ones banished from their tribes). In "The Riddle of Mohawk Valley" (*Star Spangled Comics* #102: March 1950), Tomahawk and Dan are sent on a mission to recover gold needed by Washington. Four men, each with a map piece, had set out to deliver the gold, but they were ambushed by Mohawk; three were killed, the fourth went missing. Tom and Dan are sent with Wild Jack Betts to assist them. Turns out that Betts is in disguise: he is Bud Wilson, one of the original four, and is still after the gold. Tom explains: "Bud Wilson . . . traitor! The British pay him for information an' for incitin' the Injuns to fight Americans! He put the Mohawks on his other three friends, but one o' them hid the three map parts before he died." (10). "The Unhappy Hunting Grounds" (#105: June 1950) focuses its plot on a game preservation that Tomahawk has negotiated for Indian neighbors of the settlers. The Indians use the preservation to hunt, and the settlers do not encroach upon that land. The British devise a plan to kill the animals on the preserve so that the Indians will blame the settlers and thus attack them. In a similar plot, "The Death Map of Thunder Hill!" (#111: Dec. 1950) shows the British attempt to turn the Indians against the Americans by stealing a wampum belt from the tribe while disguised as settlers.

Renegade whites and Indians also sow discord. "The Outlaw Indians" (#118: July 1951) features a group of Indians who have been banished from their tribes and so wage war on anyone, white or Indian. Similarly, "The Revenge of Raven Heart" (#120: Sept. 1951) tells of the eponymous Indian who has been banished, and so "his talents of might and cunning turned against all men" (he dies after falling from a ledge in Magua-like fashion).

The most famous renegade white appears in *Tomahawk*: Simon Girty is the featured villain of "The Traitor in War Paint" (#106: July 1950). The cover shows Tomahawk and Dan Hunter looking at a wanted poster of Girty, whose infamy carries over from the cover to the opening page: Tomahawk and Dan tied to posts, about to be burned alive as Indians dance around them. To their right and behind them, Simon Girty sits upon horseback, looking on with seeming complacency (perhaps an allusion to the story told of Colonel Crawford's execution).

Figure 4.7. Simon Girty.
Fred Ray (pencils and inks),
"The Traitor in War Paint!"
*Star Spangled Comics* #106
(July 1950). DC Comics.

The introductory narration leaves no question as to Girty's treason: "The American Revolution . . . who shall ever forget it? The new world was about to come into its own . . . and three million determined people were set to wage a savage struggle! Yet, one man . . . Simon Girty . . . would betray them!" He is "a treacherous leader known as . . . 'The Traitor in War Paint!'" According to this narration, Girty opposes those loyal American settlers, his treachery challenging the noble efforts of Americans to gain their independence. Ray emphasizes Girty's whiteness as it contrasts with his actions of leading and helping the Indians against white settlers. In one instance, as Indians attack a settlement, the script and Ray's art draw the reader's attention to one of the attackers: "But if one could look into the face of the leader of the raiders, he would see not the black eyes of a red man . . . but the cold, blue eyes of the notorious Simon Girty!" (2). His eye color marks his whiteness, while his actions and his appearance in the panel mark him as Indian. In the next panel, he meets with a British officer, removes his war paint, and thus appears white (this panel is directly below the one just described and so creates an obvious contrast on the page: see Fig. 4.7). Girty plays Indian in order to aid the British in inciting the Indians against the Americans. Such incitation involves Girty visiting various tribes and making speeches such as this one: "The Americans are your *enemies*! They wish to drive you ever back . . . away from your lands and your homes! Fight with the King . . . *kill the Americans*! Follow me in battle!" (3). This speech echoes those words that Bakeless and others cite, as well, in Girty's words preceding the Blue Licks battle.

Tom is asked to track down Girty because, according to the American officer, "nobody in America knows the wilderness and the Indians as well as" Tom and Dan (3). Tom states, "I was born among the Indians . . . and I was raised in the wilds! Indians are my brothers . . . the wilds are my home!" (3). One notable point in Tom's words is his kinship to Indians, a kinship that proceeds from birth (this statement conflicts with Tomahawk's origin story in *Star Spangled* #69, which depicts him as being captured and adopted by Indians rather than being born among them). Tom and Dan discover that various tribes are gathering in a war council. Girty addresses the gathering, urging the Indians to attack the Americans. Girty is manipulating the Indians, though. As they prepare for battle, Girty watches, thinking, "Ha! My lies have their effect! Soon, I'll have every Indian in the colony hating the Americans!" (5). This trope of white manipulation of Indians is a common one in many of these frontier and Western comics. This narrative strategy deflects blame from the Indians themselves and concentrates the villainy into a traitorous white man.

The Indians attack a fort, but Tom sets a trap and tricks the attackers, and so the advantage turns to the outnumbered colonists. Tom and Dan follow the Indians and then Girty, knowing that the attacks would proceed elsewhere, although the two heroes are discovered. With Tom thought to be dead, Girty and his Indians take Dan. Of course, Tom is not dead (he used a trick learned "from the Injuns" to play dead), and so he rescues Dan. Tom and Dan race ahead of Girty's force to warn the targeted town. Girty arrives to find himself in another trap engineered by Tomahawk (a seemingly empty town that draws the attackers into the open center, allowing the Americans to ambush the Indians). Girty escapes, though, with the promise to return and kill Tomahawk. The story ends with Washington informing Tom of a peace treaty with the Indians (10).

Another white renegade appears in "The Doom Stockade" (#119). This plot revolves around a settler, Brissom, who betrays his peers because he has discovered the settlement sits upon a gold vein. He is described as "a black-hearted renegade, who stands to profit from the darkening sun of friendship along the plains" (1). According to a son of the chief that

Tomahawk meets, Brissom has told the tribe that the white settlers plot to attack. When Tomahawk tells the Indian that Brissom is lying, the Indian responds: "Would a paleface disown his white brothers by deceiving us to no purpose?" (4). The Indian cannot comprehend that such disloyalty is possible, so he believes Brissom. This may be a minor plot point, but it speaks to the enormity of the white renegade's betrayal: is it possible that such treason is so treacherous as to be unimaginable? At least for this Indian, who might represent a kind of simplicity of honesty and honor, that seems to be the case. More importantly, this point illustrates the immensity of the renegade's betrayal.

Various stories directly link Tomahawk to assisting American efforts in the Revolutionary War. In addition to thwarting renegades and traitors who seek to defeat the American cause, Tomahawk assists the American side in assuring shipments of gunpowder and arms, many times in direct service to George Washington himself. The opening narration for "The Battle of Junction Fort!" (#116: May 1951) articulates this particular aspect of the series quite vividly:

Who shall ever forget Boston, Lexington, and Concord, the crossing of the Delaware? It was one of history's mightiest, most terrible—and most glorious wars! For out of it sprang a new nation—a nation seeking freedom for *all* men! Behind the great struggle are a hundred stories—nay, a thousand— and this is but one of them, patterned after the rest, which led to eventual victory! (1)

This issue also features a cover that perhaps most lucidly captures Tomahawk's patriotic connection to the American Revolution. Tomahawk strides up a large rock with the American flag in his left hand, a rifle in his right, leading the Americans. He towers above a group of British and Indian attackers, rifles and bows aimed at the hero. In the story itself, Washington tasks Tomahawk with assisting in taking a fort from the British. The fort occupies a strategic position, and along with that, the British are recruiting Indians. Tomahawk arrives at a plan in which he plays Indian[10]: he dyes his skin and works with a friendly tribe to accept the British recruitment. Doing so allows them entry into the fort. They are then able to attack from the inside when Washington attacks from the outside. Tomahawk plays Indian again in order to transport gunpowder through British lines in "The Ten Days That Changed a War!" (#123: Dec. 1951). Tomahawk's connection to key revolutionary moments is further

illustrated by "The Ambush at Sea!" (#128: May 1952), in which he transports arms to the Americans on the night of Paul Revere's ride.

"The Magic Tomahawk" (#126: Mar. 1952) encapsulates Tomahawk's
importance to the American cause. The tomahawk of the title is silver,
crafted by Revere and presented to Tomahawk by Washington. It bears
the inscription "Let Right Prevail," and the narrator asks, "Did some of
George Washington's genius cling to the silver-mounted hatchet he presented to Tomahawk? Did Paul Revere's ardent patriotism infuse the glittering inlays he fashioned for its blade?" (1). This image of a tomahawk
wielded by a frontiersman and blessed by Revere and Washington is a
potent one, particularly in how it fuses the symbolics of playing Indian and
American nationalism. This study has already discussed the iconicity of the
tomahawk, with its symbolic resonance of violence and strength, teetering
on the brink of savagery. Tomahawk's name itself taps into this symbolic
well. In addition, here one sees in concrete form an actual tomahawk that
fuses martial prowess (appropriated from the Indian) and nationalistic
devotion. Furthermore, as discussed in chapter 3, the tomahawk has undergone something of a whitewash in this series. "Daniel Boone—King of
the Hunters!" explicitly compares the rifle to the tomahawk, demonstrating
the latter's equal usefulness. As this comic book version of Boone says, "a
tomahawk's as good as a rifle out here—an' a rifle's as good as a tomahawk"
(8). These two stories taken together present an anchoring of the tomahawk
in white American ideology: the "magic tomahawk," with its lineage from
Revere and Washington, and Boone's blessing of the weapon operate to elevate the tomahawk from Indian weapon, and thus "primitive" or "savage,"
to an appropriate tool of the white frontiersman, as wielded by Tomahawk.
The tomahawk's symbolic status is transformed from one of Indianness to
one of patriotic Americanness.

*Tomahawk*'s patriotic strain continues into the 1960s. For example, in
"The Battle That Never Died" (Jan.–Feb. 1965), Tomahawk and his Rangers repeatedly attempt to cross a river but cannot, due to enemy gunfire.
Tomahawk protests that it is an impossible task and that his men are badly
injured: "At least 10 of the men are out of action! Others are wounded—
half-frozen" (3). His superior commands Tomahawk to continue the effort.
After another failed attempt, Tomahawk reports to the officer, who still
cannot reveal the objective of the mission. Tomahawk obeys the orders
without question, modeling the proper behavior of a soldier. Even in a situation where he is not being given the whole story of his mission, Tomahawk
conforms to military hierarchy, taking his Rangers back into the freezing

river on their futile mission. At story's end, they learn that they were creating a distraction to allow Washington to cross the Delaware. The final panel is a copy of Emanuel Leutze's *Washington Crossing the Delaware* (1851). The story depicts strict military discipline and obedience to hierarchy while placing Tomahawk in a key moment of the American Revolution.[11]

Bruce Lenthall examines the presence of race in comic strips before and after WWII and draws this conclusion: "Race became a non-factor in the popular imagination, not because the culture was racist or racialist, but because on some level it sought to hide the differences it had not overcome. In the comics immediately following World War II, then, race, disappeared" (47). Lenthall focuses on African American and Asian characters in comic strips, so it may not be fair to assume wholesale his analysis for comic books. The question of Native Americans in comic strips is one that he does not address. I would still invoke Lenthall's argument, though, to draw attention to the absence of nonwhite characters in comics, and to position the comics under study here within that argument. Generally speaking, in comics, two genres feature nonwhite characters in the postwar period: Western and jungle comics. The presence of racial difference, then, is mostly confined to the margins: temporally, in the past, and geographically, in the jungle or on the frontier. The role of the white hero in relation to the nonwhite characters is usually consistent in both genres, as well: the white hero is a paternalistic leader for the "savages," whether Indian or African. Although further comparison between the jungle and Western comics could be productive, for the purposes of my argument, I focus solely on the Western, and more specifically, the playing Indian comics.

In these playing Indian comics, the imagined Indian occupies an ambiguous status as both the ideal American and the marginalized other. For all his admirable qualities, he is still a primitive, many times speaking the pidgin English that connotes a lower intelligence or inferior status. For these reasons, the Indian is a problematic rhetorical figure in these comics and in American culture in general. He exists on the margins of "civilization." He also exists in a tempest of battles and violent attacks, a chaos of thievery and deception that the white hero must contain. Therefore, these stories articulate an important ideological function of the white hero who plays Indian: he is the one who polices the boundary between order and chaos, between wilderness and the settlement, between white and Indian. This reading is predicated on Richard Dyer's argument: "The frontier, and all the drama and excitement its establishment and maintenance entail, is about the act of bringing order in the form of borders to a land and people without them" (33). By playing Indian, the white hero functions as an attempt to neutralize the seeming problematic nature of racial difference. The white hero absorbs the best qualities of the racial other, and in his doing so, the other is no longer necessary. The white hero preserves in himself what is best of the Indian, and with that the Indian can fade away, his nobility and bravery inherited by whites, the actual Indian self erased and forgotten.

This dynamic of preservation and erasure raises an important point regarding the political context of these comics. A notable paradox emerges when one considers the playing Indian comics alongside the federal Indian policies that were being implemented during the 1950s. Termination and relocation were a two-pronged federal effort to assimilate Native Americans into the dominant white society. In short, termination sought to end federal supervision of tribal affairs, while relocation moved Native persons from their reservations to cities. Although the stated intentions and justifications for these policies might come across as positive, the effects and the implementation of termination and relocation were generally harmful, sometimes achieving the exact opposite of the stated goals. These policies resulted in the potential extinction of traditions and cultural ways. Donald Fixico articulates this point: "In everything that it represented, termination threatened the very core of American Indian existence—its culture. The federal government sought to de-Indianize Native Americans" (183). While the US government was busy with de-Indianization, comic books were busy with Indianization. How this Indianization of the comics contributes to a construction of race and cultural appropriation's role in that construction is the focus of this section.

One vivid example of how race is constructed in these comics is found in Manzar the Bright Arrow of *Indians*, discussed in passing above. To his friends and neighbors, he is Dan Carter, a trader, but when trouble arises, he becomes Manzar the Bright Arrow. The introductory blurb for Manzar offers this summary of the hero: "When smoke-sign spelled danger in the Black Hills, Dan Carter, the trader, vanished . . . and blazing along the peril-trails rode the Bright Arrow, blue-eyed son of the Sioux, shouting the battle-cry the lawless feared—'Hoka-Hai!'" This description presents evident racial clues: he is "blue-eyed," a trait that signifies his whiteness, while "son of the Sioux" marks his racial crossing. This crossing is ascribed by the tribal name, though, rather than a biological trait, like eye color. The implication, then, is that Dan Carter retains his whiteness while assuming the guise of an Indian. Dan's cross-racial identity acts as a marker of his manhood, too.

The first issue opens with posing two different perceptions of Dan Carter held by his peers. To the "wild trappers of the Black Hills," he is "only half a man," but to his "Indian brothers," he is "best and bravest of their braves." This dichotomy of his perceived manliness emphasizes that in his white persona Dan Carter is viewed as less than manly. Yet in his Indian persona he is the "best and bravest," fully displaying the characteristics of masculinity. Further notable on the opening page is how the text quoted above overlays a full-page scene depicting Indian men wielding spears and tomahawks dancing in a ring around a fire that illuminates three sets of white captives tied to totem poles. This scene depicts a typical racial dichotomy of the "savage" Indians preying upon white victims.

Dan's white/weakness and Indian/strength dichotomy develops as the story progresses, but the reader learns that Dan undertakes this dichotomy in order to protect his identity as Manzar. He acts weak so as not to reveal his true strength, a revelation that would expose his identity as the white Indian hero. This point is evident in a scene where a woman makes advances that Dan resists, but then the woman's partner, Panky Harlow, walks in and, believing that Dan has accosted the woman, punches Dan. Instead of fighting back, Dan takes the blow, thinking, "Got to fall with his blow . . . can't fight back." He refuses to fight in order to maintain his secret identity, but that refusal perpetuates the perception of him as weak and cowardly. In a following panel, Panky taunts Dan's uncle, saying, "Maul a woman, but run from a man, eh? Fine breed of skunk you raised at Cougar Pass, Pegleg." In a succeeding panel, Dan's uncle wonders about these cowardly actions, to which his wife replies, "Just redskin ways he'll soon outgrow." The comic operates on this dichotomy of perceived cowardice and racial categorization. Yet this racial characterization is false, as the reader is aware. The characters in the story see Dan as cowardly due to his Indian adoption, yet the reader knows that Dan is hiding his strength, that his Indian adoption has endowed him with those qualities that make him the hero and allow him to perform his role as defender of the innocent and upholder of justice.

Dan's embodiment of a split between his white culture and adopted Indian ways is also evident in the second issue, which shows how he changes into the Manzar persona. His costume involves not only donning Indian trappings but also darkening his skin: he changes his skin color (Fig. 4.8). In *Indians* #2 (1950), a panel shows him applying paint to his entire body,

Figure 4.8. "White blood turns red . . ." *Indians* #2 (1950). Fiction House Magazines.

saying, "Stain for my skin . . . white blood turns red . . . exit Dan Carter and enter the Bright Arrow!" (5). The preceding panel contrasts with this one in displaying Dan's whiteness before he stains his skin. The comic's color coding presents the visual marker of his racial masquerade. He not only takes on his heroic identity through costume but also undergoes a racial transformation as denoted by his reddening of his skin, a coloration that affects not only his outward appearance but his "blood" too. This color coding deserves attention in that comic art must rely on stereotypical visual cues to communicate the racial difference. This is not the first example seen in this study of this skin dyeing and will not be the last. After undergoing this transformation into his Indian identity, Dan is able to exercise fully his masculine power and strength as Manzar. While he is Dan Carter, he must, by the comic's logic, hide his strength, lest his secret identity be exposed (which is obviously akin to Superman's clumsy and inept Clark Kent persona).

Furthermore, while playing Indian in this comic adheres to the typical motif of providing strength and bravery through the masquerade, in the Manzar stories there is something of a reversal to this trope. On the surface Dan's white persona is weak, while his Indian persona is strong. Yet, since Dan was raised as an Indian, he views that self to be his true identity, and for the sake of his heroic persona, he actually plays white. Though white by skin color and birth, he views himself as Indian. Therefore, this comic, whether consciously or not, actually challenges notions of essentialized or fixed race, putting forth an image of race as a construction or as something mutable. Dan's allegiance to his Indian identity is further affirmed in issue #5 (Apr. 1951) when he abandons completely his white persona and becomes Manzar full-time, joining with a band of Arapahos to, as he explains, "serve my people in ways that I cannot serve them here." In issue #6 (June 1951), Manzar's new path is affirmed as the introductory text to his story explains how he is now a "white outcast of the Sioux" and has joined with Red Cloud, swearing together to ride "and fight for the good of our people!" In this same story Manzar proclaims, "My skin may be white, but in my heart I am Indian!"

In succeeding stories Manzar and Red Cloud operate as a duo, fighting to unite the Indian tribes while making peace with the US government and upsetting the nefarious plans of the villains, both white and Indian. Manzar's mission in these stories revolves around negotiation of a confederation between the area Indian tribes, then defending that confederation. At the end of issue #6's story, Manzar states that he and Red Cloud "must work to hold our brother Indians together in bond!" In issue #8 (Oct. 1951), Manzar and Red Cloud succeed in getting the tribes to sign a treaty, overcoming the efforts of John Caleb Nestor, a fur trader, to foil the tribes' unity. In the next issue Nestor's daughter takes up her dead father's cause to upset the tribal confederation that Manzar has arranged. In addition, succeeding stories follow a similar vein of Manzar and Red Cloud defending the Indian alliance. *Manzar the White Indian* thus becomes a story of Manzar's full embrace of his adoptive culture, completely abandoning his white identity. *Manzar* presents a sympathetic view of Native Americans, one that holds with the rest of the comic book's premise in its presentation of Native characters and nonfiction pieces on Native culture.

Like *Manzar*, *Straight Arrow* also challenges the typical racial expectations of the playing Indian trope in having its hero actually be a Comanche who is playing white. *Straight Arrow* varies the white-man-playing-Indian formula in that Steve Adams is a Comanche adopted by white settlers who has grown up white. Straight Arrow, then, is an Indian playing white in order to conceal his heroic identity. Like Manzar, Straight Arrow possesses a secret headquarters, the cave where he keeps his outfit and horse, ready for him to leap into action (Fig. 4.9). Unlike Dan Brand, Steve Adams does not conceal his strength when in his everyday identity. Steve Adams might be viewed as an example of assimilation. He has taken on a respectable

Figure 4.9. Straight Arrow's secret headquarters. Fred Meagher (pencils and inks), *Straight Arrow* #1 (Feb.–Mar. 1950). Magazine Enterprises.

profession as rancher. He owns property. He is a part of the process of settlement, transforming the wilderness into civilization.[12]

*Straight Arrow* calls attention to tribal distinctions. In the debut story, "Straight Arrow" (#1: Feb.—Mar. 1950), a new colonel, Deegan, from West Point is notified of an attack by the Osage. He responds: "Osages? What difference the name you give them? They're all the same. Sound to horse! There's a village on Cottonwood Creek that we'll teach a lesson!" A lieutenant protests: "But those are Kiowas, Colonel!" Colonel Deegan refuses to acknowledge the important national affiliations of Native Americans. While those around him attempt to explain those distinctions, he refuses to take heed. For Deegan, like many others, an Indian is an Indian. Deegan's attitude is especially alarming, given that it is one primarily responsible for many of the horrific massacres of Native peoples—such as Wounded Knee, Bear Creek, and Sand Creek—committed by the US Army. This moment highlights the complexity of diplomacy and political relations among

Native tribes, something that Steve attempts to explain to Deegan. When Deegan goes forward to attack the Kiowa village, Steve becomes Straight Arrow to locate the true perpetrators of the attack. By story's end, Deegan learns his lesson, explaining, "Straight Arrow taught me humility when my pride insisted that I continue in my blunder. Now, when I have to decide a question involving Indians—I decide it as Straight Arrow would!"

The significance of blood as racial identifier operates in *Straight Arrow*, too: "Heeding the call of the Comanche blood flowing in his veins, the legendary Straight Arrow rides once again!" ("Land of Our Fathers!" #2: Apr.–May 1950). This same story depicts Steve's defense of the Comanche as betrayal when a group of settlers grows furious, shouting, "You traitors! Injun-lovers!" In this story, as in many others of this genre, the real villains are not the Indians but crooked white men dressed as Indians. This narrative device illustrates how playing Indian can be a threatening thing, in this case being used for treacherous means.

The treachery of white men operates as the central threat in these stories, a fact made evident in the character of Black Feather in "The Battle of the Giants" (#4: Aug. 1950). Black Feather is Zeke Blower, a white man who dresses in Indian garb to carry out his thievery. He presents a mirror image of Straight Arrow; he is the white renegade, like the popular imaginings of Simon Girty, who uses Indianness as a means to serve his own selfish gain. As there are "good Indians" and "bad Indians," there are also good white Indians and bad white Indians. *Manzar* and *Straight Arrow*, then, complicate notions of racial identity and playing Indian, exposing the constructed nature of race and the proposition of cross-racial identification.

Entering into the 1960s, the critical mass of white Indian characters experienced an inevitable decline. Probably the only comic of this genre to continue into the 1960s was *Tomahawk*. Toward the end of this decade and into the next one, the white Indian in comics, much as with Western stories in other media such as the film *Little Big Man* (1970), becomes a vehicle for examinations of social issues, with the complicated relationship between race and identity as a predominant theme. Joe Kubert's Firehair illustrates the "in-between" theme of the white Indian, that character who is caught between two worlds, neither white nor Indian. *Son of Tomahawk* brings the *Tomahawk* series to a close in an effort to consider the nature of racism and prejudice. *Scalphunter* presents what is probably the last significant white Indian character (so far) in comics, taking on the conventions of its predecessors in depicting an ideal manhood while inflecting that image with a violence and aggression that echoes the larger trend in comics toward the antihero. While retaining many conventions found in playing Indian comics of the postwar period, these later characters demonstrate some of the departures in treatment of race and violence indicative of the comics being produced after the 1960s.

Joe Kubert's Firehair debuted in *Showcase* #85–87 (1969), then became a backup feature in *Tomahawk* #131–32, 134, and 136 (1970–1971). While Firehair's character arc did not develop fully, the three stories in *Showcase* establish a clear sense of direction and motivation for the white Indian. Firehair's origin follows the conventions of the white Indian story. The Blackfoot attack a wagon train of settlers, killing everyone except the red-haired infant who would become Firehair. Chief Grey Cloud spares the life of the infant and adopts him because of a prophecy delivered by the tribe's shaman (7). As is often the case, in these stories, the white Indian possesses an exceptional quality. This storyline follows the typical plot of the white Indian: adopted as a child, he then grows up to outperform his Indian peers: "Firehair had to do more than his contemporaries . . . to prove himself a chief's son! He could out-wrestle, out-run, and out-shoot (with a bow and arrow) any of the boys of his own age" (12). While Kubert follows many of the conventions of the white Indian, he also attempts to explore the complexities of acceptance and intolerance. The first story's title, "I Don't Belong Here . . . I Don't Belong There!" establishes the central theme of Firehair's middle ground status: he feels rejected by both whites and Indians, and thus his character motivation is to find his "place," to find out who he is, as he declares at the end of his first story: he will "wander the face of the earth" until he finds his "place" (22). "A Declaration of Intent," included in the comic, explains the narrative's purpose of connecting the issues of racial and cultural acceptance as set in the past to the present: "Stepping off from this basic concept [whites adopted by Indians], the problems that would present itself [*sic*] in such a situation—would *not*, we feel, differ radically from the problems we all face *today*" (16). Firehair reiterates this thematic framework in his own words in succeeding stories. Like many of his contemporaries, Kubert intends this story to grapple with social and racial issues directly relevant to the contemporary context.

*Tomahawk*'s run from 1950 to 1972 places it during a period of time in which racial awareness in the United States underwent radical change. By the last issues of the series in the early 1970s, which focus on Hawk, Tomahawk's son, Robert Kanigher (who took on writing duties with issue #119) was explicitly addressing racial issues. This attention to racism and perceptions of race follows right on the heels of Dennis O'Neil's much-touted treatment of social and political issues for the Green Lantern and Green Arrow series in the early 1970s.

In "Small Eagle . . . Brother Hawk!" (132: Jan.–Feb. 1971), Tomahawk's youngest son, Little Eagle, is accosted by racist white men in the street, with the main antagonist, Hard Rock, saying, "I'll teach that redskin pup not to walk on the sidewalk . . . but in the gutter . . . where he belongs!" (1). Little Eagle's mother (and Tomahawk's Indian wife), Moon Fawn, attacks the men as Hawk, the older brother, arrives. Hawk fights the men and wins. Later in the story two of Tomahawk's Rangers present him a gift from George Washington: a goose-quill pen that Jefferson used to write the Declaration of Independence (14). Instead of accepting it for himself, Tomahawk presents the quill to Little Eagle, saying, "[F]reedom don't come easy . . . you have to fight for it! But—you may find that a pen can be a mighty weapon . . . more potent than a lance—or—a longrifle" (14). In the final panel Little Eagle places the quill into his headband (earlier, one of the racist attackers had shot Little Eagle's feather off), with the words, "I will wear it . . . as long as I live!" This image depicts a dramatic assimilation of American national lineage: Jefferson's quill passed on from Washington to Tomahawk, a valiant hero of the Revolution, to the interracial son, Little Eagle. This transmission seems a reversal of the usual myth of white American inheritance of indigenous authenticity. The goose quill becomes a part of the Indian dress of Little Eagle, and perhaps the implication here is the value of interracial identity to national identity.

Racial identity and prejudice are also central to "Scalp Hunter" (133: Mar.–Apr. 1971), in which Hawk faces racial persecution himself at the hands of a bounty hunter (who goes otherwise unnamed). The cover features Hawk on horseback being pushed off the edge of a cliff by a bearded, muscled villain also on horseback. The man is yelling, "The only *good* Injun is a *dead* Injun!"[13] The opening splash page further epitomizes the scalp hunter's villainy. The Scalp Hunter, his name spread out before his feet, acting as title of the story but also occupying diegetic space upon the ground, stands with his right side to the audience, his right hand grips a rifle, and in his left he holds upright a pole with scalps hanging on it. He is dressed in fringed leather frontier garb, a knife holstered in his belt, his shirt sleeves ripped and tattered, with long black hair and beard. He is indeed a savage-looking man, a malicious mirror of Tomahawk (and reminiscent of the prototypical Indian hunter, like Nathan Slaughter in Robert Montgomery Bird's *Nick of the Woods* [1837], who embraces "savagery" in order to better fight it).

Hawk and Tomahawk happen by, and the Scalp Hunter, or as he's named in the story, the bounty hunter, challenges Hawk to a horse race, in which the villain sideswipes Hawk off the path and down into a river. Later that night Hawk expresses his confusion to his parents as to why the Scalp Hunter attacked him, declaring, "I'm no Indian!" Tomahawk reminds his older son to look at his mother and his brother, and Hawk, chastened, apologizes to them. His mother replies, "Red and white blood run in your veins! Like two currents! Who can tell which stronger?" Little Eagle is, in his own words, "proud to be all-Indian like his mother." Hawk reckons with his racial identity; having thought of himself as white, he sees now that others do not view him as such. Later, Hawk decides to confront the bounty hunter, leading to a chase, then a fight on a cliff in which the bounty hunter, refusing Hawk's help, falls three miles to his death. Hawk returns home and his father asks, "Did you find out how much o' you is Indian?" Hawk answers affirmatively, having accepted his Indian blood as part of his identity. This story highlights how racial identity is not always clearly signified by skin color or exterior markers. Hawk is drawn as "white," with skin color and dress that align him racially with whiteness. Yet, due to his parentage, he is viewed as an Indian. This story resolves Hawk's racial insecurity with his acceptance of his Indian blood.

On the whole, the final issues of the run represent a definite change of attitude and politics in *Tomahawk*. While the bulk of the series adheres to the typical Western's rhetoric of white American progress, *Tomahawk* ends in a decidedly different tone that echoes the social progressivism of O'Neil's *Green Lantern* and foreshadows the sort of depictions that will arrive in later comics.[14] The cancellation of *Tomahawk* in 1972 marked the end of the long-running Western comic, leaving DC with one other major Western line: the revived series *All-Star Western* became *Weird Western Tales* that year, and with that change Jonah Hex burst onto the scene. Hex, while an intriguing character, is not relevant to this study's focus. His successor as *Weird Western Tales'* lead is definitely of interest here, though. Later in the series, after Hex moved to his own comic, the new lead for *Weird Western Tales* was a white Indian named Scalphunter, aka Brian Savage, aka Ke-Woh-No-Tay.

DC's Scalphunter[15] became the sole feature for *Weird Western Tales* with issue #39 (Mar.–Apr. 1977) and remained the lead for the rest of the run, until its cancellation with issue #70 (Aug. 1980). The majority of these issues were written by Gerry Conway, with Michael Fleisher writing the initial six issues of Scalphunter's run and one more later in the series

(Fleisher had been writing the Jonah Hex stories since issue #22 and was also working on the eponymous comic during this time).[16] In 1977 Horn was observing the decline of the Western in comics. He states that the Jonah Hex–centered *Weird Western Tales* had "become the most popular Western feature among comic books in the Seventies" (111), although it would be one of the last major Western comics. The decline of popularity in comics of the Western genre reflects its general decline in American culture in the seventies and the eighties. Cawelti speaks of "the increasing obsolescence of the Western as a myth of America" (100) during this time. Slotkin marks the seventies and eighties as the period of decline of the western (*Gunfighter* 627–28). Scalphunter, then, is significant not only for his thematic relevance to this study but also as one of the last major figures in that body of Western comics immediately connected to the heyday of the genre from the fifties to the seventies.

Alas, Scalphunter as a character is not very exciting. He speaks little. His motivations are not clear at first. In general, he is a vehicle for Western action and violence but offers little competition to his counterpart Jonah Hex. *The Slings & Arrows Comic Guide* makes this assessment of Scalphunter: "Strong social concerns permeate the stories, but he's dull, and the only weird thing is how he lasted thirty-one issues" (732). His dullness notwithstanding, Scalphunter provides some variation on the white Indian comic hero model seen thus far in this study, so he merits attention in that regard.

Scalphunter's biography adheres to the typical conventions of the white Indian centered on adoption and acculturation in an Indian tribe. His introduction in "Scalphunter" (#39: Mar.–Apr. 1977) explains his origin. When his parents, Matt and Laurie Savage, are settling in Missouri, they are attacked by Kiowa. Matt is left for dead, Laurie is killed, and their son, Brian, is kidnapped to grow up as a Kiowa. Brian becomes Ke-Woh-No-Tay, or "he who is less than a human." Ke-Woh-No-Tay is, as the opening narration states, "a man who lived in two worlds." Fleisher frames Scalphunter as belonging to neither the white nor the Kiowa world; he is a man in between. The editorial page, "Trail Talk," for #39 confirms this premise: "Like his predecessor, (Jonah Hex), Scalphunter is an outcast in the days of the old west. He is shunned by the people of his birth for his Indian upbringing and hated by the Indians for this white heritage."

Like his white Indian predecessors, Scalphunter embodies a strong and physically superior manhood. Often described as "the tall man," Ke-Woh-No-Tay cuts an impressive figure, a muscular specimen who out-sizes most of the men he encounters. His first appearance on the cover of issue #39 represents his physical strength and violent nature: shown busting out of the back of a prison wagon, he swings his fists bound together in chains, knocking out two guards. When he visits New York City in "The Gangs of Old New York" (#60: Oct. 1979), he easily outmatches the urban men: "[T]o those who watch, whose lives have been spent in an urban wilderness, Ke-Woh-No-Tey's [sic][17] strength is unbelievable" (8). Scalphunter follows clearly that convention of strength through Indianness. His physical strength is also channeled into a degree of violence unseen in previous examples of the white Indian studied in this book.

Previous examples of the white Indian in comics are more than willing to fight, yet these men usually do not kill. This restraint of these comic book heroes owes partially to editorial code but also to the racial implication of savagery that accompanies murder. The trait that often defines the white Indian as more white than Indian is his ability to control himself, to succumb not to bloodlust, and, most importantly, not to scalp. This differentiation is found as far back as *The Last of the Mohicans*. Scalphunter, though, readily kills, and furthermore, he scalps. Ke-Woh-No-Tay is an example of the antihero and the move toward the more brutally violent comic book hero, a trend that was beginning to develop in the seventies, especially coming to fruition in the eighties with characters like The Punisher and Frank Miller's Dark Knight. His violence is evident, for example, in "The Mark of a Warrior" (#40: May–June 1977). In this story, Ke-Woh-No-Tay saves Miss Masefield, the editor of an abolitionist newspaper, from an attack by pro-slavery thugs. In the sequence of panels following the rescue, Ke-Woh-No-Tay proceeds to scalp the dead attackers. This exchange occurs between him and Masefield:

> MASEFIELD: *Gasp!* Wh-what are you going to do with that knife?
> KE-WOH-NO-TAY: Scalp these men, while their scalps are still fresh!
> MASEFIELD: B-But that's horrible! Barbaric!
> KE-WOH-NO-TAY: No! Scalps are strong medicine! They are the mark of a true warrior!

In the next panel Ke-Woh-No-Tay straddles the stomach of one of the men, grips the corpse's hair in his left hand, and holds the knife blade in position to scalp, saying, "When the Great Spirit looks down from his Sky Valley and sees these scalps dangling from the mane of my warpony, he will know that I am brave and that I have slain my enemies!" (5). A similar sentiment of violent accomplishment exists in the following issue's story, "The Black Seer of Death Canyon!" (#41: July–Aug. 1977). Ke-Woh-No-Tay happens upon a group of men torturing a prospector for information about his claim and kills one of the attackers. One panel depicts the slamming of the tomahawk into the head of one of the bandits with a "thwack." In the next panel, Ke-Woh-No-Tay looks upon the corpse, its feet splayed out toward the viewer, thinking, "To have killed an enemy silently—and face to face is strong medicine! But there will not be time to take his scalp!" (3).

This theme of violent warrior-hood reaches a fuller articulation in "Death Stalk" in #42 (Sept.–Oct. 1977) while crystallizing a motivation for Scalphunter's character: the attainment of true warrior status in his tribe. His father had remarked earlier about the Kiowa restriction against a white man becoming a warrior, and this prohibition seems to fuel Ke-Woh-No-Tay's quest in these early issues to prove himself as one. "Death Stalk" brings this conflict into the open when Ke-Woh-No-Tay does not prevent the murder of a Kiowa boy and thus is accused of cowardice by members of his tribe. The chief sends Ke-Woh-No-Tay on a mission of vengeance, a "death stalk." Ke-Woh-No-Tay must kill each of the white murderers or face execution himself: "[Y]ou will bring the blood-drenched scalps of the evildoers to my tepee as proof you have fulfilled your mission! Fail in your mission, and you will die at the stake in the evildoer's stead!" (12). This issue, then, accentuates how Ke-Woh-No-Tay's desire to achieve warrior status is barred by his whiteness. In the typical playing Indian trope, the hero's whiteness acts to enrich his Indianness; he is a better Indian due to his whiteness. In the case of Scalphunter, his whiteness is his weakness. Try as he might, he will not achieve full warrior status within the tribe. He still endeavors toward that status, and thus killing and scalping are nearly an obsession for him: the more men he scalps, the closer he is to warrior-hood.

In issue #58 (Aug. 1979), Conway's story "Weep, the Widow" has Ke-Woh-No-Tay aid a widow and her son. The widow's misguided pacifism results in their being assaulted and robbed by Union Army deserters. The deserters leave the widow and son, with Ke-Woh-No-Tay unconscious and tied up, to burn alive in their home. Ke-Woh-No-Tay escapes and saves the woman and boy. As the hero leaves to find the Union deserters, the boy wants to join him but is held back by his mother's protest. The narration describes the following silent exchange between the eleven-year-old boy and Ke-Woh-No-Tay: "The boy is silent, but his face is in agony. He looks at the tall man, seeking an answer . . . and perhaps he finds an answer in the tall man's cool grey eyes . . . no words pass between them: Ke-Woh-No-Tey [*sic*] understands—the boy's place is here for now . . . sometimes a man becomes a man by rejecting the 'duties' of manhood" (16–17). This line suggests an alternate conception of manhood, perhaps one not founded upon violence and warrior-hood. Perhaps visible here is a difference in philosophies between Fleisher and Conway. Whatever the case, this scene provides for some complexity to the perception of ideal manhood. This scene is but a glimmer of such an alternative, though, for this panel is inlaid over a full-page scene (the last page of the story) that shows Ke-Woh-No-Tay walking away from the bodies of the three dead deserters around a campfire. He walks away, his back to the viewer, toward the sunrise shining bright from beyond a mountain range with birds flying upward. In his left hand is a knife, and in his right hand scalps. The previous words that account for a manhood that rejects the perceived "duties" of vengeance and violence give way to a scene that visually glorifies the accomplishment of vengeance and violence. Ke-Woh-No-Tay is defined by a drive to kill. This drive to kill clearly demarcates him from the typical white Indian examined so far. The convention of playing Indian allows for violence but stops short of murder. To murder and to scalp crosses the line into savagery. Ke-Woh-No-Tay crosses that line willingly. His white surname, in a not-so-subtle hint, marks him as "savage," as well. The characters of Kubert's Firehair, the son of Tomahawk, and Scalphunter approach a more nuanced and complex understanding of racial identity, as compared to the postwar comics, while retaining many of the recurring conventions of playing Indian.

While white Indians as comic book heroes may be but a small segment of the Western genre in comics, and in comics overall, their existence speaks to an ongoing fascination with and attraction to the idea of playing Indian. The white Indian persists as a powerful image and symbol into the twentieth century, and these comics attest to that phenomenon. Yet playing Indian is not confined to the Western genre in comic books. The superhero genre has also delved into the playing Indian trope: first appearing in the forties and fifties as a reaction to the popularity of Westerns, and then in following decades and on into the twenty-first century, the superhero as Indian has made occasional appearances. The superhero as Indian, then, engages in some of the common rhetoric already examined but also adds further considerations of symbolism and imagery. The next chapter explores this phenomenon of superheroes playing Indian.

## CHAPTER FIVE

# WHEN SUPERHEROES PLAY INDIAN

*Heroic Masculinity, National Identity, and Appropriation*

THE PREVIOUS CHAPTER FOCUSED ON COMIC BOOKS OF THE WESTERN genre, but in superhero comics playing Indian also finds rhetorical purchase. In the late 1940s and early 1950s, Plastic Man, Captain Marvel, Superman, and Batman play Indian. Later, in the 1970s, Green Arrow's Indian masquerade intersects with the social consciousness of Dennis O'Neil's *Green Lantern*. Then, in the early 2000s, Captain America mingles his traditional role as nationalist superhero and representative of US identity with the conventions of playing Indian. In Neil Gaiman's *1602* (2003–2004) and Tony Bedard's one-shot story *What If? Featuring Captain America* (2006), these reimagined visions of the Captain America mythos appropriate and perform Indianness in order to possess virile masculinity and physical strength. These examples of the superhero appropriating Indianness emphasize the ideological strain of heroic masculinity within the comics conventions of superheroism. While the male superhero is already a paragon of manly physical vigor, the superhero as Indian accentuates that vigor, drawing attention to male physicality as the embodiment of heroic masculinity, as well as situating the superhero within the conventions of frontier myth and American idealism. This framing of the superhero as Indian, then, follows a typical pattern of performing Indianness (while marginalizing Native peoples) in order to establish and perpetuate an authentic white American identity.

As seen in chapter 4, the period from the 1940s into the 1950s saw a number of comics premised upon the white hero as Indian. During this same period, superhero comics flirted with similar storylines. Plastic Man in *Police Comics* #16 (Feb. 1943), Captain Marvel in *Captain Marvel Adventures* #83 (Apr. 1948), Superman in *Action Comics* #148 (Sept. 1950), and Batman in *Detective Comics* #205 (Mar. 1954) and *Batman* #86 (Sept. 1954)

Figures 5.1, 5.2, and 5.3. Superheroes as Indians, details from covers. C. C. Beck (pencils and inks), *Captain Marvel Adventures* #83. Fawcett. Win Mortimer (pencils and inks), *Batman* #86 (Sept. 1954). DC Comics. Al Plastino (pencils and inks), *Action Comics* #148 (Sept. 1950). DC Comics.

play Indian. The cover images for the latter three superheroes feature each wearing a headdress, while in their respective costumes (Figs. 5.1, 5.2, and 5.3). These images clearly embody the conflation of the imagined Indian trope with the superhero. The images of Batman and Superman even present them in conflict with Indians, while the Captain Marvel cover reduces the Indian characters to barely visible figures in the background. These cover images appropriate the headdress as the sign of Indianness while imposing the white superhero as superior to the Indian characters. These stories echo much of the paternalist and imperialist rhetoric found in the Western comics of the same premise. This paternalism is especially pronounced in the superhero, whose authority and power already predispose that figure to such a role. This paternalism is most evident in the examples of Captain Marvel and Superman under study here. These comics also perpetuate a perception of Indianness as a past stage of human development, Indianness as a condition of savagery or primitiveness. Indianness also operates in these comics as a condition created by environment rather than inherited and developed through cultural heritage and family. The hero can easily become Indian through the wearing of certain clothes and practice of certain skills, as easily as he can switch from one identity to another through a change of outfit. Furthermore, Indianness is understood as an absence of "civilization"; whites act or become Indian, or Indians remain "Indian," without exposure to civilization. This assumption dictates, then, that Indianness is a state of lack, of not being exposed to "proper" ways of living. Therefore, the view that these particular stories espouse (whether consciously or not) is that Indianness is a condition that must be "fixed."

Jack Cole's Plastic Man story opens with the hero applying grease paint to disguise himself as an Indian and enter a "pow wow" (Fig. 5.4). As the panels depicting Plastic Man's becoming "Indian" detail, Chief Great Warrior of the Blackfoot is inciting his tribe to "revolt against the U.S.A." (2). Plastic Man is careful not to blame the members of the tribe, though, but identifies a single individual, a "rabblerouser," as the problem. In the next panels, Great Warrior voices his imputation to revolt: "I repeat now is the time to overthrow the accursed whites! We, the rightful owners of America must strike while the nation is busy with foreign wars! This is our moment!!! Let us act!!" (2) Any legitimate protest of these Indians has been undercut by the framing of Great Warrior as a "rabblerouser." His words speak to a fear of domestic weakness as the United States focuses on the war overseas. Such an environment, some would say, calls for an increased vigilance for loyalty and unity, a sentiment that Plastic Man voices in his

Figure 5.4. Plastic Man disguising himself as Indian. Jack Cole, "[The Revenge of Chief Great Warrior]" *Police Comics* #16 (Feb. 1943). Comic Magazines.

Indian guise when he appears at the meeting and responds to Great Warrior: "This is no time for back-stabbing! Unity is the watchword today! You're trying to fan a personal grudge into a civil war!" (2). Plastic Man casts Great Warrior's protest as a "personal grudge" rather than a perhaps genuine reaction against systemic issues.

Great Warrior questions Plastic Man's authority to speak, so he transforms himself into a totem pole, stating, "I speak by this authority!!" (3). Because of this display, the Indians demur to Plastic Man and reject Great Warrior's argument, driving him out of the village. The ousted chief runs into a bog, where he sinks, letting himself drown, but curiously calls attention to the fact that he has no reflection. The importance of this fact will be revealed soon in the story.

This opening sequence possesses a few significant points to consider. Plastic Man's disguising himself as an Indian is most notable for this study's purposes. He colors his skin a dark brown with grease paint, wears fringed pants but no shirt, along with a headband with a single feather: all the typical markers of Indianness. He plays Indian in order to infiltrate the tribe and head off a potential revolt against the United States. Cole, then, is depicting white intervention in tribal affairs. Plastic Man intrudes upon this political process because it is viewed as flawed due to the perceived power of an individual in swaying the tribe's decision. Furthermore, Plastic

Figure 5.5. Hypnotized by Chief Great Warrior. Jack Cole, "[The Revenge of Chief Great Warrior]" *Police Comics* #16 (Feb. 1950). Comic Magazines.

Man's intervention is couched in the rhetoric of unity during wartime: Great Warrior's "personal grudge" against the United States due to its treatment of Indians must be subordinate to the needs of the nation.

A few days after this opening, Will Hawes is introduced, "common, ordinary, inconspicuous Will Hawes" (4). His significance to the story becomes evident when Great Warrior appears in Hawes's mirror at home and hypnotizes him, ordering him to set bombs and traps that will kill a number of city officials, although Plastic Man survives the attempt on his life (5–6). Note as well how this scene of Hawes seeing the Indian in the mirror echoes the comic's second panel, in which Plastic Man peers into the mirror as he disguises himself as an Indian (Fig. 5.5). Later, Hawes sees the Indian in the mirror again. Great Warrior chastises Hawes for failing to kill Plastic Man. Hawes smashes the mirror and leaves but sees the Indian again in a store window. Hawes smashes the window until police arrive, taking him to the station, where he confesses: "It was I who planted those death traps!! I was hypnotized by the reflection of an Indian!! He tried to force me under his will again today!" (9).

For the moment, Hawes is thought to be insane. Plastic Man then sees Great Warrior reflected in a store window and falls under the Indian's command. Great Warrior sends Plastic Man on a destructive rampage around the city. Eventually the police apprehend and subdue Plastic Man and arrest him. At the police station Woozy, Plastic Man's sidekick, brings Great Warrior's son and asks for a mirror. The son speaks to the mirror, "Appear oh father! Your son vows a life of shame unless you clear the innocent name of Plastic Man!" (13). Great Warrior appears and exonerates

Plastic Man, then disappears. Plastic Man's name is cleared. The Indian chief is gone, "to rest with his body forever," as the son explains (13).

This image of the Indian in the mirror hypnotizing the white man to kill and destroy is a powerful one, especially in the context of playing Indian. Great Warrior, in an obvious way, represents the dark side of humanity, a mirror self who embodies destruction and chaos. Even the hero falls under the sway of the vengeful Indian. Earlier in the story, Plastic Man had controlled his Indianness, the mirror reflecting back his conscious transformation; in this case, he has no control: the Indian in the mirror dominates Plastic Man's will. Furthermore, the mirror Indian represents discord and dissent that would disrupt national unity. He instigates the murder of city officials, including the mayor and the police commissioner. At the mirror Indian's command, Plastic Man crashes trains, tears down telephone lines, and explodes a truck carrying TNT. The actual physical Indian is subjugated in this story. Yet his spirit lives on to wreak havoc upon the city, an Indian spirit working through the actions of white men. Cole's story, then, provides a rich symbolism that represents the perceived power of Indianness as a potential destructive force in America. Great Warrior as the mirror Indian embodies a "heart of darkness," that feared inner savagery to which any man may fall prey. The potential for the white man to succumb to savagery also appears in Captain Marvel.

In "Indian Chief" from *Captain Marvel Adventures* #83, Captain Marvel encounters a group of white people who have become stuck in the past and behave in the manner of the "savage" Indian. The story commences with Billy Batson, Marvel's alter ego, reporting on the dedication of the Hidden Valley Reservation for Indians, a previously unexplored area now made a reservation. This reservation has, according to Billy, "all the comforts of civilization . . . like any other small town in the country." This description accompanies an aerial shot of the town, with a typical small-town look: homes, stores, and a church with a steeple sit near the center of the panel. The language and the visuals convey the homogeneity of the town. Like the town, its residents appear in dress and physical appearance similar to the supposed typical American. Billy describes the Indians in the next panel: "The Indians of today are quite civilized and up-to-date, like all other American citizens! The day of savage, painted redskins is gone!" They have assimilated, and this panel shows them from a perspective from behind and over Billy's right shoulder as he speaks to them from the stage. The audience of Indians gathers: men in suits, ties, and button-down shirts, and women in dresses. They appear no different from "other American citizens."

The "civilized" appearance of the reservation residents contrasts sharply with a group of attacking "Indians," who arrive on horseback, dressed in buckskins and headdresses, with bows and arrows. This group fulfills the stereotypical appearance and behavior of Indians. Billy transforms into Captain Marvel and punches the lead attacker, Chief Crooked Jaw, to discover that the Indian is actually white. Marvel thinks, "What a reversal of history this is! Wild white men attacking a village of civilized Indians!" The novelty and premise of the story lies in this reversal: savage whites attacking civilized Indians. With Marvel's intervention, the attacking whites retreat, and so Marvel follows them.

Transforming back to Billy, the hero surveys the village, thinking, "It's just like an old-time Indian village, tepees and all! But they're two hundred years behind the times!" and, "These people, who are *not* Indians, have adopted all the ancient customs and ways of the redmen!" He then meets Phyllis, daughter of the chief. She is a blonde girl who speaks in pidgin English. She takes him to an ancient rock with an English inscription that she cannot read. Billy reads it, to learn that a group of settlers was lost in the valley in 1754. Billy explains to Phyllis, "A band of pioneers got lost here, almost two centuries ago! Surrounded by wilderness, they forgot civilization and adopted the life of the Indians! Your people have stayed in that primitive stage ever since!"[1] He tells Phyllis that her people belong in the modern world, something to which her father would never consent.

A new chief would consent, though, so Captain Marvel takes it upon himself to challenge the chief for his position. Of course, Marvel wins the contests (even though at one point he reverts to Billy and escapes beheading when Phyllis defends him in an obvious nod to the Pocahontas–John Smith myth) and becomes chief. His "first and only command" is for the tribe to join with the modern world. Later, Billy sees Phyllis, who says, "My people are all happy to be out of the wilderness! This is where we belong!" The closing panel shows Crooked Jaw in suit and tie, speeding along on a scooter, thoroughly enjoying his newfound civilized life, saying, "Wheee! Why didn't someone tell me civilization was like this? Yippeeee!" The white Indians have been de-Indianized.

A central assumption of this story is that the twentieth-century, American model of "civilization" (depicted as suburban homes and modern technology) is a preferable condition. In this regard, Indianness is not a cultural or ethnic identity but a performed identity, something that represents disconnection from "civilization," and something that is superficial and can be purged or stripped away. Assimilation into mainstream society is the preferred state of being, and something that Indians are capable of performing. The reverse is true, too: whites are capable of losing their civilization and reverting to a primitive state if they separate from "civilization." What seems to be of value in this story is not a racial identity (white vs. Indian) but an identity defined by assimilation into the "modern" world. Conformity to suburban life, to the dominant styles of dress and housing, to the use of modern technology defines the citizen's place in American society. Indian or white, one must ascribe to the conventions and expectations of the modern world in order to be a full-fledged member.

In contrast to a dominant theme in other white Indian stories, Captain Marvel's playing Indian operates not to reinvigorate his manhood. The performance of masculinity operates on a different level in the superhero story, anyway. Instead, in this instance, playing Indian is the means for Marvel to right a perceived wrong (the resistance of these white Indians to assimilation). In this way, Marvel as chief functions in a paternalistic way, assuming the headdress only to guide these wayward people to where he thinks they should be in the civilized world. He becomes chief in order to terminate the tribe.

This story appears during a period in which federal policy was moving toward terminating federal tribal jurisdiction. During the postwar period, movement toward termination and relocation began; a movement that sought to assimilate Native Americans into mainstream American life. This story's language of modernity, civilization, and assimilation especially adheres to the rhetoric of the postwar period concerning the continuance of tribal sovereignty and Native cultural traditions within American society. Whether the comic's rhetoric is intentionally conversant with the political context of the period or not, that rhetoric still stands and channels a recurring attitude toward Native culture, an attitude as old (or even older) than the United States itself. A similar paternalism emerges in Superman's turn as Indian in a story that raises the issues of treaty rights and land ownership.

"Superman, Indian Chief!" is the lead story for *Action Comics* #148. Like Captain Marvel, Superman becomes an Indian chief, although he travels back in time to do so. The lead-in text establishes the story's premise: Metropolis is on land sold by Indians to whites, but "a clever schemer" now claims ownership of that land and of Metropolis, so Superman must travel back in time three hundred years to discover the truth of the original sale. Henry Meecher claims that the original land sale was illegal, since the Indian representative, Gray Wolf, who signed the sales document was not the chief. Since Meecher is, as he says, "last part-descendant of the tribe," then the land belongs to him.

With the papers' legitimacy confirmed, the judge rules that Meecher is the owner of Metropolis. Meecher is not a benevolent property owner: he charges one hundred thousand dollars for a month's rent on a building, and since the owner cannot pay, Meecher orders the razing of the building. Cue Superman. He moves rocks to form new land out on the water, to which Meecher will have no claim, and then moves the building onto that land. Meecher still owns the rest of Metropolis, though, so Superman decides to travel back in time to verify the land claim.

He arrives in 1644. In the Indian village, Gray Wolf is arguing for sale of the land to acquire guns in order to "conquer all the northern tribes." Superman intercedes to argue against such aggression, since the tribe has agreed to peaceful relations with the other tribes. Gray Wolf orders his men to attack Superman, because "he pleads for peace . . . he must be a coward." The weapons are ineffective, of course, and one of the Indians observes, "The stranger has mighty magic powers!" Gray Wolf then declares that their medicine man will observe omens to decide whether they should decide on peace or war. Superman realizes that Gray Wolf and the medicine man are conspiring together to produce omens that will point toward war. Superman alters each of the omens to suggest peaceful action.

Gray Wolf's tribe deposes him due to the omens being against him, so he leaves and then sells the land to the white settlers, who still believe him to be chief. He returns to the village with the guns while a tribal council discusses who will be the next chief. Superman fights off Gray Wolf and his attackers. Conferring with the European settlers, Superman discovers that Meecher is correct about the illegal sale. The tribe names him "Flying Eagle" and afterward offers Superman a "belt of honor" for this help, but he declines, since he cannot take it with him in his return to his present day.

Returning to the present, Superman confirms that the sale was illegal, and at the higher court deliberations, a new detail emerges. The actual chief at the time was Flying Eagle. Superman interrupts before the final ruling, asking for a recess. He then leaves to find the belt.

He discovers that the "tribe preserved a wampum belt as a relic of a great benefactor—and the belt is now in Metropolis Museum!" In court the wampum belt is read aloud: "We name Flying Eagle our chief—and we hereby sell the island to the white men in his name!" With this evidence, the judge decides that the island was sold legally, and Meecher's claim is invalid. The final panel closes the story with a punch line between Clark and Lois. Clark, wearing a headdress, says, "Lois, I thought I'd go to the reporters costume ball tonight as an Indian!" Lois replies, "Oh, no, Clark, you'd look silly! You're just not the type!"

Before Superman alters history through time travel, Meecher has a legitimate claim. Furthermore, the situation described in the story is one that typifies the problematic nature of how many treaties and land sales occurred between Native peoples and Europeans. The story verges on presenting a more accurate depiction of the disingenuous negotiation of many treaties by Europeans. Meecher's characterization, though, undercuts any such critical awareness of the problematic process of such treaties, and so, too, preempts any potential sympathy for the validity of his claim. He is introduced as a "schemer," and his demands for exorbitant rent cast him as the villain of the piece. The Indian descendant who possesses valid claim to the land is cast as the bad guy. Superman, then, alters history in order to protect the modern city of Metropolis from the economic invasion, in this case, of the Indian. In addition, like Captain Marvel, Superman becomes chief only to effectively usurp the rights and sovereignty of the tribe. Both of these stories obviously enact an ideology that privileges mainstream modern society (read as white) over Indian claims for tradition or autonomy. While Chief Crooked Jaw's band does not represent an authentic depiction of Native tradition, the Captain Marvel comic assumes that their way of life is inherently inferior to modern notions of civilization. Superman's comic makes a similar assumption about the privileging of modern urban life over the legal claims of the land's indigenous inhabitants.

In 1954 Batman too plays Indian, not once but twice. "The Origin of the Bat-Cave" first appeared in *Detective Comics* #205 (Mar. 1954) and was reprinted in *Batman Annual* #1 (1961). Written by Bill Finger, this story relates Batman and Robin's time travel to discover the origin of the Bat-Cave. As Chris Sims notes, this is one of a few Batman tales during the fifties in which he fights Indians; another one, also appearing in 1954, is discussed below. This story's significance for this study lies in its repetition of elements found in other playing Indian comics as well as its precedence for the "Batman—Indian Chief!" which follows a few months later.

The plot begins with the discovery of a pottery shard in the Bat-Cave. Bruce Wayne and Dick Grayson visit a professor, who translates an inscription on the shard: "Death to the Man of Two Identities" (42). Their curiosity piqued, Bruce and Dick visit Professor Nichols, who has devised a method of time travel using hypnosis and a machine. Reaching their destination three hundred years in the past, the two heroes quickly change into their

Figures 5.6 and 5.7. Staining skin. Bill Finger (script), Sheldon Moldoff (pencils), and Charles Paris (inks), "The Origin of the Bat-cave." *Detective Comics* #205 (Mar. 1954). DC Comics. *Indians* #2 (1950). Fiction House Magazines.

costumes as Batman and Robin, whereupon they see a white frontiersman being chased by two Indians on horseback. Batman and Robin intervene, diving at the Indian pursuers as Batman proclaims, "No scalps today, fellows—if you don't mind" (43).

After chasing off the Indians, the heroes assist the injured frontiersman. His name is Jeremy Coe, and he leads Batman and Robin to his "secret headquarters." Jeremy then explains his mission: he has been disguising himself as an Indian to spy on the tribe and find out their attack plans (45–46). Notably, he stains his skin to do so. One panel depicts this skin staining, a panel that echoes visually and thematically a panel discussed in the previous chapter: Manzar's "white blood turns red" scene (Fig. 5.6 and 5.7). The visual similarities are obvious: both men apply stain to their right arm with their left hand, and both men stand in a cave, facing the viewer. Since the Manzar scene appeared in 1950, it is possible that Moldoff had seen it. Regardless of any potential direct copying by Moldoff for the Batman story, the repetition of this scene vividly illustrates its thematic power of depicting the white man becoming Indian.

Because Coe is injured, Batman volunteers to take his place and spy on the Indians (after providing some upgrades to Coe's "Bat-Cave"). Like Coe, Batman dyes his skin (he removes his costume, since he is not worried about anyone in the 1600s knowing his identity): "And so it is that Batman becomes an Indian of three centuries ago!" (48). Batman joins a tribal war council and learns of an attack, but before he can slip out, a rainstorm washes his dye away (48). His identity revealed, he changes into the Batman costume (which he had brought along in a quiver) and attempts to beguile the Indians with "Batarang magic" (49). After sending bat-shaped smoke signals to Robin, the sidekick arrives on horseback to rescue Batman from the rampaging Indians. After warning the white settlement, Batman and Robin return to their own time, having discovered the "origin of the Bat-Cave" (50).

The prejudiced depiction of the Indians is obvious here. As Chris Sims writes, "Sorry, Finger and Moldoff, I know you guys probably didn't know any better, but holy buckets, when you've got a dude actually saying 'white men—thank heavens!' and talking about how he needs to rid the world of the 'redman savages,' there's not a lot I can do here." Beyond the inappropriate treatment of Native Americans, this comic further demonstrates how the playing Indian trope has spread into superhero comics. This demonstration is even more evident in the fact that Batman plays Indian yet again in the following months.

"Batman—Indian Chief!" likewise demonstrates many of the conventions and perceptions of Indianness that frequently recur in the comics of this period. In this story, Batman meets his Indian counterpart, Chief Man-of-the-Bats, along with his sidekick, Little Raven (whose actual identities are Great Eagle and Little Eagle). Due to an injury inflicted by the villainous Black Elk upon Great Eagle, he cannot appear as Man-of-the-Bats lest his secret identity be revealed. Batman agrees to take the chief's place to preserve his secret. Batman puts on Man-of-the-Bats' headdress, wields an eagle-imprinted shield, and dyes his skin (as has been seen in other examples), while Robin takes on Little Eagle's identity. As they leave, Man-of-the-Bats tells his surrogate, "You must perform only in the Indian fashion! If not, people will guess immediately that you are stand-ins for us!" (22). Batman and Robin then run across Black Elk and his crew attempting to rob an armored car. The usual heroics occur, but Black Elk escapes. Batman and Robin follow, with the sidekick suggesting they take their Batplane (in which they had arrived) in pursuit. Batman responds, "No! We've got to handle this like Indians—remember!" (25). The Dynamic Duo then track the villains "like Indians." They follow the trail but lose it, to which Robin laments, "No! Not yet! Again we've got to play Indian!" (25). Eventually, they locate Black Elk and his gang; a final confrontation occurs, Great Eagle shows up, and Black Elk gives up on the notion that Great Eagle is Man-of-the-Bats.

One immediately noticeable feature of this story is the fact that although it is set in Batman's contemporary time (he has a plane, there is an armored car), the Indians appear as if they had time-traveled from the past, riding horses, wearing buckskins, and using bows and arrows and spears. Man-of-the-Bats is contemporary to Batman, yet the former is drawn as a primitive copy of the latter, with a Bat-canoe instead of Batmobile, torch-lit cave, and drum with the Bat insignia. In addition, the idea that Batman can simply become "Indian" through dyeing his skin and donning a headdress conforms to the notion that Indianness is but a masquerade, a metonymic performance of iconic visual objects, a masquerade that the white man can put on and take off at will. The story perpetuates the notion of "Indian" performance: "You must perform only in the Indian fashion," "We've got to handle this like Indians," and "[W]e've got to play Indian!" This performance constitutes eschewing modern technology (like the Batplane) and using tracking skills. Overall, the story fixes its Indians in the past. While this story does not follow the empowerment-through-playing Indian trope seen in other playing Indian stories, it represents Indianness as something that whites can perform, and perform convincingly.

These "golden age" superheroes clearly reflect the consensus culture of the postwar period. These comic books adhere to a faith in the progress of American civilization and expectations for its citizens to adhere to the supposed standards and lifestyles of modern America. Indianness plays its role as symbol of the past and of a bygone primitive phase of America. Plastic Man encourages the subordination of individual dissent to maintaining the unity of the nation. With Captain Marvel, a group of white people has reverted to Indianness in their separation from society. Superman travels to the past to right a perceived wrong. Batman's stories either take place in the past or present Indian characters that are stuck in the past. These comics of the forties and fifties depict Indianness in a manner that is firmly rooted in the predominant ideology of consensus and progress. By the seventies, though, the potential of the superhero to question consensus becomes apparent.

In response to social movements of the 1960s, mainstream comics, especially represented by Marvel and DC, made gestures toward politically minded storylines along with recasting superheroes as rebels against the establishment. Wright shows how Marvel sought to imbue its comics with a countercultural edge, with characters like Spider-Man, the Hulk, and Silver Surfer affecting antiestablishment poses (230–31). In regard to Marvel in the 1960s, Costello argues, "As the dissents of the 1960s became more vocal and more overt, the moral certainty of Marvel's Cold War would gray into increasing ambiguity; even while continuing to assert the orthodoxy of the American consensual identity, the characters, stories, and art would begin to render that orthodoxy problematic" (61). A similar move toward questioning of American orthodoxy also occurs in DC comics, a move that is most apparent in Dennis O'Neil's work on *Green Lantern/Green Arrow* (Wright 233). Jesse T. Moore argues, "The *Green Lantern/Green Arrow* comic series calls for a reordering of America's political affairs, while simultaneously urging a reform of the consciousness of its citizens" (267). O'Neil's *Green Lantern/Green Arrow* takes on a multitude of social causes and concerns, and Native rights are among those. *Green Lantern/Green Arrow* #79 tackles Native land rights in "Ulysses Star Is Still Alive" (Sept. 1970), featuring Green Arrow in Indian masquerade.

"Ulysses Star Is Still Alive" was the fourth story of the O'Neil-scripted *Green Lantern/Green Arrow* series. With art by Neal Adams and Dan Adkins, this story picks up from the previous issue that found the two heroes in Washington state rescuing Black Canary from a cult. Still in Washington, the story opens with Green Lantern, Green Arrow, and the Oa watcher around a campfire. In the opening narration, O'Neil reiterates their purpose: "These three men . . . have vowed to find America . . . to learn why this land of the free has become the land of the fearful!" (83). As the preceding issues have established and developed, the trio are traveling through America, searching for what makes the country special, what defines the nation. Their quest brings them into encounters with various incidents that epitomize hot-button issues prevalent in the United States during the time. The stories preceding "Ulysses Star" dealt with issues of wealth and poverty, the rights of workers, and cults. "Ulysses Star" addresses Native land rights.

The cover of *Green Lantern/Green Arrow* #79 presents a surprising and curious scene: Green Arrow, in Indian headdress, aims his bow and arrow at Green Lantern, tied to a totem pole. In the background, Indian men look on. Green Lantern's ring lies on the ground, aglow beneath Green Arrow's foot in the bottom left corner of the cover. Green Arrow's words fill the middle empty space between him and Green Lantern: "My redskin brothers find you guilty! And I am your executioner!" Neal Adams's art captures an arresting moment that performs the work of the cover: to catch the attention of a comic book buyer, present a dramatic scene that will cause one to linger, open the book, and buy it. While this scene does not actually occur in the story itself, as an image it conveys significant themes that are central to this study. Green Arrow dons the iconic headdress, a single visual marker that defines his identification with the Indians of the story. This image transforms him from the Robin Hood archetype into a force of Indian vengeance. Green Lantern occupies the position of the establishment figure; his unidentified guilt in this image might be associated with the history of injustices and wrongs inflicted upon Native peoples by white settlers and the US government.

The action of the story begins when Green Lantern and Green Arrow rescue a Native man from being shot by two white attackers. These two men are Theodore Rudd, head of the Lumbermen's Union, and Pierre O'Rourke, who supposedly owns the lumber. O'Neil casts this encounter in historically evocative terms:

> GREEN ARROW: Okay, you bargain-basement Custers—drop the weapons . . .
> GREEN LANTERN: or we make like a couple of Sitting Bulls! (85)

The heroes align themselves with the Indian cause, invoking Custer's defeat. Their sympathy with Indian rights first appeared in the previous story, "A Kind of Loving, a Way of Death" (*Green Lantern* #78: July 1970). After bringing to justice a gang who was terrorizing an Indian restaurant owner, the conversation turns to white treatment of Indians, which the owner describes: "The white-eyes swiped our land, broke treaties, herded us like animals onto reservations . . . now, the big-bellies in the capital are talking about taking away our fishing rights! Next, they'll want the marrow from our bones!" (68). O'Neil brings this theme to the forefront in "Ulysses Star," placing Lantern and Arrow in the midst of a dispute over lumber rights.

The dispute centers on missing documentation. Pierre claims ownership of the land, but that claim is dubious, since the land was ceded to the tribe by the US government during Ulysses Star's time as chief a century earlier. Like "Superman, Indian Chief!" this comic delves into the problematic history of treaty documentation, but O'Neil's story will arrive at a far different resolution that favors indigenous rights. The problem is that any documents proving this land cession are missing: the government's copy and local copy are gone. The only possible remaining copy might be with the son of Ulysses, but he has moved to the city. The two heroes propose, as usual, differing strategies to address the problem. Arrow wishes to force the issue through physical means, if necessary, while Lantern argues for going through the legal system. The two men split up, Lantern to the city to locate the chief's son and his copy of the land agreement, and Arrow to "stay . . . and fight!" (86). By this point in the series, the two heroes' divergent philosophies have been well established: Lantern attempts to maintain faith in legal means, in the system, for protecting rights and addressing injustice. Arrow espouses skepticism of the system, arguing for open conflict with those forces that would manipulate the system to serve their own selfish ends.

Having established the conflict in the prologue, the story divides into three chapters; the first two follow Lantern and Arrow individually, then chapter 3 brings everyone back together to resolve the story. Chapter 1 follows Lantern as he searches for Ulysses Star's son. Searching through city records, he finds the son's address, but when he arrives the apartment building is on fire. Lantern rescues Abe, the son, but learns that the paperwork is lost in the fire. Lantern leaves, thinking, "There must be another way . . . a way I can help—legally!" (93). He decides to go to Washington and speak to his friend Congressman Sullivan.

Chapter 2 follows Arrow as he learns more about life in the Indian town. Black Canary is there, providing medical aid to the residents, as she recovers from her traumatic experience with the cult in the previous issue. Lantern asks her what the Indian people need; she explains, "They've been under the white man's heel for so long they've lost faith in themselves—they no longer believe in themselves as a tribe—a society—or even as human beings!" (95). Arrow determines that he can help with that. Hours later, two white men sneak into a melon field, trespassing on Indian land. A ghostly figure confronts them, identifying himself as "the spirit of Ulysses Star" (95). The story switches scene to a bar where the white lumbermen are gathered. The spirit appears, warning them to "stop persecuting my people" (96). The spirit then appears to a group of Indian men, proclaiming, "You were once a proud people . . . a great people . . . and you can be again! First, though, you have to stop playing doormat for O'Rourke and Pudd . . . and be willing to fight for your rights!" (98).

Chapter 3 opens with the groups of whites and Indians in open conflict with each other. As the spirit of Ulysses enters the fray, Green Lantern calls for a halt to the fight. With him is the congressional representative who will be investigating the land claims. The spirit, who in this moment is obviously Green Arrow, challenges Lantern's deferral to legal process: "Sure . . . go home—sit on your hands!—Like always! Be nice while you're being robbed blind! Can it, Lantern! Go, crawl back to your pals, the guardians!" (100). Lantern takes the bait of those fighting words, dropping his ring since Arrow has painted himself in yellow, and the two heroes slam into each other. O'Neil paints the fight in symbolic terms: "The elemental struggle between two men—each fired by a belief in justice! . . . The masks fall, and they look, they see, and they know they are looking upon their nation, their world, in the agonized expression of a friend's face" (101). O'Neil incorporates a quote from Norman Mailer's *The Armies of the Night* at this point, as Lantern remembers it: "Brood on that country who expresses our will . . . she is America—once a beauty of magnificence unparalleled, now a beauty with leprous skin . . . God writhes in his bonds. Rush to the locks . . . deliver us from our curse" (102). At this moment, Lantern and Arrow are knocked unconscious by logs in the river where they are fighting.

Later, Lantern, Arrow, and Canary debrief each other, Arrow explaining why he took on the guise of Ulysses Star. Two Native men parallel Lantern and Arrow in their beliefs on how to proceed with the fight for tribal rights. One will go with Congressman Sullivan to present their case to Congress. The other argues for action that is more urgent: Congress might "get around to passing a law in ten years or so—meantime, our kids go shoeless . . . our old folks don't have decent medical attention" (103). He will stay and fight. Sullivan enters and states that "the judicial process is slow . . . but in some cases it's far-reaching!" (103). The men follow him outside to see O'Rourke and Pudd being arrested for their involvement in the fire of the tenement where Abe Star lived. While local justice may be served, the larger problem remains. The story closes with continuation of Mailer's words: "Deliver us from our curse. For we must end on the road to that mystery where courage, death, and the dream of love give promise of sleep" (104).

In terms of the story's treatment of Native–white relations, O'Neil has produced a relatively more sympathetic and progressive depiction of Native peoples and their rights, especially as compared to most of the examples examined in this study. While O'Neil's work is commendable, some of the white paternalism found in those other comics retains its hold. Green Arrow acts as a savior to the tribe, donning an Indian disguise; he still acts as the paternal white man that a supposedly dispirited people need to spur them to action. Green Arrow's actions even parallel those of Tomahawk in "The Buffalo Brave from Misty Mountain!" (#31: Mar. 1955). An imposter poses as a government land agent to swindle an Indian tribe out of their land. To expose the scheme, Tomahawk disguises himself as an Indian warrior to inspire the tribe, because, in the words of Running Wolf, one of the tribal members, "My people are so downcast that mere words would never convince them that they have dealt with evil imposters! Someone will have to stir them with action—not words!" And that someone must be "a champion they can trust!" Tomahawk acts as that "champion." This story presents a paradox, though: the villain poses as a land agent to swindle the Indians, while the hero poses as an Indian warrior to expose the villain and inspire the Indians. Both the white villain and white hero practice deception to achieve their ends, although the white hero does so for an assumedly righteous cause.

In these stories, then, the white hero masquerades as an Indian warrior to encourage and protect the tribe. Implicit in this plot, although probably not intended, especially in O'Neil's case, is the belief that Indians require white assistance, that they are too weak or beaten down to be able to fend for themselves. Viewed in this way, this story overlooks the agency and activism of Native Americans throughout history, an activism especially visible during the period that O'Neil's *Green Lantern* is being published. Vine Deloria's *Custer Died for Your Sins* appears in 1969 with its cogent examination of Native issues and activism of that time. The occupation of Alcatraz, by the Indians of All Tribes, occurs from 1969 to 1971 in what Dean Rader calls "one of the most important instances of American resistance since the American Revolution" (10). In addition, although following the publication of O'Neil's series, the American Indian Movement's protest at Wounded Knee in 1973 embodies the building momentum of Native activism during this time. O'Neil's engagement with Native issues, although not perfect, represents this context and calls attention to the efforts of those fighting for Native civil rights.

Paralleling the decline of the Western during the 1970s, depictions of or attention to Native peoples in comics saw a decline, too. In fact, it would seem that popular-culture interest in Native Americans depends upon the popularity of the Western genre, rather than a genuine interest in the peoples and cultures themselves. In the 1990s a seemingly more authentic interest in Native cultures emerged, although that interest, while perhaps proceeding from a place of good faith, retained many of the conventions and expectations of earlier depictions of Indians and playing Indian. The decade of the 1990s opened with *Dances with Wolves* (1990), and thus a definite turn in attitude occurred in popular treatments of Native Americans as well as something of a revival of playing Indian as a dominant trope in American culture. Superhero comics also took up this more sensitive attempt to portray Native cultures. The following pages examine some notable examples of the attempt to root superheroes in American history, especially via a connection to Native peoples and ancestry. *Legends of the Dark Knight* #1–5 (1989–1990, collected as *Batman: Shaman* 1993) slightly precedes the release of *Dances with Wolves* to relate a "Year One" story of Batman that intertwines his origins with indigenous culture and ritual. *The Kents* #1–12 (1997–1998, collected as *The Kents* 1999) roots Superman's adopted ancestry in the history of Bleeding Kansas while incorporating a Native great-grandmother.[2] Into the twenty-first century, Captain America will be the focus in his turns at playing Indian.

*Legends of the Dark Knight* (1989–2007) featured non-continuity stories set during Batman's "Year One." In the opening story arc (issues 1–5), Dennis O'Neil reframes Batman's origin as arising from Bruce Wayne's encounter with a north Alaskan medicine man (and noticeable here is O'Neil's interest in Native issues as evident earlier in *Green Lantern*). This story opens with Bruce Wayne tracking down a murderer, Thomas Woodley, in northern Alaska. In a struggle between Wayne and the murderer, the latter seemingly falls to his death from a cliff (later in the story we learn that he survived), while Wayne is left injured and exposed to the cold. He is found by a medicine man and his granddaughter, members of an Indian tribe (the name of the tribe, as well as the names of the medicine man and granddaughter, is never given).

The medicine man heals Wayne through telling a story about how Bat gains his wings in order to heal Raven. When he is well enough, Wayne leaves and the medicine man's granddaughter commands him, "[D]o not ever repeat the story to anyone. It is sacred to our tribe. We believe it is part of the healing process. You are the first outsider to hear it" (1:13). Although a white outsider, Wayne has been given access to a sacred tribal story, yet he does not seem to appreciate this fact, exhibiting scientific skepticism about the power of the story as well as later sharing it with an anthropologist in Gotham City.

After returning to Gotham, Wayne goes out on his first night of vigilantism, and, as with the usual telling of Wayne's initial foray into crime fighting, he is not as successful as he desired to be. While sitting in his study, a bat crashes through the window, and Wayne has a flashback to the medicine man's mask, inspiring Wayne: "I shall become a bat" (1:16–17).

This origin follows a pattern present in other stories examined in this study: the white man nearly dies in the wilderness (a wilderness he is not fully prepared for), to be healed by an Indian character. This plot informs the opening story of *White Indian*, for example. The Civil War Captain

America (see below) follows a similar pattern of the nearly dead white protagonist being healed through an Indian ritual. O'Neil further develops Batman's complicity with his Indian caregivers when Wayne returns to Alaska.

In part 3 Wayne returns to Otter Ridge, Alaska, the location of the tribe that had saved him. He finds a different world there: it has been developed, and upon entering town, he sees the medicine man who had healed him. The medicine man is dancing in the street, panhandling for alcohol. While driving Wayne and her grandfather home, the granddaughter explains what has happened: the anthropologist that Wayne funded to study the tribe traded alcohol and drugs for the tribe's stories, even drugging the medicine man with a "truth drug" to get him to share even the most guarded stories (3:22–23). Wayne is complicit in the encroachment upon Indian land and the degradation of indigenous traditions.

The granddaughter provides Wayne with this exposition until their truck is run off the road by an oncoming car into a river. Wayne retrieves the medicine man and his granddaughter from the truck and starts a fire to warm them up, yet the woman is suffering from hypothermia. When Wayne asks the medicine man to heal her, as he had done with Wayne, the medicine man says, "I gave away my healing power when I disgraced myself—but you know the healing story. You can tell it" (4:5). In the last panel of the page, Wayne falters: "Me? I'm not a shaman. I don't have the mask or— " (5). On the following page, the top panel depicts the shaman's hand pointing to the Batman cowl in Wayne's open suitcase (4:6). The shaman tells Wayne: "You have the mark in your eyes" (4:6). Wayne is skeptical but goes ahead and puts on the cowl. The narration describes the change Wayne feels upon donning the mask: "And when the mask hides his face, he feels something surge— " (4:6). A succession of five narrow panels spans the width of the top of the next page: Batman tells the story of Bat healing Raven, each panel a close-up of his masked face from different angles. Wayne is still uncertain after the story: "No good. I'm not a shaman, I'm not even a doctor like my father . . ." (4:7). Regardless of Wayne's uncertainty, his telling the story worked; the woman has been saved. Wayne's becoming Batman aligns him with the healing power of a shaman; the cowl takes the place of the traditional mask.

A subplot of the narrative involves a mysterious figure named "chubala," who is controlling drug trade in Gotham City and is based on the traditions of Santa Prisca (the fictional Caribbean island of the DC universe). "Chubala" practices human sacrifice, wearing a vulture mask as a dark version of the bat identity Wayne has adopted. Wayne discovers that Carl

Fisk, a white banker from Gotham, has taken on the chubala disguise, as he explains:

> Fisk had taken control of the Santa Priscan narcotics operation and was using his bank to launder the profits. But he needed a way to control his dealers and runners—so he adopted the guise of what those dealers and runners fear most, a chubalan shaman—and brought the hideous ritual of human sacrifice to Gotham City (5:9)

Fisk appropriates a fictionalized indigenous tradition to spread fear and advance his own profits. Fisk's appropriation mirrors Wayne's appropriation of the northern Alaskan Indian tradition. Fisk steals the tradition and manipulates it for his self-gain and for nefarious purposes. Wayne's appropriation occurs via the blessing of the indigenous shaman (who will be dead by story's end). The transmission from the Alaskan medicine man to Wayne follows the typical pattern of the vanishing Indian in American culture: Chingachgook or Hiawatha passing his blessing and power onto the white man. This transmission is confirmed in the final sequence of the comic. Wayne has returned to Alaska to return the stolen bat mask. He converses with the granddaughter:

> WAYNE: There's a question and I don't have the words . . . look, you don't know me, not very well, but I want to . . .
>
> GRANDDAUGHTER: Get better acquainted? Keep company?
>
> WAYNE: Yes.
>
> GRANDDAUGHTER: Poor, poor Mr. Bruce Wayne. You *are* struggling, aren't you? Telling yourself you're the rich man from Gotham who might get married, have a family. That's not what you are.
>
> WAYNE: You're saying no.
>
> GRANDDAUGHTER: You don't really have to ask. In a moment, I will leave you and I will never see you again. But first, listen to me—something marked you, wounded you, when you were a child. You have a choice . . . either let go of it or *use* it. Stop fighting. Surrender and let its power transform you.
>
> WAYNE: I guess that means wearing a mask.
>
> GRANDDAUGHTER: Much more. It means *becoming* the mask. But the choice was made years ago. You know that.
>
> WAYNE: Now I do. I want to give you this—the mask . . .
>
> GRANDDAUGHTER: Keep it. (5:24)

This exchange exhibits two significant tropes that have been recurring throughout this study. One is the transmission of indigenous power to white possession, as was mentioned just above. This transmission occurs earlier in the story when the shaman acknowledges his loss of healing power, and Wayne finds that he has inherited it through wearing the mask. This exchange with the granddaughter further confirms that transmission, even materially in her allowing Wayne to keep the sacred mask of her tribe. The second significant theme in this exchange involves the rejection of domesticity found here, except it is not Wayne who explicitly rejects it himself but the potential romantic partner who gives him permission to turn away from home and family. In order to be Batman, he cannot be a family man. While he cannot see this yet at this point of the story, his romantic interest sees it for him. Perhaps there is a parallel of blessings: the medicine man as representative Indian gives his blessing for Wayne to become the Bat and take on indigenous power, and the granddaughter as representative woman gives her blessing for Wayne to eschew the obligations of home and family. The succeeding page, and final one of the story, shows Batman putting on the tribal mask over the cowl, then removing the mask and placing it in a display case. The cowl supersedes the traditional mask, now an artifact in a display case. Batman is the successor to the indigenous shaman, the healer replaced by vigilante, the primitive mask replaced by the modern cowl. The final panel depicts Batman in an iconic pose: the reader views him from behind, as he stands upon a gargoyle, his cape fluttering out to his right while he surveys the cityscape.

*The Kents* (1997–1998) was a twelve-part series written by John Ostrander that relates the history of the first Kents to settle Kansas. With art from a variety of artists (Timothy Truman, Tom Mandrake, and Michael Bair), Ostrander constructs the narrative around Jonathan Kent passing on information to Clark from a collection of family documents that Jonathan found buried on the farm. Jonathan writes to Clark, "You have amazing abilities but that is only part of what has made you the man you are. This makes up the other part—the heritage that has helped shape you" ("Bleeding Kansas: Part 1"). Clark Kent, though an alien, has grown up a Kent, and this story especially seeks to emphasize his Americanness, incorporating Superman's family heritage into a crucial juncture of American history: the conflict between abolitionist and pro-slavery forces in Kansas preceding and during the Civil War. After this opening with Jonathan, the story shifts to 1854: Silas Kent, with his sons Nathaniel and Jebediah, are working with the Underground Railroad. Later that year, the three men move to Kansas to support the abolitionist movement there. The narrative continues in this vein, with the Kents participating in vital moments of Kansan and American history, with Nathaniel and Jebediah taking opposing sides, the former continuing his father's fight for abolition, and with appearances by actual historical persons and characters from other DC comics.

Ostrander integrates into the story various historical figures such as Wild Bill Hickok, Buffalo Bill, and Jesse James, as well as DC Western characters such as Jonah Hex and, notably for this study, Scalphunter. Nathaniel meets Brian Savage, Scalphunter, while serving as a scout for Custer. Scalphunter, or Ke-Woh-No-Tay, is "a white man raised by the Kiowa," as Nathaniel explains. Later, Scalphunter would serve as a liaison between Nathaniel and Mary Glenowen. Nathaniel and Savage witness Custer's massacre of Black Kettle's camp on the Washita River in 1868. Both men quit after the attack.

Of particular interest to this study is the character of Mary Glenowen. She is half Delaware (white father and Delaware mother), and she eventually marries Nathaniel. Early on, though, their romance is forestalled, although her significance to Nathaniel is early revealed when she nurses him back to health after he is shot. Nathaniel, while defending a free African American family that he has befriended, is shot by his brother. Mary cares for him, and when he awakes he is covered by a blanket with numerous designs on it. He says, "Thought I knew . . . a lot of the symbols . . . but this one . . . got me beat." This symbol is on the blanket over Nathaniel's chest. And the reader will recognize it as Superman's S-shield. Mary explains the symbol:

> Iroquois sign. The five lines represent each of the five tribes of the confederacy; my mother's people is one of them. The symbol inside is a snake— one of the medicine animals. It represents healing and making whole. Deganawidah, the lawgiver and prophet who helped forge the Iroquois confederacy, spoke of a great hero to come from the sky who would unite east and west into one nation.

The blanket is "a powerful healing blanket," as well, and that is what Mary says Nathaniel needs at the moment. Once Nathaniel is better, Mary gives him the blanket. In the final panel, Jonathan Kent is shown with the blanket.

This scene presents themes similar to those found in other examples in this study. The white man escapes death through the healing of a Native character. Like *White Indian*, like Batman in *Shaman*, Nathaniel Kent, as ancestor to Superman's adopted family, undergoes such healing. A sacred indigenous object is the medium of this healing, an object that the Native woman gives to Nathaniel (much like the Alaskan Indian giving Bruce Wayne the sacred mask). As argued above, this gifting represents a transmission from the Native to the white, an inheritance by the white male of indigenous power and sovereignty. Furthermore, the original Native symbol is transformed into and superseded by the superhero's symbol: the sacred mask becomes Batman's cowl, and the "Iroquois sign" becomes recognizable as Superman's emblem.

Later in the series, in "To the Stars by Hard Ways: Part Two," Mary tells Nathaniel that she was wrong about the Delaware being one of the tribes of the Iroquois confederacy. Her confession of this error comes on the heels of her recognition of her in-between state of identity, neither Indian nor white, as she laments to Nathaniel: "With my father's people, I'm too much an Indian. With my mother's people, I'm too much a white." She questions where she belongs, prompting Nathaniel's marriage proposal. Mary's interracial lineage makes her feel outcast from either side, but within the narrative development, this lack of identity sets her up for marriage to the white protagonist. In addition, Mary not being full-blooded Indian makes her, perhaps, a more appropriate mate for Nathaniel. Soon after, Nathaniel becomes sheriff of Smallville.

Ostrander's narrative places Clark Kent's adoptive family at a central point of American history and geography: the Civil War and frontier settlement. This story ensconces Superman, albeit by adoption, in what purports to be a "true" American lineage. The integrating of Native ancestry into this lineage works, as it typically does, to authenticate more strongly the heritage as "American." Superman's Americanization in this story takes on a more profound symbolism through the introduction of the Native ancestor, a symbolism that links vividly to the pervasive white American fascination with Indians and with the desire to claim an authentic connection to the continent via indigenous inheritance.

A similar dynamic is at work in Grant Morrison's *Batman: The Return of Bruce Wayne* (2011). In his work on Batman, Grant Morrison revived quite a few of the Western elements seen in the 1950s comics. The two stories examined above from 1954 find some of their elements reappear in Morrison's hands: Man-of-the-Bats (in *Batman Incorporated*), Professor Nichols and his time machine, and the Bat-Cave's structure existing since the days of the earliest inhabitants of the land that would become

Gotham (the latter two in *Return*). This last plot point functions to anchor Batman's history to an indigenous one. In the same way that Ostrander's *The Kents* seeks to incorporate Superman into American history, so too does Morrison's *Return* incorporate Batman. In Morrison's case, though, he originates Batman's line of descent in the earliest inhabitants of the land that would become Gotham. *Return*'s premise is that Darkseid has sent Bruce Wayne forward from the dawn of time to the present day in order to accumulate omega energy, an accumulation that will explode and end the world when Wayne arrives at the present. *Return* follows Wayne's time skips, from prehistory onward, with stops along the way wherein Wayne finds himself a caveman, a Puritan witch hunter, a pirate, a cowboy, and a private detective. Throughout the years, a group of people has inhabited the catacombs beneath land that would become Wayne Manor, protecting a box connected to Batman. Martha Wayne provides this information on the caves: "The whole pile [Wayne Manor] sits on top of an immense maze of caves that's been associated with buried treasure and all kinds of romantic and deadly characters. Jeremy Coe, the Frontiersman, the Black Pirate, the Hellerite Sect, and even ancient Bat-People" ("Masquerade"). The Bat-People become known as the Miagani, "who claim direct descent from the first boy" ("The Bones of Bristol Bay"). This "first boy" assists Bruce Wayne in the first part of the series, acting as a proto-Robin. Thus, from the time of the caveman, the Bat-People have existed, safeguarding possessions of Batman in the caves beneath Gotham. Morrison, like Ostrander, performs that work of incorporating the superhero into an indigenous legacy of America. Batman acts as a keystone figure throughout the history of the continent that would become America: he is there at the earliest appearance of humans on the land. Through the vehicle of time travel, Morrison's Batman predates the United States and predates the first European settlers. In this narrative, Batman becomes an indigenous figure.

In these stories, Ostrander and Morrison weave the stories of Superman and Batman into American history. These stories imagine a world where these superheroes have actual roots, an actual heritage in American history. Captain America has also been treated with such reimaginings, placing him at key moments in the history of North America and the United States.

As 2003 was winding to a close, Marvel premiered its eight-part series *1602*, which transfers major heroes of the modern Marvel universe to the year of the series' title. At exactly the halfway mark of the inaugural issue, a two-page spread presents three panels arching from left to right. In the middle panel, a young girl with white hair and blue eyes rests her chin upon her arm, gazing at something in the distance, something that seems just over the reader's right shoulder. Behind her a blonde-haired man stands, his arms crossed and his torso bare. He is a white man, yet he is dressed as an Indian. This center spread is the first appearance of Virginia Dare and Rojhaz, who, as is revealed six pages later, are on their way to London to gain support for the Roanoke colony. Rojhaz is Virginia's protector, and his second appearance echoes his first: a white Indian with arms crossed and a stoic expression. Moreover, as revealed in the series' final issue, Rojhaz is Steve Rogers, or Captain America.

Throughout the first seven issues of *1602*, Captain America's actual identity remains unknown, although but thinly concealed. Known as Rojhaz, he accompanies Virginia Dare to England, serving as her bodyguard. The peculiarity of Rojhaz's racial identity receives explicit attention in the second issue when Virginia Dare meets Queen Elizabeth. Astonished that Virginia refers to him as an Indian, the queen remarks, "We had thought them all black of hair and red of skin." Virginia relates her father's explanation that Rojhaz is a descendant of early Welsh visitors to the New World. "Sir Indian Welshman," the Queen addresses Rojhaz, then telling him of Indians who had visited and provided entertainment but had died. This scene reveals that within the story Rojhaz possesses a unique racial appearance: his physical features mark him as white, while his dress, mannerisms, speech, and self-identification signify him as Indian. Within this same issue Rojhaz is referred to as "savage" and "wild man," as well, and one can't help but see parallels between this scene and stories such as that of Pocahontas, whose fatal visit to England was met with much fanfare and attention. Later in issue 4, Virginia Dare explains to Dr. Strange how Rojhaz came to the colony with Indians from an unnamed tribe. He brought food and stayed with the colony after the other Indians left. He became the colony's protector and taught them how to survive. In that role he became Virginia Dare's guard and confidant, sharing and protecting her secret (her ability to metamorphose into animals).

At the beginning of part 8, Rojhaz reveals that he is actually Captain America ("Rojhaz" being a phonetic approximation of Captain America's real last name, Steve Rogers). Finding himself resisting a tyrannical government during his original timeline, he is arrested and executed. The execution is meant to obliterate him but instead transports him back four hundred years. This event creates a temporal rip that destabilizes the entire world (and threatens to obliterate all known universes), while triggering the emergence of mutants and superheroes hundreds of years too soon. He awakens from the time transport on the American continent and is adopted into a tribe. His story then joins with Dare's account from part 4: he takes on the Roanoke colony as his charge to protect and serve. This charge is embodied by Virginia Dare, of whom he states, "I knew I had to protect her. To guard her. To fight for her, if I had to. I wasn't going to let her die. I failed before. I wasn't going to fail again." Virginia Dare, with white hair and blue eyes, represents the promise of a new world. Furthermore, Rojhaz views his being at this moment in history as an opportunity to guide and protect the American ideals that he was unable to preserve in his original timeline. He was unable to stop the tyranny that had taken over his original America, but now, in being transported back to 1602, he sees the opportunity for a second chance to make things right.

Rojhaz reveals his desire to safeguard a new beginning for his still-to-be-formed nation: "This is my *country*. They need me. I *can't* leave them. We don't have to make the same mistakes again. We're here at the birth of a nation . . . of a dream. Nobody has to *die*. We can work together to *protect* them. My *people*." Before we attend to the rhetoric in this speech, the visuals of this scene deserve attention. In the panel at the bottom of the preceding page, Rojhaz stands atop boulders. The page-width panel's point of view looks upward to him as he towers over the viewer. The panel bleeds to the page's outer edge, striking tension with the upper panels on the page that are all bordered by black lines. In this unframed panel, Rojhaz is an imposing presence, his head puncturing the panel's top border and overlaying the lower borders of the middle panels. This composition emphasizes Rojhaz's defiance and physical presence. Then, on the next page in the top panel, which fills the top half of the page, he makes his "birth of a nation" speech (Fig. 5.8). In the left top quarter of the panel, Rojhaz's words appear in a descending chain of five speech balloons. The rest of the panel presents a close-up of his face, with his forehead and cheeks painted in blue, a solid white "A" stretching from his scalp to his eyebrows. This image refigures the iconic Captain America helm as "Indian" face paint, a stark visualization of Captain America as Indian.

Threatened with return to his original present, Captain America argues for remaining at the beginning of an "America" that will not be built on the "same mistakes" of dispossession and death. Rojhaz envisions the possibility of an alternate course of American history with him as its guide and protector. Rojhaz stands upon the cusp of creating what he believes will be a better America than the one he inherited, but he cannot remain, because

Figure 5.8. Captain America as Indian. Neil Gaiman (script), Andy Kubert (art), and Richard Isanove (digital painting), *1602: Part Eight* (June 2004). Marvel Comics.

there will not even be an America, and a world, to save if he stays. With Rojhaz's return to his present, the normal continuity of history resumes its course. Yet return to these words: "We're here at the birth of a nation . . . of a dream. Nobody has to *die*. We can work together to *protect* them. My *people*." Reading these lines in the context of this study, one has to ask: Whose nation? Whose people? Does Rojhaz view himself as protector of a nation and people that includes the rarely seen and anonymous indigenous inhabitants of the continent along with the newly arrived European settlers? Or other races or ethnicities who have no presence at all in this series? If Virginia Dare is somehow the embodiment or seed of the nation, where does that leave the people who first took Rojhaz in and taught him how to survive in his new world (something that he would then pass on to the colonists)? Rojhaz's speech here is ambiguous about just whom he sees himself as representing in his guardianship. This speech's rhetoric conveys a sentiment of inclusiveness, yet the actual details of the story belie such inclusiveness. The unnamed Indian tribe that takes in Rogers is marginal, barely seen in the comic. The impetus of the plot is the preservation of the future (usually viewed as destined for white succession, as Native peoples are usually perceived as existing in the past). This preservation centers on the world returning to its "normal" course and not the alternate one as imagined by Rojhaz and as described as proceeding in Uatu the Watcher's possession.

In *1602*'s alternate history the poignancy of what could have been highlights the necessity of what should be in our own world. The series concludes with the knowledge that this Rogers-altered world ("Earth-311") continues on in the possession of Uatu the Watcher. In this alternate universe the Roanoke colony will declare its independence to be, in the words of Javier (*1602*'s version of Charles Xavier, founder of the X-Men), "a place where people—people of *all* shapes and talents—can prosper." This ideal speaks to inclusion and tolerance, a theme that develops throughout the series in its treatment of the persecution of the mutants. This inclusive and tolerant place comes into being due to a Captain America who plays Indian. In this series Captain America is reborn as an Indian, and with his exit he leaves behind a world that will be based on the inclusion and tolerance Javier describes above. This alternate world remains merely a what-if scenario, though. The implications of *1602*'s resolution are that history will proceed as it already has, and thus the violence and oppression will duly proceed as well. And so, what could have been remains simply that; and so too the implications of Captain America's playing Indian in this story adhere to the typical patterns of appropriation in service of advancing a white national identity. This same dynamic of appropriation and white nationalism plays out similarly in Bedard's *What If? Featuring Captain America*. In this one-shot comic, the Indianization of Captain America spurs an alternate American history that is imagined to adhere more closely to American ideals of equality and freedom.

The premise of the comic is that the reader has access to an alternate Earth in which Rogers is a corporal in the Union Army. His own journal entries relate his story. As the story proceeds, Rogers ends up caught in the reins of two stampeding horses. While being dragged by the horses, Rogers enters into a hallucinatory state in which an eagle spirit tells him: "Wake up, Union man. Protect my children." Like Rojhaz's "my people" discussed above, this "my children" is somewhat ambiguous: are "my children" all Americans? The implication seems to be yes if one reads the eagle spirit as being a manifestation of the nation. After receiving this charge, Rogers awakens to see an African American soldier in US uniform. He is Private Wilson of the Third Indian Guard, "an all-volunteer regiment" composed of "Cherokee, Osage, Delaware, Quapaw, and Shawnee."[3] Wilson is an adopted Shawnee, as well. Wilson and his regiment represent an ideal of racial crossing, an African American Shawnee who is part of a Native American regiment fighting to end slavery.

Wilson's role in this alternate origin story of Captain America is analogous to that of Reinstein (or Erskine) in the official origin. Instead of the scientific use of sera and technology, though, in this story Wilson performs an "Indian" ceremony. Wilson's function in the story adheres to the trope of the "magical negro" in assisting the white Rogers in achieving his purpose and then dying once his work is done. As critics like Matthew W. Hughey and Nnedi Okorafor-Mbachu have shown, the "magical negro" serves only to assist or heal the white protagonist, often disappearing or dying once that black character has served his or her purpose. *What If?* follows this trope. Wilson explains that a medicine man (who goes unnamed and unseen) had prophesied to Wilson that he would "find a soldier who could bring union to all people" and that "the spirit of We-Pi-Ahk the Eagle Chief" would show him that soldier. Recall the prophecy in *The Kents* of "a great hero to come from the sky who would unite east and west into one nation": these superheroes are being imagined as national saviors. Wilson's ceremony transforms the nearly dead Rogers into a revitalized, muscular hero with "Indian"-style headdress and shield (Fig. 5.9). After Rogers becomes Captain America, Wilson is murdered, having served his purpose. Admittedly, Wilson's death must occur in order for this reimagining to adhere to the canonical origin of the Captain. Yet one cannot ignore the echo in Wilson's role of the "magical negro," especially given the comic's publication during a period when multiple films had featured that stock character (for instance, John Coffey in *The Green Mile*, Morpheus in *The Matrix*, and Bagger Vance in *The Legend of Bagger Vance*). More importantly, though, Wilson and the medicine man's role in Captain America's origin recalls the myth of national inheritance in which the "primitive" races pass on their blessings to white heirs, then quickly get out of the way.

After his revival from near death and transformation into an Indianized warrior, Captain America delivers a speech that nullifies any deference to Native inhabitation of the continent and suggests a racial line of inheritance in the United States: "[A]ll of us, even the Indians, came to this land from somewhere else . . . drawn here by a unique opportunity—a chance to pursue our dreams and reinvent ourselves. . . . And so a Red man taught a Black man to find a White man who would bring us all back together." The final statement falls into a typical racial hierarchy: the white man is the ultimate end, the one who will bring order and harmony to the world. The "Red man" serves as that primal source, the origin of wisdom and

Figure 5.9. Captain American
as Indian during the Civil War.
Tony Bedard (script), Carmine
DiGiandomenico (pencils), and John
Stanisci (inks), *What If? Featuring
Captain America* #1 (Feb. 2006).
Marvel Comics.

power; the "Black man" serves as a subordinate who assists the "White
man" in obtaining the wisdom and power to unite the nation. The course
of this inheritance in the comic echoes an ideology of historical progress in
which "primitive" races pave the way for the more advanced and "civilized"
races. The line of transmission as described in the comic follows a racialized progress that positions the white man as final heir and beneficiary
of the gifts passed down to him, a transmission that echoes the myth of
inheritance found in works such as Longfellow's *The Song of Hiawatha* and
Cooper's *The Last of the Mohicans*.[4] Through absorption of Indianness, and
the aid of a black helper, Captain America becomes even more "American"
due to his incorporation of an "authentic" indigenous identity. As suggested
above in *1602*, this same trope of inheritance is at work in how Rojhaz has
to disappear, has to leave in order for that alternate universe to survive

but also to allow for the Europeans who have settled at Roanoke to build a democratic society independent of England.

In *What If?* this transmission performs the work of legitimizing Captain America's role as *the* representative "American," having received the blessings of Native and African American representatives. Although this Captain America integrates within himself the strength and virtue of the Indian and black races, his iconography in the comic represents only the Indian and the white. His initial appearance after the transformation conveys a primitive look: he is shirtless, with pants torn at mid-thigh, but his skin color remains unmistakably white, and if not for the shield and headdress, there would be little visual indication of his newfound role as representative of racial unity and harmony born from a racially fragmented United States.

These stories of Captain America becoming Indian not only seek to fortify or enrich his representative status but also to invigorate a weak physical body. In the same way that numerous predecessors in US culture, like the examples from the 1950s surveyed above, become Indian in order to become physically tougher and stronger, so too does Captain America in the stories above. The Captain America mythos is rooted in the fantasy of physical improvement, and upon adding the white Indian trope, another nuance of this analysis reveals itself.

While the preceding discussion has focused on playing Indian as a rhetorical maneuver to accentuate Captain America as a representative of national identity, one must not ignore the display of his physical body as marker of his heroic manhood. Relevant to this point, Aaron Taylor observes the way that superhero bodies are constructed by the reader: "In reading a superhero comic, s/he is engaged in the *reassemblage* of the fractured, objectified body mentioned above [bodies in comics are fragmented due to paneling and page composition]—reunifying the panels (and the bodies) into their personal totalities" (349). While Taylor refers specifically to the reader's construction of the body in comics here, this concept can be applied to the process of reassembling Steve Rogers as Captain America in *1602* and the *What If?* story. In both of these stories, Captain America's body is reassembled from either a body completely disintegrated (*1602*) or a torn and battered body near death (*What If?*).

In *1602* the modern Captain America is executed, then his body evaporated (the powers that be "didn't even want [his] ashes left behind," he explains). A panel shows an explosion of white specked with red and Captain

America's narration: "And then I just remember the pain." On the following page the image of Captain America awaking outdoors leads to his adoption into an unnamed Indian tribe. The first panels of the Captain's arrival in the past call attention to his body, here not even clothed, though discreetly shadowed. Captain America's body is fit and muscular, although not outlandishly so. Rojhaz goes shirtless throughout the whole series, and until the final book he is, as far as anyone else knows, an Indian. His dress calls attention to his difference from the white Anglo characters in the story, and this difference largely revolves around the exposure of his physical body and his Indianness. *1602: Part Two* offers a striking contrast in which we see Rojhaz standing guard outside Virginia's door, as tall as the doorframe, with arms crossed (his signature pose throughout the series). In a six-panel sequence, Peter Parquah arrives to deliver a message to Virginia, standing barely stomach-high to Rojhaz. The top three panels feature Rojhaz in the same pose, unmoving, stoic, and forbidding in his physicality. This repetition of his posture from panel to panel emphasizes his considerable physical presence.

In *What If?* a similar dynamic is at play. Images of Stephen Rogers show him bloodied and bandaged after being dragged by a pair of horses. From this state of bodily disrepair, Rogers undergoes Wilson's ceremony and is revived, with body fully healed and renewed as the Indianized Captain America. The top three-quarters of the page provides an almost complete view of the new Rogers's body (only his feet are not shown). Shirtless, his muscled torso and arms emphasize his renewal and physical vigor. On the following page one sees a panel focused on his right arm outstretched with the eagle spirit perched on it, and half of his upper body, a frame that fragments his body (per Taylor's discussion) and draws the reader's attention to the chiseled musculature of this Captain America. The Indian accoutrements lend further associations of physical vitality and strength to these images of the body. This very connotation informs *What If?*'s imagining of Captain America's birth during the Civil War. Captain America's masquerade as Indian in these stories emphasizes his body as a marker of his superior ability, his heroic masculinity.

The physical body exposed in this way also marks a certain primitiveness or savagery (clothing, or lack of it, long being associated with the perception of civilization). While the lack of dress accentuates the sculptured physique of the superhero, it also divides that hero from "normal" society. For example, *White Indian*'s Dan Brand undergoes a similar sartorial transformation in his Indianization: going from the well-dressed city dweller to the Indian-costumed wilderness hero, Brand often wears nothing but leggings and a headband. The racial dimensions of the superhero's body receive treatment by Jeffrey Brown and his argument that "[a]s much as the body has been related with the 'virtues' of masculinity, it has also been associated via racial and class prejudices with the insensitive, the unintelligent, and the animalistic. Moreover, the more one's identity is linked to a hypermasculine persona based on the body, the more uncultured and uncivilized, the more bestial, one is considered to be" (30). Brown's point here of how the racialized body connotes brutishness in its emphasized physicality applies to the image of the white hero's body performed as Indian. Brown's discussion of the combination of "duality and performative masquerade" found in the superhero males (and specifically for Brown's purposes, the ramifications for perceptions of African American masculinity) applies as well to the images of Captain America as Indian. The original Captain America's birth from weakling Steve Rogers needs little further explanation on this point: the duality of weakling and superhero, the performance of superheroics as Captain America juxtaposes to the seemingly inept Rogers non-superhero persona.

This physical transformation so often found in superhero comics (usually via scientific or supernatural means) is translated in the comics under study here as Indianization: the weak protagonist gains his power through playing Indian. Dan Brand metamorphoses into a wilderness hero after taking up a tomahawk and putting on leggings and a headband. Tom Hawk becomes a valiant warrior for the Revolution via his adoption of Indian ways. A Civil War Steve Rogers goes from ineffectual private to superpowered soldier through an "Indian" ritual. In addition, a Captain America transported back to 1602 undergoes a literal rebirth, a resurrection of a disintegrated body that takes on the trappings of Captain America's adopted Indian tribe.

The physical transformation from weak to strong, from puny to muscular bears an obvious relation to the depiction in much advertising of the twentieth century (and the twenty-first) of the ideal male body. Especially visible in comic books, the classic Charles Atlas advertisement, and its ilk, denigrated the weak and thin male body in order to elevate the muscular male body. Brian E. Hack connects these muscle ads to Captain America specifically, observing how "such ads capitalized on the vicarious desires of its young male readers to become as muscle-bound as their comic book heroes" (82). The transformation of Rogers into Captain America enacts that fantasy of instantaneous metamorphosis from weakling to superhero.

While such ads are not present in the early-twenty-first-century Captain America stories examined above, the Rogers transformation from weak to strong still remains as a key component of the Captain America mythos. Furthermore, the postwar comics mentioned earlier did actually share space with such muscle ads, and so their publication contexts tie them quite vividly to that Charles Atlas ideal. Such proximity to that idealized Atlas male body further indicates the significance of physical strength to the white Indian characters of the fifties, a physical strength that they obtain through becoming Indian.

These comics rest within a triangulation of race, manhood, and nationhood: by playing Indian, these white males obtain a physical superiority that solidifies their manhood and anchors them to national service. As Dana D. Nelson has demonstrated, the perception of Indian masculinity as a standard for white masculinity is implicated in the white inheritance of national identity from indigenous forebears. In this imagined course of inheritance, the "vanishing Indian" willingly releases his land to and bestows his authentic "Americanness" upon the advancing "new" Americans. Moreover, along with that transmission of land and identity, the Indian provides an admirable model of manliness for white males. This white appropriation, then, redeems Indianness for proper and acceptable use in service of nationalist authenticity and representation.

While the imaginings of Captain America discussed above present him as an unproblematic embodiment of American diversity, earlier stories in the continuity challenge Steve Rogers as Captain America on the grounds of the actual racial division that exists in the United States. In J. M. DeMatteis's *Captain America* #292 (Apr. 1984), Jesse Black Crow, a Native American,[5] and in Robert Morales's *Captain America: Truth* (2003), Isaiah Bradley, an African American, challenge the seemingly exceptional status of Steve Rogers as Captain America.

In the climax of *Captain America* #292, the Captain and Black Crow meet in a second encounter in which Black Crow emerges as the dominant fighter (16–22). DeMatteis depicts the contrast between these two characters on multiple levels: as a racial divide of white vs. Indian; as a temporal divide of "old" vs. "new"; and as a divide of values of "traditional" vs. "modern." The fight culminates in the Captain falling to his near death. Upon regaining consciousness, instead of continuing the fight, he kneels before Black Crow. The latter lifts Captain America, and both men embrace: a symbolic joining of the old and new Americas. With that embrace, Black Crow disappears in a flash of light, declaring, "The Earth Spirit . . . is pleased" (22). On this scene, David Walton argues that Black Crow "reasoned that Rogers' blood atonement would create a new America for all peoples" (167). Captain America's surrender affords a "harmony," that Black Crow earlier in the story describes, in which "the past and the present can merge . . . become transformed . . . and this land we love so can birth a future worthy of both our peoples" (18).

The fantasy of merging and transformation described here echoes in the alternate-Earth version of Captain America presented in the *What If?* story. Captain America serves as a focal point in these narratives to seek some space of unity, some embodiment of integration between races. Captain America undergoes a near-death experience, and upon his reawakening he emerges as a savior of America's hopes and ideals. The Civil War Captain made way for a course of American history unblemished by racism, while DeMatteis places him at a turning point in American history: the "past was born of dreams and blood: savage nobility—and civilized barbarism" and the "present is equal parts violence and ideals unfathomable despair—and unfathomable hope" (22). DeMatteis resolves Black Crow's challenge with hope for racial harmony that acknowledges the sacrifices of the past while looking forward to a better world. The final page of Morales's *Truth*, with Rogers and Bradley standing side by side, sounds a similar note of optimism, although getting there lays painfully bare America's brutal and cruel history of racism.

The challenge to Captain America's representative status drives the narrative of *Truth* in its revelation of the secret history of the super-soldier serum, of experimentation upon African American soldiers resulting in disfigurement and death. The one survivor, Isaiah Bradley, lives on as a reminder of the cruel prejudice, racism, and neglect suffered by him and his fellow soldiers. Steve Rogers learns of the sacrifice of blood and sanity made by others in the attempts to replicate the super-soldier serum, a sacrifice unrecognized by official history (although a wall of photographs in Bradley's home attests to his recognition by prominent African Americans of the late twentieth century). Isaiah Bradley's existence undermines the exceptional status of Steve Rogers as Captain America. On this point, another way to read his Indianization in Gaiman's and Bedard's stories is as a decentering of Captain America: an argument that Captain America's whiteness is not inherent or essential to his becoming a superhero, but that Steve Rogers was a fortunate recipient of his powers due to his social status.

While DeMatteis and Morales may seek to challenge the essential nature of the Captain as white, they must still concede to the fact that Captain

America is a white man meant to represent multiple ethnicities and races in his role as America's protector and hero. These historical revisions (whether canonical or not) reveal the admirable attempt to maneuver the Captain America mythos into a discourse recognizing the troubled and problematic racial history and present of the United States. All the while, these stories never lose sight of heroic masculinity and physical strength as essential characteristics of the superhero. In addition, while these stories may decenter race as a foundation for the male hero, they maintain the male body as the locus for representative power.

Although *Captain America* #292 and *Truth* may provide for the possibility of challenging the status of a white Captain America as *the only* Captain America, the dominant discourse underlying these stories points more definitely toward that assemblage of American identity as described by critics such as Slotkin and Deloria. As Deloria argues, "Indianness provided impetus and precondition for the creative assembling of an ultimately unassemblable American identity" (5). Indianness acts as a rough sketch of white American identity that is soon revised and forgotten. In the same way that Steve Rogers's body is fragmented in order to be made stronger and better, one might see the fragmentation and reassemblage of Indian identity into something perceived as better and improved. To put the matter into the language of the Captain America mythos, the "Indian" is a frail body of strong spirit that, when injected with the super-serum of white civilization, is transformed into a stronger, more admirable figure. In this way the Captain America mythos provides an apt analogy for the postcolonial formation of American identity in its appropriation and marginalization of Indianness. In *1602* the Indian tribe adopts and revives Steve Rogers, then disappears from the story as Rojhaz/Rogers becomes the central locus of American identity. In *What If?* Bedard explicitly describes a line of transmission that approves of the colonial succession and inheritance of America by whites: Captain America absorbs the best qualities of his racial predecessors, while they disappear from view. Similarly, in *Captain America 292*, the final scene between Black Crow and the Captain enacts a fantasy of the Indian's blessing of white inheritance of the nation. Captain America's identity as the representative American rests upon this "persistent tradition in American culture" (Deloria 7) in which whites appropriate Indianness to register an authentic and indisputable American identity.

Captain America as Indian in the 2000s invokes much of the same symbolism and ideology of masculinity and heroism as the white Indians of earlier comics, albeit with an awareness of the problematic nature of race in the Captain's mythos. There is an extraordinary and resilient power in the image of the white man playing Indian in US culture. The stories examined above reveal the potency of Indianness as imagery and symbol. A multifaceted system of metaphor revolves around the popular imagining of Indianness that, when channeled into comics, reifies the appropriation of Indianness as a vehicle for heroic masculinity and national identity. When we add Captain America to the mix, this appropriation's valorization of physical strength and martial power as markers of masculinity and national identity becomes remarkably visible.

Throughout this range of superhero stories, playing Indian functions in a variety of ways. In the mid-century comics, appropriation acts as a sort of exotic play, a novelty of the white superhero as Indian. After the 1960s, playing Indian provides an opportunity for the comic writer to interrogate American assumptions about race and representation. In addition, these later imaginings of indigenous ancestry or origins for the superheroes seem to reach toward a more authentic vision of the superhero as American. This latter phenomenon is perhaps complicated by the fact that two of the authors doing this indigenous Americanization of the hero are British (Gaiman and Morrison). In all, these superhero stories of playing Indian encapsulate many of the themes and concerns raised throughout this study and thus make for a fitting point of closure.

# CONCLUSION

---

*"Stain for my skin . . . white blood turns red . . .*
*exit Dan Carter and enter the Bright Arrow!"*
—MANZAR THE WHITE INDIAN, *INDIANS* #2

"WHITE BLOOD TURNS RED." CONSIDER THE IMAGE ITSELF: RED AS THE color of blood, and blood as vigor, as life, so the movement from the anemic "white" to the vital "red." The racial metaphor, though, is evident: from white to Indian. And in that racial transformation, the transformations from weak to strong and from average to heroic. On another level, this metaphor is one of appropriation, an act of co-opting Native cultures that runs rampant throughout US history. While perhaps not always inherently a malicious act, too many times appropriation produces derogatory and damaging consequences, regardless of intent. This book has sought to examine the seemingly eternal recurrence of "white blood turns red" in American culture, a recurrence vividly represented in comic books of the last half of the twentieth century and even into the twenty-first century, inherited from cultural productions of the nineteenth century.

The literature and art of the nineteenth century in the United States that focus on the frontier and the Indian harbor recurring themes and tropes: the Indian as savage, the Indian as physical ideal, as hero, the white frontiersman as counterpart to the Indian, the frontiersman's heroism and savagery. A recursive dynamic exists in these depictions intertwining race, gender, and nationalism. The white man plays Indian and becomes a hybrid of the perceived best parts of the Indian and the white. The Indian male body becomes frozen as statuary, harmless in its aesthetic stasis. During this period, groundwork is laid of frontier tropes and romanticized Indianness. Into the twentieth century, these tropes remain, carried by the dime novels to popular media, and emerging with much vivacity in comics. While finding these themes in a comic of the Western genre comes as no surprise, to find these tropes in superhero comics highlights and magnifies some of the resident ideological strains of those tropes.

The superhero as Indian accentuates the masculine ideal of playing Indian, the whitening of romanticized Indian qualities, and the appropriation of the imagined Indian as American superhero. Sometimes as outright appropriation and sometimes as a politically correct attempt at diversity, the superhero as Indian promulgates that dynamic of race, gender, and nationalism found in the older Westerns, passed down from nineteenth-century antecedents. A definite evolution is visible, though: the white Indians of 1950s comics strike a different tone from the Indianized Captain America of the twenty-first century. Even so, there are sympathetic and sincere treatments of Native peoples in the earlier comic books. While Superman or Batman as Indian communicates problematic depictions and assumptions about Native peoples, a series like *Indians* intends a sincere appreciation of Native cultures rooted in history, aiming for accuracy. In fact, an exchange in the letters column of *Indians* in 1950 highlights the ugliness of racism and the socially conscious response to it.

While most letters printed in the column conveyed admiration for the comic book, one letter takes a particularly nasty and hateful view. Gerald P. Algerton writes, "By accident, and to my regret, I read your magazine, and I am very disgusted at your attempts to glorify Indians, who were just rough savages. The Indians were cruel, uneducated, and very uncultured and lived like animals. Only very stupid people could enjoy reading stories about them." Algerton's comments are such that one wonders if they are written simply to aggravate or if he sincerely believes them (this comment is so egregious, one might wonder if the letter is an editorial fabrication designed to enlist reader response or sympathy to the comic). The following issue (#3: Fall 1950) prints a reply to Algerton, "one of many, many letters replying" to him, according to the editors. Jean Brockman responds: "This show-off, who probably just wants to feel superior to somebody, simply succeeds in proving that he is the stupid and uneducated one. He calls the Indians cruel and savage—but in these things they were actually innocents compared to the torturing, slaughtering, slave-keeping white men of their day who boasted of their so-called civilization." Brockman also references Logan's speech that the editors print in full. The fourth issue (Winter 1950) has another letter directly responding to Algerton. The Bennings from Oklahoma describe moving to the state and befriending Indians. In reference to Algerton, they write, "As it is, he showed his own ignorance to write as he did—and also a lack of any religious feeling." Another letter writer,

Alan Wheelock, states: "[I]t's my opinion that anyone who detests Indians doesn't think much of the heritage and glory of his country."

Indians are equated with "the heritage and glory of [the] country" in Wheelock's letter, and this equation participates in a popular ideology that views Indians as the ancestral lineage of the United States. This ideology circulates throughout the mythology of American culture's roots in the frontier. The romanticized national lineage runs from Indian to frontiersman to citizen. The stories, art, and comic books examined in the preceding chapters testify to the power and persistence of the playing Indian trope. The ability to "turn red" stands as an admirable one, a superheroic switching of identity, sloughing off the weakness of the normal self and taking on the empowerment of the heroic alter ego. While the superhero genre has made this fantasy commonplace in American culture, seeing it synchronized with the fantasy of playing Indian draws out the nuances of racial and gender identities interwoven with national identity.

This book, then, has sought to illustrate the triangulation of race, gender, and national identities found in American culture, a triangulation that follows a logic in which playing Indian strengthens manhood and that improved manhood strengthens the nation. Playing Indian is integral to American identity in these comic books (as in the culture at large). This triangulation is readily apparent not only in the Western and frontier genres (as it obviously would be) but also in superhero comics in their utilization of the playing Indian trope. This transmission of the frontier myth and playing Indian from nineteenth-century literature and art to comic books demonstrates the staying power of these tropes. Through adaptations and allusions, through appropriations and borrowings, later media sustain the ideological power of the frontier and playing Indian. From Westerns to superheroes, the frontier and playing Indian demonstrate their malleability as symbolic phenomena in American culture, and while their symbolism may shift and change, they remain rooted in ideals of masculinity and nationalism. These ideals endure in American culture, continually informing popular perceptions of national, racial, and gender identities.

# NOTES

## INTRODUCTION

1. Gerald Vizenor introduces this term in *Manifest Manners* (1994), describing it in the preface to the 1999 edition as "an active sense of presence, the continuance of native stories, not a mere reaction, or a survivable name. Native survivance stories are renunciations of dominance, tragedy, and victimry" (vii). Vizenor elucidates this concept in *Fugitive Poses* (1998): "[S]urvivance, in the sense of native survivance, is more than survival, more than endurance or mere response; the stories of survivance are an active presence" (15). This connotation of "active presence," of agency and resistance, informs and motivates my use of "survivance" here.

2. The appropriate terminology for referring to indigenous peoples and cultures continues to be a point of debate and discussion. Both "Indian" and "Native" have their respective criticisms and merits. Amanda Blackhorse, in *Indian Country Today*, surveys a range of views on which term is preferable. Blackhorse concludes that the important factor in this issue of naming is the indigenous person's ability to choose which term to use. In much of what I study in this book, that choice does not exist and has been imposed from outsiders to indigenous culture. With that in mind, I use "Indian" to refer to fictional depictions or within the conventional usage of the time period being discussed. "Native" refers to actual peoples, as well as affirming the contemporary existence of Native peoples and cultures. My intent is to demarcate between the fictional, imagined depictions and the actual, living peoples. Further, tribal names found in this book are usually used according to the primary texts in which they appear. These tribal names may not reflect any authenticity or accuracy of actual Native affiliations or group titles. I adhere to the fictional use of these names in order to illustrate the perception of Native peoples and their traditions as found in these primary texts, as inaccurate as those perceptions may sometimes be. In fact, many times, the tribal names in these texts take on an exotic or evocative quality in themselves, detached from historical or actual reference.

3. The headdress is a recurring item of appropriation even today, appearing in fashion shoots, atop non-Native celebrities or reality stars, on T-shirts, and so on. See Adrienne Keene's *Native Appropriations* for a relentless and incisive cataloging and disputation of these inappropriate uses of the headdress, as well as other appropriations of Indianness in popular culture.

4. This point would seem to confirm McCloud's contention that the further we move from realistic images toward abstraction, to the icon as cartoon, the more universal the appeal of the image and the more involved the viewer becomes with the image (28–31).

5. Hatfield's breakdown and application of Peirce's theory in *Hand of Fire* has especially influenced my utilization of this theory (37–45). Daniel Chandler's explanation of Peirce's system is also useful (290–47).

## CHAPTER 1

1. While not a focus of my argument, the Indian female body should be mentioned, too, for its appeal in American culture. A similar dynamic is work in the sexualization of the exotic Indian female, along with the potential for miscegenation.

2. As Roy Harvey Pearce noted, "The Indian who was important to Americans setting out to make their new society was not the person but the type, not the tribesman but the savage, not the individual but the symbol. The American conscience was troubled about the death of the individual. But it could make sense of his death only when it understood it as the death of the symbol" (73).

3. Elizabeth Hallam et al. (1999) argue for "hybrids" that combine features of both life and death, such that they "confuse the cultural categories of life and death." (1). Hallam et al. also argue that these "hybrids" "are perceived as unstable, dangerous and marginal within dominant social and cultural orders" (2). This study of the social identity of the dead argues that identity does not end at death, but that the "dead" persist as part of society.

4. "This statue was exhibited in the Capitol Rotunda at the time of Abraham Lincoln's funeral in 1865 and later in the Crypt. By the Act of July 20, 1868 prohibiting the exhibition of works of art in the Capitol not government property, the statue was transferred to the Corcoran Gallery of Art in 1878, where it remained until 1916, when it was transferred to the National Museum" (*Compilation of Works of Art and Other Objects in the United States Capitol* 390). Also see *National Museum of American Art*, 30.

5. Modern audiences might be tempted to associate this pose with Auguste Rodin's *The Thinker*, yet Rodin's sculpture was conceived and sculpted years later, in the 1880s. Crawford's use of the thinking pose might have some precedence, though, in Michelangelo's sculpture of Lorenzo de Medici (1526–1531).

6. Canova's *Endymion* is especially notable here, since he was a popular influence on US sculpture in the early nineteenth century (Kasson 1). More specifically for Pettrich, his father was a follower of Canova (Craven 68). Moreover, while *Endymion* does not represent a dying male, it does show a male locked in eternal sleep, impassive, powerless, and subject to Selene's sexual advances.

7. Todd Smith's analysis of Morse's painting is cogent here. Smith argues that *The Dying Hercules* represents a weakened America during the War of 1812, and due to this connection, the painting fared poor among American audiences (241–42). *The Dying Tecumseh* seems a literal reversal of Morse's painting: a dying Indian instead of dying white man that demonstrates the strength of the United States, especially in its vanquishing of Tecumseh, a foe in the War of 1812. *Dying Tecumseh* works to prop white

manhood; the white male sees not himself lying supine (as Smith argues with Morse's Hercules), but his own empowerment through the death of this Indian. We should remember, too, the significance of Hercules to white national identity in the United States. Fliegelman relates a comparison of the United States as an infant nation to Hercules in his cradle playing with snakes (224). On the left side of Greenough's *George Washington* appears this same image of Hercules (Fryd 83).

8. See Kasson's (1990) analysis of Edward Brackett's *Shipwrecked Mother and Child* (1850), 101–40. Of the *Dead Pearl Diver*, Wayne Craven (1968) argues that it epitomizes "the Romantic, hypersentimental preoccupation with death" (281).

9. According to Bil Gilbert, Tekamthi's proposed confederacy would have done away with the existing Indian power structures, eliminating the village chiefs and routing power into the hands of the warriors (209–10).

10. See Sugden 397 for a list of titles. Tecumseh has been popular beyond the United States, as well. For references to Canadian titles, see Sugden, 391–93. And for German titles, see Sugden, 393–95.

11. Harrison's "campaign reminded voters of his battles with Tecumseh and the British through ballads, biographies, almanacs, and numbers of *The Log Cabin*. It was launched at a Whig rally which reputedly drew thirty thousand people to the battlefield of Tippecanoe" (Sugden 397).

12. In addition to Johnson and Harrison, Andrew Jackson, Zachary Taylor, and Lewis Cass ran their political campaigns on fighting Tecumseh. The Battle of Thames "helped create one president, one vice president, three state governors of Kentucky, three lieutenant-governors, four United States senators, and a score of congressmen" (Sugden 396–97). See also Thomas G. Mitchell (2003), 45–68, for the influence of Indian fighting in the War of 1812 on subsequent US politics.

13. Lepore quotes one critic who hopes that the applause at *Metamora*'s end is for Forrest and not for the "savage" he plays (210). Emmons leaves absolutely no room for ambiguity concerning the death of Tecumseh.

## CHAPTER 2

1. Bryan's poem is significant in its epic appropriation of Boone, see Slotkin, 348–54. Peck's biography is significant as the source for Ranney's painting.

2. Faragher offers a comprehensive review of the various incarnations of Boone from the late eighteenth century into the twentieth century in the chapter "Left until I'm Put in the Ground: Myth and Memory." The relevant pages for the antebellum period are 320–38.

3. In his later years, Boone would visit the Shawnee village near Femme Osage. According to a grandson, the Shawnee men who had known Boone during his captivity would recount stories from that time in good spirits (Faragher 313–14).

4. See John Mack Faragher (1992), 327–30, for depictions of Boone as a natural man.

5. For the concept of the "middle ground," see Richard White (1991). My thoughts here owe much to James Axtell's chapters on "white Indians" in *The European and the Indian*, 168–206.

6. The neoclassical style was also a self-conscious linkage of the new US republic with the republics of ancient Greece and Rome. See Castiello, 75. The fear of instability due to ratification and post-ratification dissensus would intensify the need of white male citizens to embrace a vision of order and predictability. David J. Siemers argues that the legitimation of the Constitution occurred due to a fear of instability, that Federalists, Madisonians, and Anti-Federalists legitimated the Constitution due to this fear. See his chapter "Consensus, Dissensus, and Interpretation," 1–24. Sheldon Wolin provides additional support for this embrace of a unified order over the potential of pluralistic difference in his *"E Pluribus Unum:* The Representation of Difference and the Reconstitution of Collectivity" in *The Presence of the Past*, 120–36. Underlying my linking of neoclassical form to political stability is Dana Nelson's suggestion in "Representative/Democracy" that singularizing "representative symbolic" of the Constitution "conjoins aesthetics and politics and offers unity and harmony as its goal" (219). Neoclassical unity and harmony reflects or assures white males of political unity and harmony.

7. Although Slotkin does not specify when this association occurred, he implies that it was contemporaneous to the statue's initial exhibition. Faragher specifies that *The Rescue* was explicitly associated with Boone in an 1874 lithograph "in which the figures were copied and retitled *Daniel Boone Protects His Family*" (337). With Boone's popularity in the antebellum period and his image as civilizer and defender, it is safe to assume that the association was at least implicit in white viewers' minds well before 1874.

8. Nathalia Wright offers a similar view. She argues that Greenough's "pioneer merely restrains his Indian, without wielding the rifle against the tomahawk. . . . Most significantly, the pioneer is characterized by a composure intended to express not only self-confidence but compassion for his enemy" (164).

9. Art historians have supplied the foundational reading of the statuary as representing white domination and triumph over Indian peoples. Nathalia Wright, Greenough's biographer, sees the statue as a representation of the power of civilized man in settling the continent (177). Fryd similarly views it as "the triumph of Anglo-Saxon civilization over the subservient native population" but adds that this sculpture reverses the captivity tradition with an Indian male being held captive rather than a white female (94, 95). Lubin elaborates the theme of white domination in stressing the destructive power of the frontiersman who kills Indians out of service to white expansion (83).

10. Although any argument about the composition of *The Rescue* must bear in mind that the statue may not be assembled as Greenough intended it. Fryd relates a claim that Robert Mills assembled the statue incorrectly: that the mother and child should have been in front of the men (101). If this were so, the mother and child would be foregrounded as the target of the Indian's raised tomahawk. Still, this alternate composition does not change the physical relationship of the two men.

11. For other readings of this painting, see Mark Thistlethwaite, 51–55, and Estill Curtis Pennington, 27–28. Critics generally agree that Ranney modeled this scene on John Peck's description of Boone's first view of Kentucky; see, for instance, Glanz, 16.

12. Glanz's reasoning for this identification is that the figure pointing would have to be John Finley, the only member of the group who had been in that area (18).

13. For specifics about the painting's composition and exhibition, see John F. McDermott, 83–86, and E. Maurice Bloch, 120–28.

14. E. Maurice Bloch asserts that Boone was modeled after the *Doryphoros*, and the male tying his shoe after the *Jason* or the *Cincinnatus* (128). As Lubin relates, Cincinnatus is a significant reference, since he "was a powerful symbol for the Whigs of republican modesty, duty, and circumspection" (101). As an interesting side-note, Winckelmann argued that the original statue was of Jason, since "nudity would have been incongruous for Cincinnnatus" (Haskell and Penny 184).

15. This particular depiction of Boone changes from one that Bingham had proposed in 1844 for a Whig banner that would have "old Daniel Boone himself engaged in one of his death struggles with an Indian" (*Letters* 13). This depiction certainly echoes Causici's Boone.

16. See Scheckel, 137, and Castiello, appendix 9, 139, and appendix 8, 135–36.

17. See especially Smith, 92–100.

18. The likelihood of McClung being a source for Bennett comes from two factors. One is the popularity of McClung's *Sketches of Western Adventure*. The other that is Bennett's hero has the surname of Reynolds, whereas McClung relates a story of a man named Reynolds who named his dog "Simon Girty" "in consequence of his striking resemblance to the man of that name" (77).

19. My attention came to this essay through Pearce and I draw my basic reading from his interpretation, that "although the frontier meant freedom from the business of the civilized world . . . such a life could not long endure, that the higher life called for the fireside, society, a sense of social obligation" (222–23).

## CHAPTER 3

1. Barker and Sabin date this adaptation as 1940–1941. According to the Grand Comics Database and my own examination of the comic, the publication dates are in 1942. The descriptions of the comic in Barker and Sabin match the comic that I examine here, so I can only conclude that we are addressing the same adaptation. With that, I am assuming the 1942 dates as the publication dates.

2. The HRN for the copy that this study uses is 141 (which would put its publication at November 1957). According to William B. Jones, Jr., there were twenty-two printings of *Mohicans*. The Ramsey version first appeared in August 1942 and was reprinted through November 1957. Starting in May 1959, the second version by Severin, Cole, and Addeo was published and was reprinted multiple times until 1969.

3. Barker and Sabin connect the composition of this fight scene to that of N. C. Wyeth's illustration of Magua and Heyward (187).

4. In his biography of Boone, Meredith Mason Brown (2008) cites Butterfield's claim about the probable fiction of Girty's speech (320 n.25).

## CHAPTER 4

1. Frank M. Young notes that this sort of stereotyping was very rare in John Stanley's Lulu comics, providing an important contextual reminder that "[t]he kids' fantasies are fueled by the Hollywood crap that encouraged these stereotypes" (2012).

2. While claiming a "first" is always a precarious endeavor, and perhaps not always a productive form of criticism, *White Boy* is the earliest title that I have found in the comics medium that features a white Indian character.

3. That the hard/soft dichotomy acts as a pervasive rhetorical device during the time can also be seen in Marine Colonel Lewis "Chesty" Puller's speech to his troops in Korea: "Tell 'em there's no secret weapon for our country but to get hard, to get in there and fight. . . . Our country won't go on forever if we stay as soft as we are now" (qtd. in Slotkin 1992, 363).

4. In addition to Cuordileone's trenchant study, Barbara Ehrenreich's *The Hearts of Men* has greatly informed my understanding of the conversation about masculinity and its supposed decline in the 1950s, especially chapter 3, "Early Rebels: The Gray Flannel Dissidents." Elaine Tyler May also addresses this rhetoric of masculinity in *Homeward Bound* (94–95). Rupert Wilkinson provides concise summaries of Riesman's and Whyte's arguments (16–21).

5. If one has not noticed yet, quite a few characters in these comic books are named "Dan," most likely an echo of Daniel Boone.

6. Notable in this plot point is the "women in refrigerators" trope, too. In this trope, named by Gail Simone, death of or harm to a female character motivates the male hero to action.

7. A female going Indian is not in itself an unusual story in American culture. Women captives and adoptees heavily populate US historical records and literature. Primarily, though, these women are depicted in submissive or secondary roles, with their Indianization often depicted as victimization. Rarely do we see a female who goes Indian as the hero and as being strengthened or invigorated in that transformation as we do with Firehair.

8. For more on the relationship between comics of the late forties and early fifties and the Cold War, see Bradford W. Wright, 109–34. William W. Savage, in his chapter "The Cowboy Crusade," provides a closer look at anticommunist sentiment found in the cowboy comics of this period.

9. This episode is set during the French and Indian War (1754–1763), which is odd, since Brand became the White Indian in 1770.

10. In an earlier story, "The Lost Men of Fort Chance" (#90), Tomahawk also plays Indian, although this time not in connection to the Revolution. In order to infiltrate a Seneca tribe and stop them from attacking a white settlement, Tom shaves his head and dyes his skin with berries. He is discovered but then finds out that Dan has also sneaked in and taken the chief's place, thus protecting Tom.

11. *Tomahawk*'s evident patriotism finds further illustration in the character of Miss Liberty, in issues #81 and 88. Miss Liberty is actually Bess Lynn, a nurse, who dons the patriotic garb of Miss Liberty to assist Tomahawk in completing his missions for

the Americans during the Revolution. Miss Liberty represents the necessity and the capability of domestic actors (wives and nurses) in aiding the war effort.

12. Straight Arrow's radio show and the comic anticipate *Devil's Doorway* (1950) and its protagonist Lance Poole, a Shoshone who is a cattle rancher.

13. An obvious echo of the infamous words often attributed to Philip Sheridan in 1869, although the saying more likely originated with Rep. James Cavanaugh.

14. This change of tone is further amplified in Rachel Pollack's 1998 retelling of Tomahawk's origin. Pollack emphasizes Tomahawk's appropriation of Indianness as the catalyst for his strength and power. Pollack's retelling depicts an essential transformation of Tomahawk: he has become a hybrid of white and Indian, his time in the wilderness acting as a purgation of his former self (that is more in line with the post–*Dances with Wolves* style of appropriation of the 1990s).

15. Not to be confused with Marvel's Scalphunter, a Comanche who is a villain mutant in the X-Men universe. His first appearance is in *Uncanny X-Men* #210 (Oct. 1986).

16. After *Weird Western Tales'* cancellation, *Scalphunter* became a back-up feature for *Jonah Hex* in issues 40, 41, and 45–47 (with Conway as writer). In later years Scalphunter would make occasional reappearances in the DC universe: *Crisis on Infinite Earths* (1985), *Jonah Hex* #57 (2006 series), and a special issue of *Weird Western Tales* (#71: March 2010) during the *Blackest Night* event.

17. It appears that Conway sometimes spells the name with "Tey" instead of "Tay."

## CHAPTER 5

1. This plot gets a retread in *Tomahawk 82* (Sept.–Oct. 1962). In "Lost Land of the Paleface Tribe," Tomahawk and Dan Hunter happen into a valley that has been disconnected from the rest of the world. There a group of whites has taken on Indian dress and customs. The story ends with the group remaining in the valley, "a tribe that time forgot."

2. See also Marco Arnaudo's reading of *Batman: Shaman* and *The Kents* as reflecting a shamanistic tradition (23–25).

3. This "Third Indian Guard" reflects actual history (although, perhaps, not this particular composition of nations described in the story). Native Americans fought on both sides of the Civil War for a variety of political, social, and geographical reasons. See Laurence M. Hauptman.

4. See Brian Dippie, Lora Romero, Susan Scheckel, and Birgit Brander Rasmussen.

5. Black Crow would have obtained an even grander place in the Captain America mythos if DeMatteis had gotten his way. DeMatteis wrote a plot for issue 300 in which Black Crow would take Captain America's place. His logic for this replacement: "Who better to represent America than one of the first Americans?" The change was rejected (due not to the proposed replacement, but to separate issues involving Captain America's character). See Brian Cronin.

# WORKS CITED

Note: For the comics citations, this bibliography follows the recommendations of the Comic Art and Comics Area of the Popular Culture Association located at comics-research.org. In keeping with this format, information in brackets is not supplied by the primary material. I have consulted the Grand Comics Database (comics.org) for information on creators and publishers when this information is not present in the original sources. Citations for *Classics Illustrated* entries rely upon William B. Jones's *Classics Illustrated: A Cultural History* for additional information. Publication dates for comics usually do not represent when the comic was actually for sale; most comics are available before the listed publication date.

Adare, Sierra S. *"Indian" Stereotypes in TV Science Fiction: First Nations' Voices Speak Out*. Austin: University of Texas Press, 2005. Print.

Arnaudo, Marco. *The Myth of the Superhero*. Baltimore: Johns Hopkins University Press, 2010. Print.

Averill, Esther (w), and Feodor Rojankovsky (i). *Daniel Boone*. New York: Harper & Row, 1945. Print.

Axtell, James. *The European and the Indian: Essays in the Ethnohistory of Colonial North America*. New York: Oxford University Press, 1981. Print.

Bakeless, John. *Daniel Boone: Master of the Wilderness*. 1939. Lincoln: University of Nebraska Press, 1989. Print.

Bakeless, John (original), [Ken Fitch (adaptation), and Alex Blum (p, i)]. *Classics Illustrated: Daniel Boone* #96 [HRN 134] (June 1952), Gilberton. Print.

Barker, Martin, and Roger Sabin. *The Lasting of the Mohicans: History of an American Myth*. Jackson: University Press of Mississippi, 1995. Print.

Barnett, Louise K. *The Ignoble Savage: American Literary Racism, 1790–1890*. Westport: Greenwood Press, 1975. Print.

Beaty, Bart. *Fredric Wertham and the Critique of Mass Culture*. Jackson: University Press of Mississippi, 2005. Print.

Bedard, Tony (w), Carmine DiGiandomenico (p), and John Stanisci (i). *What If? Featuring Captain America* #1 (Feb. 2006), Marvel Comics. Print.

Bennett, Emerson. *The Renegade: A Historical Romance of Border Life*. Cincinnati: Robinson & Jones, 1848. *Early American Fiction Collection*. Web. 6 Nov. 2013.

Berger, John. *Ways of Seeing*. New York: British Broadcasting Corporation and Penguin, 1991. Print.

Bergland, Renee. *The National Uncanny: Indian Ghosts and American Subjects.* Hanover: University Press of New England, 2000. Print.

Berkhofer, Robert. *The White Man's Indian: Images of the American Indian from Columbus to the Present.* New York: Alfred A. Knopf, 1978. Print.

[Bernstein, Robert (w), and Sam Citron (p, i).] "Menace of the Renegades." *Exploits of Daniel Boone* #6 (Oct. 1956), Comic Magazines [Quality Comics]. Digital.

[Binder, Otto (w), and Pete Costanza (a).] "Indian Chief." *Captain Marvel Adventures* #83 (Apr. 1948), Fawcett. Digital.

Bingham, George Caleb. *The Emigration of Daniel Boone.* 1851–1852. Washington University Gallery of Art, St. Louis, Missouri.

———. Bingham, George Caleb. "Letters of George Caleb Bingham to James S. Rollins." Ed. C. B. Rollins. *Missouri Historical Review* 32:1 (Oct. 1937): 3–34, and 32:2 (Jan. 1938): 164–202. Print.

Bird, Robert Montgomery. *Nick of the Woods.* 1837. New York: American Book Company, 1939. Print.

Bird, S. Elizabeth, ed. *Dressing in Feathers: The Construction of the Indian in American Popular Culture.* New York: Westview, 1996. Print.

Blackhorse, Amanda. "Do You Prefer 'Native American' or 'American Indian'? 6 Prominent Voices Respond." *Indian Country Today Media Network.* 21 Mar. 2015. Web. 25 June 2015.

*Blazing West* #3 (Jan.–Feb. 1949), B & I. Digital.

*Blazing West* #4 (Mar.–Apr. 1949), B & I. Digital.

Bloch, E. Maurice. *George Caleb Bingham: The Evolution of an Artist.* Berkeley: University of California Press, 1967. Print.

Boyd, Thomas. *Simon Girty: The White Savage.* New York: Minto, Balch, 1928. Print.

Brown, Bill. "Reading the West: Cultural and Historical Background." *Reading the West: An Anthology of Dime Westerns.* Ed. Bill Brown. Boston: Bedford Books, 1997. 1–40. Print.

Brown, Jeffrey A. *Black Superheroes, Milestone Comics, and Their Fans.* Jackson: University Press of Mississippi, 2001. Print.

———. "Comic Book Masculinity and the New Black Superhero." *African American Review* 33.1 (Spring 1999): 25–42. Print.

Brown, Meredith Mason. *Frontiersman: Daniel Boone and the Making of America.* Baton Rouge: Louisiana State University Press, 2008. Print.

Butterfield, Consul Willshire. *History of the Girtys.* Cincinnati: Robert Clarke, 1890. *Historic Pittsburgh General Text Collection.* Web. 29 Sept. 2014.

Byrd, Jodi A. *The Transit of Empire: Indigenous Critiques of Colonialism.* Minneapolis: University of Minnesota Press, 2011. Print.

[Cameron, Lou (a).] "Daniel Boone in the Shawnee Ambush." *Heroes of the Wild Frontier* #2 (Apr. 1956), Ace. Digital.

———. "Golden Warrior and the Raiders of Terror Canyon." *Pawnee Bill* #3 (July 1951), Story Comics. Digital.

Castiello, Kathleen Raben. *The Italian Sculptors of the United States Capitol: 1806–1834*. Diss. University of Michigan, 1975. Ann Arbor: UMI, 1982. 76-9362. Print.

Castronovo, Russ. *Necro Citizenship: Death, Eroticism, and the Public Sphere in the Nineteenth-Century United States*. Durham: Duke University Press, 2001. Print.

Causici, Enrico. *Conflict of Daniel Boone and the Indians*. 1826–1827. US Capitol Rotunda, above south door.

Cawelti, John G. *Adventure, Mystery, and Romance: Formula Stories as Art and Popular Culture*. Chicago: University of Chicago Press, 1976. Print.

———. *The Six-Gun Mystique*. 2nd ed. Bowling Green: Bowling Green State University Popular Press, 1984. Print.

———. *The Six-Gun Mystique Sequel*. Bowling Green: Bowling Green State University Popular Press, 1999. Print.

[Certa, Joe (p, i).] "Born to the Frontier." *Dan'l Boone* #1 (Sept. 1955), Sussex [Magazine Enterprises]. Digital.

———. "Peril Shadows the Forest Trail." *Dan'l Boone* #4 (Dec. 1955), Sussex [Magazine Enterprises]. Digital.

———. "Renegade on the River." *Dan'l Boone* #4 (Dec. 1955), Sussex [Magazine Enterprises]. Digital.

———. "Sell-Out." *Dan'l Boone* #8 (Sept. 1957), Sussex [Magazine Enterprises]. Digital.

———. "Simon Girty Worst of the Renegades." *Dan'l Boone* #7 (Mar. 1956), Sussex [Magazine Enterprises]. Digital.

———. "Spirit of the Frontier." *Dan'l Boone* #5 (Jan. 1956), Sussex [Magazine Enterprises]. Digital.

Chandler, Daniel. *Semiotics: The Basics*. London: Routledge, 2007. Print.

Clifton, James, ed. *The Invented Indian*. New Brunswick: Transaction, 1990. Print.

Cole, Jack. "[The Revenge of Chief Great Warrior]." *Police Comics* #16 (Feb. 1943), Comic Magazines. Digital.

Colton, George Hooker. *Tecumseh; or, The West Thirty Years Since*. New York: Wiley and Putnam, 1842.Print.

*Compilation of Works of Art and Other Objects in the United States Capitol*. Washington: United States Government Printing Office, 1965. Print.

Conway, Gerry (w), Dick Ayers (a), and Luis Dominguez (a). "Hanging for a Scalphunter." *Weird Western Tales* #51 (Jan. 1979), DC Comics. Print.

Conway, Gerry (w), Dick Ayers (a), and Romeo Tanghal (a). "A Cold Way to Die!" *Weird Western Tales* #70 (Aug. 1980), DC Comics. Print.

———. "The Gangs of New York." *Weird Western Tales* #60 (Oct. 1979), DC Comics. Print.

———. "Weep, the Widow." *Weird Western Tales* #58 (Aug. 1979), DC Comics. Print.

Coogan, Peter. *Superhero: The Secret Origin of a Genre*. Austin: MonkeyBrain Books, 2006. Print.

Cooper, James Fenimore. *The Last of the Mohicans: A Narrative of 1757*. 1826. New York: Signet Classic, 1962. Print.

Costello, Matthew J. *Secret Identity Crisis: Comic Books and the Unmasking of Cold War America*. New York: Continuum, 2009. Print.

Craven, Wayne. *Sculpture in America*. Rev. ed. Newark: University of Delaware Press, 1984. Print.

de Crèvecoeur, J. Hector St. John. *Letters from an American Farmer*. 1782. New York: Penguin, 1986. Print.

Cronin, Brian. "Comic Book Urban Legends Revealed #94." *Comic Book Resources*. 15 Mar. 2007. Web. 1 Apr. 2012.

Cuordileone, K. A. "'Politics in an Age of Anxiety': Cold War Political Culture and the Crisis in American Masculinity, 1949–1960." *Journal of American History* 87.2 (Sept. 2000): 515–45. *JSTOR*. Web. 15 May 2013.

Davis, Jack (p, i). "The Last of the Mohicans!" Adapted from James Fenimore Cooper. *Two-Fisted Tales* #40 (Dec. 1954–Jan. 1955), EC Comics. Digital.

Dean, Janet. "Stopping Traffic: Spectacles of Romance and Race in *The Last of the Mohicans*." *Doubled Plots: Romance and History*. Ed. Susan Strehle and Mary Paniccia Carden. Jackson: University of Mississippi Press, 2003. 45–66. Print.

DeLay, Harold (p, i). "The Last of the Mohicans: Parts 1–10." Adapted from James Fenimore Cooper. *Target Comics* v. 2 #12, v. 3 #1–9 (Feb. 1942–Nov. 1942), Novelty Press. Digital.

Deloria, Philip J. *Playing Indian*. New Haven: Yale University Press, 1998. Print.

DeMatteis, J. M. (w), Paul Neary (p), and Ed Barreto (i). *Captain America* #292 (Apr. 1984), Marvel Comics. Print.

Denning, Michael. *Mechanic Accents and Working-Class Culture in America*. New York: Verso, 1998. Print.

DeVoss, Dànielle Nicole, and Patrick Russell LeBeau. "Reading and Composing Indians: Invented Indian Identity through Visual Literacy." *Journal of Popular Culture* 43.1 (2010): 45–77. Print.

DeVoto, Bernard. *The Year of Decision: 1846*. Boston: Little, Brown, 1943. Print.

Dippie, Brian. *The Vanishing American: White Attitudes and U.S. Indian Policy*. Middletown: Wesleyan University Press, 1982. Print.

Draper, Lyman C. *The Life of Daniel Boone*. 1856. Ed. Ted Franklin Belue. Mechanicsburg: Stackpole Books, 1998. Print.

Drinnon, Richard. *Facing West: The Metaphysics of Indian-Hating and Empire Building*. Minneapolis: University of Minnesota Press, 1980. Print.

Duncan, Randy, and Matthew J. Smith. *The Power of Comics: History, Form, and Culture*. New York: Continuum, 2009. Print.

Dyar, Jennifer. "Fatal Attraction: The White Obsession with Indianness." *Historian* 65.4 (Summer 2003): 817–36. Print.

Dyer, Richard. *White*. London: Routledge, 1997. Print.

Edmunds, R. David. *Tecumseh and the Quest for Indian Leadership*. Boston: Little, Brown, 1984. Print.

Ehrenreich, Barbara. *The Hearts of Men: American Dreams and the Flight from Commitment*. New York: Anchor, 1984. Print.

Faragher, John Mack. *Daniel Boone: The Life and Legend of an American Pioneer*. New York: Henry Holt, 1992. Print.

Fiedler, Leslie. *Love and Death in the American Novel*. 1960. Rev. ed. New York: Stein and Day, 1975. Print.

Filson, John. *The Discovery, Settlement and Present State of Kentucke (1784): An Online Electronic Text Edition*. Ed. Paul Royster. *Electronic Texts in American Studies*. Digital Commons at University of Nebraska–Lincoln. Web. 6 Nov. 2013.

Finger, Bill (w), Sheldon Moldoff (p), and Charles Paris (i). "Origin of the Bat-Cave." *Giant Batman Annual* #1 [1961]. New York: DC Comics, 1999. Print.

[Fitch, Kenneth (w), and Alex A. Blum (a).] *Daniel Boone* (June 1952), Gilberton. Digital.

Fixico, Donald L. *Termination and Relocation: Federal Indian Policy, 1945–1960*. Albuquerque: University of New Mexico Press, 1986. Print.

Fleisher, Michael (w), Dick Ayers (a), and George Evans (a). "Death Stalk." *Weird Western Tales* #42 (Sept.–Oct. 1977), DC Comics. Print.

———. "The Mark of a Warrior." *Weird Western Tales* #40 (May–June 1977), DC Comics. Print.

———. "Scalphunter." *Weird Western Tales* #39 (Mar.–Apr. 1977), DC Comics. Print.

Fleisher, Michael (w), Dick Ayers (a), and Frank Springer (a). "The Black Seer of Death Canyon!" *Weird Western Tales* #41 (July–Aug. 1977), DC Comics. Print.

Fleisher, Michael (w), Dick Ayers (a), and Romeo Tanghal (a). "The Search." *Weird Western Tales* #59 (Sept. 1979), DC Comics. Print.

Fleming, James R. "Incommensurable Ontologies and the Return of the Witness in Neil Gaiman's *1602*." *ImageTexT: Interdisciplinary Comics Studies* 4.1 (2008): n. pag. Web. 8 Feb. 2010.

Fliegelman, Jay. *Prodigals and Pilgrims: The American Revolution against Patriarchal Authority, 1750–1800*. Cambridge: Cambridge University Press, 1982. Print.

Flint, Timothy. *Indian Wars of the West*. Cincinnati: E. H. Flint, 1833. Print.

[Fox, Gardner (w), and Fred Meagher (p, i).] "Land of Our Fathers." *Straight Arrow* #2 (Apr. –May 1950), Magazine Enterprises. Digital.

———. "Straight Arrow." *Straight Arrow* #1 (Feb.–Mar. 1950), Magazine Enterprises. Digital.

Frazetta, Frank (a). "Brothers of the Wilderness." Apr.–May 1950. *The Complete Frazetta White Indian*. Ed. J. David Spurlock. Lakewood: Vanguard, 2011. 9–15. Print.

———. "White Indian." Oct.–Nov. 1949. *The Complete Frazetta White Indian*. Ed. J. David Spurlock. Lakewood: Vanguard, 2011. 9–15. Print.

Frazetta, Frank. *The Complete Frazetta White Indian*. Lakewood: Vanguard, 2011. Print.

Fryd, Vivien Green. *Art and Empire: The Politics of Ethnicity in the United States Capitol, 1815–1860*. 1992. Athens: Ohio University Press/United States Capitol Historical Society, 2001. Print.

Gabilliet, Jean-Paul. *Of Comics and Men: A Cultural History of American Comic Books*. Trans. Bart Beaty and Nick Nguyen. Jackson: University Press of Mississippi, 2010. Print.

Gaiman, Neil (w), Andy Kubert (a), and Richard Isanove (digital painting). *1602: Part One* (Nov. 2003), Marvel Comics. Print.

———. *1602: Part Two* (Nov. 2003), Marvel Comics. Print.

———. *1602: Part Four* (Jan. 2004), Marvel Comics. Print.

———. *1602: Part Eight* (June 2004), Marvel Comics. Print.

Galt, John. *The Life of Benjamin West*. 1816–1820. Gainesville: Scholars' Facsimiles and Reprints, 1960. Print.

Gilbert, Bil. "The Dying Tecumseh and the Birth of a Legend." *Smithsonian Magazine*. July 1995. Web. 17 Sept. 2015.

———. *God Gave Us This Country: Tekamthi and the First American Civil War*. New York: Atheneum, 1989. Print.

Glanz, Dawn. *How the West Was Drawn: American Art and the Settling of the Frontier*. Ann Arbor: UMI Research Press, 1982. Print.

Goulart, Ron. "Introducing *White Boy*." *Comics Journal* 266 (Feb. 2005): 135–36.

*Grand Comics Database*. 2012. Web. 1 Apr. 2012.

Greenough, Horatio. *Letters of Horatio Greenough: American Sculptor*. Ed. Nathalia Wright. Madison: University of Wisconsin Press, 1972. Print.

———. *The Miscellaneous Writings of Horatio Greenough*. Ed. Nathalia Wright. Delmar: Scholars' Facsimiles and Reprints, 1975. Print.

———. *The Rescue*. 1837–1853. Photograph taken before 1920, showing the work in situ to the right of the staircase on the east facade of the US Capitol. In storage since 1958.

Hack, Brian E. "Weakness Is a Crime: Captain America and the Eugenic Ideal in Early Twentieth-Century America." *Captain America and the Struggle of the Superhero: Critical Essays*. Ed. Robert G. Weiner. Jefferson: McFarland, 2009. 79–89. Print.

Hallam, Elizabeth, Jenny Hockey, and Glennys Howarth. *Beyond the Body: Death and Social Identity*. London: Routledge, 1999. Print.

[Hamilton, Edmond (w), and Al Plastino (a).] "Superman, Indian Chief!" *Action Comics* #148 (Sept. 1950), National Comics Publications [DC Comics]. Digital.

Harvey, Robert C. *The Art of the Comic Book: An Aesthetic History*. Jackson: University Press of Mississippi, 1996. Print.

Haskell, Francis, and Nicholas Penny. *Taste and the Antique: The Lure of Classical Sculpture 1500–1900*. New Haven: Yale University Press, 1981. Print.

Hatfield, Charles. *Alternative Comics: An Emerging Literature*. Jackson: University Press of Mississippi, 2005. Print.

———. *Hand of Fire: The Comics Art of Jack Kirby*. Jackson: University Press of Mississippi, 2013. Print.

Hauptman, Laurence M. *Between Two Fires: American Indians in the Civil War*. New York: Free Press, 1995. Print.

*Hawkeye and the Last of the Mohicans* #884 (1958), Dell. Print.

Herman, Daniel J. "The Other Daniel Boone: The Nascence of a Middle-Class Hunter Hero, 1784–1860." *Journal of the Early Republic* 18.3 (1998): 429–57. *JSTOR*. Web. 1 Jan. 2015.

Herron, France (w), Sheldon Moldoff (p), and Stan Kaye (i). "Batman—Indian Chief!"
    Sept. 1954. *Batman: The Black Casebook.* New York: DC Comics, 2009. 19–28. Print.

[Herron, France (w), and Fred Ray (a).] "The Battle That Never Died." *Tomahawk* #96
    (Jan.–Feb. 1965), National Periodical Publications [DC Comics]. Print.

———. "Lost Land of the Paleface Tribe." *Tomahawk* #82 (Sept.–Oct. 1962), National
    Periodical Publications [DC Comics]. Print.

———. "Miss Liberty Rides Again." *Tomahawk* #88 (Sept.–Oct. 1963), National
    Periodical Publications [DC Comics]. Print.

———. "The Secrets of Sgt. Witch Doctor." *Tomahawk* #87 (July–Aug. 1963), National
    Periodical Publications [DC Comics]. Print.

Holmberg, Ryan. "Shigeru Sugiura and His Mohicans." Afterword. *The Last of
    the Mohicans.* By Shigeru Sugiura. Ed. and trans. Ryan Holmberg. New York:
    PictureBox, 2013. 120–57. Print.

Horn, Maurice. *Comics of the American West.* New York: Winchester, 1977. Print.

Hughey, Matthew W. "Cinethetic Racism: White Redemption and Black Stereotypes in
    'Magical Negro' Films." *Social Problems* 56.3 (Aug. 2009): 543–77. Print.

Huhndorf, Shari M. *Going Native: Indians in the American Cultural Imagination.*
    Ithaca: Cornell University Press, 2001. Print.

Inge, M. Thomas. *Comics as Culture.* Jackson: University Press of Mississippi, 1990.
    Print.

Jackson, Jack (w and a). *The Last of the Mohicans.* Adapted from James Fenimore
    Cooper (1992), Dark Horse Comics. Print.

Jillson, Willard Rouse. *The Boone Narrative.* Louisville: Standard Printing, 1932. Print.

Johns, Elizabeth. "The 'Missouri Artist' as Artist." *George Caleb Bingham.* Ed. Michael
    E. Shapiro. New York: Harry N. Abrams/Saint Louis Art Museum, 1990. 93–139.
    Print.

Jones, Daryl. *The Dime Novel Western.* Bowling Green: Popular Press, Bowling Green
    State University, 1978. Print.

Jones, William B., Jr. *Classics Illustrated: A Cultural History.* 2nd ed. Jefferson:
    McFarland, 2011. Print.

Kammen, Michael. *American Culture, American Tastes: Social Change and the 20th
    Century.* New York: Alfred A. Knopf, 1999. Print.

Kanigher, Robert (w), and Frank Thorne (a). *Tomahawk* #132 (Jan.–Feb. 1971), National
    Periodical Publications [DC Comics]. Print.

———. *Tomahawk* #133 (Mar.–Apr. 1971), National Periodical Publications [DC Comics].
    Print.

———. *Tomahawk* #136 (Sept.–Oct. 1971), National Periodical Publications [DC
    Comics]. Print.

———. *Tomahawk* #140 (May–June 1972), National Periodical Publications [DC
    Comics]. Print.

Kasson, Joy S. *Buffalo Bill's Wild West: Celebrity, Memory, and Popular History.* New
    York: Hill & Wang, 2000. Print.

——. *Marble Queens and Captives: Women in Nineteenth-Century American Sculpture*. New Haven: Yale University Press, 1990. Print.

Keene, Adrienne. *Native Appropriations*. 2010–2015. Web. 1 Apr. 2012.

[Kiemle, H. W. (a)], and Everett Raymond Kintsler (cover art). *White Chief of the Pawnee Indians* (1951), Avon. Digital.

Kilpatrick, Jacquelyn. *Celluloid Indians: Native Americans and Film*. Lincoln: University of Nebraska Press, 1999. Print.

King, C. Richard. *Unsettling America: The Uses of Indianness in the 21st Century*. Lanham: Rowman & Littlefield, 2013. Print.

Kubert, Joe. "A Declaration of Intent." *Showcase* #85 (Sept. 1969), National Periodical Publications [DC Comics]. Print.

——. "I Don't Belong Here . . . I Don't Belong There." *Showcase* #85 (Sept. 1969), National Periodical Publications [DC Comics]. Print.

——. "River of Gold." *Showcase* #86 (Nov. 1969), National Periodical Publications [DC Comics]. Print.

——. "The Shaman." *Showcase* #87 (Dec. 1969), National Periodical Publications [DC Comics]. Print.

Lawrence, D. H. *Studies in Classic American Literature*. 1923. Ed. Ezra Greenspan, Lindeth Vasey, and John Worthen. New York: Cambridge University Press, 2003. Print.

Lears, Jackson. "A Matter of Taste: Corporate Cultural Hegemony in a Mass-Consumption Society." *Recasting America: Culture and Politics in the Age of Cold War*. Ed. Lary May. Chicago: University of Chicago Press, 1989. 38–57. Print.

Lenthall, Bruce. "Outside the Panel: Race in America's Popular Imagination: Comic Strips before and after World War II." *Journal of American Studies* 32.1 (Apr. 1998): 39–61. *JSTOR*. Web. 19 Apr. 2013.

Lepore, Jill. *The Name of War: King Philip's War and the Origins of American Identity*. New York: Alfred Knopf, 1998. Print.

Lubin, David M. *Picturing a Nation: Art and Social Change in Nineteenth-Century America*. New Haven: Yale University Press, 1994. Print.

MacDonald, J. Fred. *Television and the Red Menace: The Video Road to Vietnam*. New York: Praeger, 1985. Print.

Mailer, Norman. *The Armies of the Night: History as a Novel, the Novel as History*. New York: Plume, 1968. Print.

Marienstras, Elise. "The Common Man's Indian: The Image of the Indian as Promoter of National Identity in the Early National Era." *Native Americans and the Early Republic*. Ed. Frederick Hoxie, Ronald Hoffman, and Peter Albert. Charlottesville: University Press of Virginia, 1999. 261–96. Print.

May, Elaine Tyler. *Homeward Bound: American Families in the Cold War Era*. New York: Basic Books, 2008. Print.

McCloud, Scott. *Understanding Comics: The Invisible Art*. New York: Harper Perennial, 1993. Print.

McClung, John A. *Sketches of Western Adventure*. Philadelphia: Grigg & Elliot, 1832.

McDermott, John Francis. *George Caleb Bingham: River Portraitist*. Norman: University of Oklahoma Press, 1959. Print.

[Meagher, Fred (p, i).] "The Battle of the Giants." *Straight Arrow* #4 (Aug. 1950), Magazine Enterprises. Digital.

———. "The Buffalo Hide of Peace!" *Straight Arrow* #4 (Aug. 1950), Magazine Enterprises. Digital.

Miettinen, Mervi. "Men of Steel? Rorschach, Theweleit, and *Watchmen*'s Deconstructed Masculninity." *PS: Political Science and Politics* 47.1 (Jan. 2014): 104–7. Print.

Mihesuah, Devon A. *American Indians: Stereotypes and Realities*. Atlanta: Clarity, 1996. Print.

[Millard, Joe (w), and Sam Citron (p, i).] "Assault on Boonesborough." *Exploits of Daniel Boone* # 1 (Nov. 1955), Comic Magazines [Quality Comics]. Print.

———. "Doom at the Stake." *Exploits of Daniel Boone* #1 (Nov. 1955), Comic Magazines [Quality Comics]. Print.

———. "Raid on the Scioto." *Exploits of Daniel Boone* #1 (Nov. 1955), Comic Magazines [Quality Comics]. Print.

———. "The Web of the White Savage." *Exploits of Daniel Boone* #2 (Jan. 1956), Comic Magazines [Quality Comics]. Print.

[Millard Joe (w), Edmond Good (p), and Sam Citron (i).] "The Pilgrims from Pennsylvania." *Exploits of Daniel Boone* #4 (May 1956), Comic Magazines [Quality Comics]. Digital.

———. "Rescue from the Redskins." *Exploits of Daniel Boone* #3 (Mar. 1956), Comic Magazines [Quality Comics]. Digital.

Miller, Angela. "The Mechanisms of the Market and the Invention of Western Regionalism: The Example of George Caleb Bingham." *American Iconology: New Approaches to Nineteenth-Century Art and Literature*. Ed. David C. Miller. New Haven: Yale University Press, 1993. 112–34. Print.

Mitchell, Thomas G. *Indian Fighters Turned American Politicians: From Military Service to Public Office*. Westport: Praeger, 2003. Print.

Moebius, William. "Introduction to Picture Book Codes." *Children's Literature: The Development of Criticism*. Ed. Peter Hunt. London: Routledge, 1990. 131–47. Print.

Moench, Doug (w), and Sonny Trinidad (a). *The Last of the Mohicans*. Adapted from James Fenimore Cooper (1976), Marvel Comics Group. Print.

Moore, Jesse T. "The Education of Green Lantern: Culture and Ideology." *Journal of American Culture* 26.2 (June 2003): 263–78. *ProQuest Direct*. Web. 14 May 2013.

Morales, Robert (w), and Kyle Baker (a). *Captain America: Truth*. New York: Marvel, 2009. Print.

Morrison, Grant. *Batman: The Return of Bruce Wayne*. New York: DC Comics, 2011. Print.

Moses, L. G. *Wild West Shows and the Images of American Indians: 1883–1933*. Albuquerque: University of New Mexico Press, 1996. Print.

*National Museum of American Art*. Boston: Smithsonian Institution, 1995.

Nelson, Dana D. *National Manhood: Capitalist Citizenship and the Imagined Fraternity of Men*. Durham: Duke University Press, 1998. Print.

——. "Representative/Democracy: The Political Work of Countersymbolic Representation." *Materializing Democracy: Toward a Revitalized Cultural Politics*. Ed. Russ Castronovo and Dana D. Nelson. Durham: Duke University Press, 2001. 218–47. Print.

Nolan, Michelle. "Collecting the Western Genre!" *Comic Book Marketplace* 2.61 (July 1998): 23–26. Print.

Nyberg, Amy Kiste. *Seal of Approval: The History of the Comics Code*. Jackson: University Press of Mississippi, 1998. Print.

Okorafor-Mbachu, Nnedi. "Stephen King's Super-Duper Magical Negroes." *Strangehorizons.com. Strange Horizons: A Weekly Speculative Fiction Magazine*, 25 Oct. 2004. Web. 20 Oct. 2012.

O'Neil, Dennis (w) and Neal Adams (p). *The Green Lantern/Green Arrow Collection*. Vol. 1. New York: DC Comics, 2004. Print.

O'Neil, Dennis (w), Edward Hannigan (p), and John Beatty (i). *Batman: Shaman*. New York: Warner Books, 1993. Print.

O'Rourke, John H. (w), and Henry C. Kiefer (a). *Classics Illustrated #72: The Oregon Trail* (June 1950), Gilberton Company, Inc. Print.

Ostrander, John (w), Timothy Truman and Tom Mandrake (p), and Michael Bair and Tom Mandrake (i). *The Kents*. New York: DC Comics, 1999. Print.

Palmer, Lorrie. "The Punisher as Revisionist Superhero Western." *The Superhero Reader*. Ed. Charles Hatfield, Jeet Heer, and Kent Worcester. Jackson: University Press of Mississippi, 2013. 279–94. Print.

[Parker, Bill (w), and Pete Costanza (p, i).] "Golden Arrow." *Whiz Comics* #2 (Feb. 1940), Fawcett. Digital.

Parkman, Francis. *The Oregon Trail*. 1849. New York: Penguin, 1982. Print.

——. *The Oregon Trail; The Conspiracy of the Pontiac*. New York: Library of America, 1991. Print.

Pearce, Roy Harvey. *Savagism and Civilization*. Baltimore: Johns Hopkins Press, 1965. Print.

Peck, John M. *Daniel Boone*. 1846. *The Makers of American History*. New York: University Society, 1904. *Kentuckiana Digital Library*. 2002. Web. 29 June 2004.

Peirce, Charles Sanders. *Philosophical Writings of Peirce*. Ed. Justus Buchler. New York: Dover, 1955. Print.

Pennington, Estill Curtis. *Passage and Progress in the Works of William Tylee Ranney*. Augusta: Morris Museum of Art, 1993. Print.

Petchesky, Barry. "Harry Reid's Office Is Laughing at the Sad #RedskinsPride Campaign." *Deadspin*. 29 May 2014. Web. 30 May 2014.

Pettrich, Ferdinand. *The Dying Tecumseh*. 1856. National Museum of American Art. Transfer from the US Capitol.

Pike, Albert. "Life in Arkansas: The Philosophy of Deer Hunting." *American Monthly Magazine* 7 (Feb. 1836): 154–59. *American Periodicals Series Online 1740–1900*. 2004. Web. 27 May 2004.

*Pioneer West Romances* #7 (Spring 1951) [Fiction House Magazines]. Digital.

Plowright, Frank, ed. *The Slings & Arrows Comic Guide*. Great Britain: Slings and Arrows, 2003. Print.

Pollack, Rachel (w), and Tom Yeates (a). *Tomahawk* #1 (July 1998), Vertigo Visions/DC Comics. Print.

Prats, Armando José. *Invisible Natives: Myth and Identity in the American Western*. Ithaca: Cornell University Press, 2002. Print.

[Premiani, Bruno (p), and Ray Burnley (i).] "The Buffalo Brave from Misty Mountain." *Tomahawk* #31 {*Tomahawk* #140} (Mar. 1955), National Comics Publications [DC Comics]. Print.

Price, Garrett. *White Boy*. *The Comics Journal* 266 (Feb. 2005): 137–68. Digital.

Rader, Dean. *Engaged Resistance: American Indian Art, Literature, and Film from Alcatraz to the NMAI*. Austin: University of Texas Press, 2011. Print.

Ramsey, Ray (a). *Classic Comics: The Last of the Mohicans* #4. Adapted from James Fenimore Cooper. (Aug. 1942), Gilberton. Cover. Print.

Ramsey, Ray (interior art). *Classics Illustrated: The Last of the Mohicans* #4. Adapted from James Fenimore Cooper. (Nov. 1957), Gilberton. Print.

Rash, Nancy. *The Painting and Politics of George Caleb Bingham*. New Haven: Yale University Press, 1991. Print.

Rasmussen, Birgit Brander. *Queequeg's Coffin: Indigenous Literacies and Early American Literature*. Durham: Duke University Press, 2012. Print.

"The Real Renegade." *Dan'l Boone* #7 (Mar. 1956), Sussex. Digital.

Richter, Daniel K. *Facing East from Indian Country: A Native History of Early America*. Cambridge: Harvard University Press, 2001. Print.

Riesman, David, and Nathan Glazer. *The Lonely Crowd: A Study of the Changing American Character*. 1950. New Haven: Yale University Press, 2001. Print.

Romero, Lora. "Vanishing Americans: Gender, Empire, and New Historicism." *Subjects and Citizens*. Ed. Michael Moon and Cathy N. Davidson. Durham: Duke University Press, 1995. 87–105. Print.

[Samachson, Joe (w), and Edmond Good (a).] "Flames along the Frontier." *Star Spangled Comics* #69 (June 1947), National Comics Publications [DC Comics]. Digital.

Samuels, Shirley. *Romances of the Republic*. New York: Oxford University Press, 1996. Print.

Savage, Kirk. *Standing Soldiers, Kneeling Slaves: Race, War, and Monument in Nineteenth-Century America*. Princeton: Princeton University Press, 1997. Print.

Savage, William W. *Commies, Cowboys, and Jungle Queens: Comic Books and America, 1945–1954*. Middletown: Wesleyan University Press, 1990. Print.

Sawyer, Michael. "Albert Lewis Kanter and the Classics: The Man behind the Gilberton Company." *Journal of Popular Culture* 20.4 (1987): 1–18. Print.

Sayre, Gordon M. *The Indian Chief as Tragic Hero: Native Resistance and the Literatures of America, from Moctezuma to Tecumseh*. Chapel Hill: University of North Carolina Press, 2005. Print.

Scheckel, Susan. *The Insistence of the Indian: Race and Nationalism in Nineteenth-Century American Culture*. Princeton: Princeton University Press, 1998. Print.

Schimmel, Julie. "Inventing the 'Indian.'" *The West as America: Reinterpreting Images of the Frontier, 1820–1920*. Ed. William Truettner. Washington: Smithsonian Institution Press, 1991. 149–89. Print.

Schlesinger, Arthur, Jr. "The Crisis of American Masculinity." 1958. *The Politics of Hope*. Boston: Houghton Mifflin, 1963. 237–46. Print.

———. *The Vital Center: The Politics of Freedom*. Boston: Houghton Mifflin, 1949. Print.

Seelye, Elizabeth Eggleston. *Tecumseh and the Shawnee Prophet*. Chicago: M. A. Donohue, 1878. Web. 1 Dec. 2014.

[Severin, John (p), and Stephen Addeo (i).] *Classics Illustrated: The Last of the Mohicans* #4 [May 1959] (June 1964), Gilberton. Print.

Sheardy, Robert. "The White Woman and the Native Male Body in Vanderlyn's *Death of Jane McCrea*." *Journal of American Culture* 22.1 (Spring 1999): 93–100. Print.

Sheyahshe, Michael A. *Native Americans in Comic Books: A Critical Study*. Jefferson: McFarland, 2008. Print.

Shoemaker, Nancy. "Body Language: The Body as a Source of Sameness and Difference in Eighteenth-Century American Indian Diplomacy East of the Mississippi." *A Centre of Wonders*. Ed. Janet M. Lindman and Michele L. Tarter. Ithaca: Cornell University Press, 2001. 211–22. Print.

Siemers, David J. *Ratifying the Republic: Antifederalists and Federalists in Constitutional Time*. Stanford: Stanford University Press, 2002. Print.

Sims, Chris. "CA Classic: Batman in the Worst Thanksgiving Ever." *Comics Alliance*. 22 Nov. 2012. Web. 15 Sept. 2014.

Singer, Marc. "'Black Skins' and White Masks: Comic Books and the Secret of Race." *African American Review* 36.1 (2002): 107–19. Print.

Slotkin, Richard. *Gunfighter Nation: The Myth of the Frontier in Twentieth-Century America*. 1992. Norman: University of Oklahoma Press, 1998. Print.

———. *Regeneration through Violence: The Mythology of the American Frontier, 1600–1860*. Norman: University of Oklahoma Press, 1973. Print.

Smith, Henry Nash. *Virgin Land: The American West as Symbol and Myth*. Cambridge: Harvard University Press, 1950. Print.

Smith, Todd. "The Problematics of Absence: Looking for the Male Body in the War of 1812." *A Centre of Wonders*. Ed. Janet M. Lindman and Michele L. Tarter. Ithaca: Cornell University Press, 2001. 237–54. Print.

Sollors, Werner. *Beyond Ethnicity: Consent and Descent in American Culture*. New York: Oxford University Press, 1986. Print.

Solomon-Godeau, Abigail. *Male Trouble: A Crisis in Representation*. New York: Thames and Hudson, 1997. Print.

[Stanley, John (w and layouts), and Irving Tripp (a).] "Indian Uprising." *Four Color* #120 (Oct. 1946), Dell. Digital.

Starr, John (w). "'Hoka-Hai!' In the Sky above the Black Hills . . ." *Indians: Picture Stories of the First Americans* #2 (1950), Wings [Fiction House Magazines]. Digital.

Starr, John (w), and [Bob Lubbers (a)]. "Prowlers of the Wild." *Rangers Comics* #40 (Apr. 1948), Flying Stories [Fiction House Magazines]. Digital.

———. "Two-Face Traps a Lynx." *Rangers Comics* #42 (Aug. 1948), Flying Stories [Fiction House Magazines]. Digital.

Starr, John [John Mitchell] (w), [Bob Webb (p), and David Heames (i).] "Heartbreak Range." *Pioneer West Romances* #3 (1950), Flying Stories [Fiction House Magazines]. Digital.

———. "Siren of the Silver Sage." *Pioneer West Romances* #3 (1950), Flying Stories [Fiction House Magazines]. Digital.

———. "You've Cheated Me for the Last Time, Firehair!" *Pioneer West Romances* #6 (1950), Flying Stories [Fiction House Magazines]. Digital.

Starr, John (w), and L[ee] Elias (a). "It Happened Yesterday . . ." *Rangers Comics* #21 (Feb. 1945) [Fiction House Magazines]. Digital.

Starr, John (w) and [Lee Elias (a)]. "It Was Little Ax . . ." *Rangers Comics* #22 (Apr. 1945), Flying Stories, Inc. [Fiction House Magazines]. Digital.

———. "Tomahawk Trail." *Firehair Comics* #1 (Winter 1948–1949), Flying Stories [Fiction House Magazines]. Digital.

———. "Triumph Swelled . . ." *Rangers Comics* #26 (Dec. 1945), Flying Stories [Fiction House Magazines]. Digital.

Steckmesser, Kent Ladd. *The Western Hero in History and Legend.* Norman: University of Oklahoma Press, 1965. Print.

"Straight Arrow 'Injun-uity' Manual." *Straight Arrow* #2 (Apr.–May 1950), Magazine Enterprises. Digital.

Sugden, John. *Tecumseh: A Life.* New York: Henry Holt, 1997. Print.

Taylor, Aaron. "'He's Gotta Be Strong, and He's Gotta Be Fast, and He's Gotta Be Larger than Life': Investigating the Engendered Superhero Body." *Journal of Popular Culture* 40.2 (2007): 344–60. Print.

Thistlethwaite, Mark. *William Tylee Ranney: East of the Mississipi.* Chadds Ford: Brandywine Museum, 1991. Print.

Thomas, Roy (w), Steve Kurth (p), and Cam Smith (i). *The Last of the Mohicans.* Adapted from James Fenimore Cooper. New York: Marvel, 2008. Print.

Townshend, Kim. "Francis Parkman and the Male Tradition." *American Quarterly* 38.1 (Spring 1986): 97–113. *JSTOR.* Web. 19 May 2013.

"Trail of the Ambush Killers." *Pawnee Bill* #3 (July 1951), Story Comics Inc. Digital.

Truettner, William, ed. *The West as America: Reinterpreting Images of the Frontier, 1820–1920.* Washington: Smithsonian Institution Press, 1991. Print.

Trumbull, Henry. *The Adventures of Col. Daniel Boon.* 1786. 17–31. Willard Rouse Jillson. *The Boone Narrative.* Louisville: Standard Printing Company, 1932. Print.

Vaughan, Alden T. "From White Man to Redskin: Changing Anglo-American Perceptions of the American Indian." *American History Review* 87 (1982): 917–53. Print.

Versaci, Rocco. *This Book Contains Graphic Language: Comics as Literature.* New York: Continuum, 2008. Print.

Vizenor, Gerald. *Fugitive Poses: Native American Indian Scenes of Absence and Presence.* 1998. Lincoln: University of Nebraska Press, 2000. Print.

———. *Manifest Manners: Narratives on Postindian Survivance*. 1994. Lincoln: University of Nebraska Press, 1999. Print.

Walker, Jeffrey. "Deconstructing an American Myth: Hollywood and *The Last of the Mohicans*." *James Fenimore Cooper: His Country and His Art*. Proceedings Of the 10th Cooper Seminar, July 1995, State University of New York College at Oneonta. *James Fenimore Cooper Society Website*. 1999. Web. 11 June 2013.

Walton, David. "'Captain America Must Die': The Many Afterlives of Steve Rogers." *Captain America and the Struggle of the Superhero: Critical Essays*. Ed. Robert G. Weiner. Jefferson: McFarland, 2009. 160–75. Print.

Weltzien, Friedrich. "Masque-*ulinities*: Changing Dress as a Display of Masculinity in the Superhero Genre." *Fashion Theory* 9.2 (2005): 229–50. Print.

Wertham, Frederic. *Seduction of the Innocent*. 1954. Introd. James E. Reibman. Laurel: Main Road, 2004. Print.

White, Richard. "Frederick Jackson Turner and Buffalo Bill." *The Frontier in American Culture*. Ed. James R. Grossman. Berkeley: University of California Press, 1994. 6–65. Print.

———. *The Middle Ground: Indians, Empires, and Republics in the Great Lakes Region, 1650–1815*. New York: Cambridge University Press, 1991. Print.

Whyte, William H. *The Organization Man*. 1956. Philadelphia: University of Pennsylvania Press, 2002. Print.

"The Wild River." *Frontier Scout, Dan'l Boone* #11 (Mar. 1956), Charlton Comics Group. Digital.

Wilkinson, Rupert. *The Pursuit of American Character*. New York: Harper & Row: 1988. Print.

Witek, Joseph. *Comic Books as History: The Narrative Art of Jack Johnson, Art Spiegelman, and Harvey Pekar*. Jackson: University Press of Mississippi, 1989. Print.

Wolin, Sheldon S. *The Presence of the Past: Essays on the State and the Constitution*. Baltimore: Johns Hopkins University Press, 1989. Print.

[Wood, Dave (w), and Fred Ray (p, i).] "Miss Liberty—Frontier Heroine." *Tomahawk* #81 (July–Aug. 1962), National Periodical Publications [DC Comics]. Print.

Wright, Bradford W. *Comic Book Nation: The Transformation of Youth Culture in America*. Baltimore: Johns Hopkins University Press, 2001. Print.

Wright, Nathalia. *Horatio Greenough: The First American Sculptor*. Philadelphia: University of Pennsylvania Press, 1963. Print.

Wylie, Philip. *Generation of Vipers*. 1942. New York: Rinehart, 1955. Print.

Young, Frank M. 2012. "Tootling Tubas, Iodine Indians, and Fatal Cookies: Three Stories from the Fourth *Little Lulu* One-Shot Comic, 1946." *Stanley Stories*. 13 Feb. 2012. Web. 29 Apr. 2013.

# INDEX

Page numbers in **bold** indicate illustrations.

CPSIA information can be obtained
at www.ICGtesting.com
Printed in the USA
LVHW092313130819
627584LV00002B/267/P